University Library

Date of Return - Subject to Recall

THE
RISK
MANAGEMENT
HANDBOOK
for *HEALTHCARE PROFESSIONALS*

THE
RISK
MANAGEMENT
HANDBOOK
for *HEALTHCARE PROFESSIONALS*

EDITED BY

JOSEPH S. SANFILIPPO, MD, MBA
Department of Obstetrics, Gynecology & Reproductive Sciences,
University of Pittsburgh School of Medicine,
Magee-Womens Hospital, Pittsburgh, PA

and

CLAYTON L. ROBINSON, JD
Jenkins Pisacano Robinson & Bailey, Lexington, KY

The Parthenon Publishing Group
International Publishers in Medicine, Science & Technology

A CRC PRESS COMPANY
BOCA RATON   LONDON   NEW YORK   WASHINGTON, D.C.

Published in the UK and Europe by
The Parthenon Publishing Group Ltd
23-25 Blades Court
Deodar Road
London SW15 2NU, UK

Published in the USA by
The Parthenon Publishing Group Inc.
One Blue Hill Plaza
PO Box 1564, Pearl River
New York 10965, USA

British Library Cataloguing in Publication Data
The risk management handbook for healthcare professionals
    1. Hospitals - Risk management
    I. Sanfilippo, J. S. (Joseph S) II. Robinson, Clayton L. N.
    362.1'1'068

    ISBN 1842140698

Library of Congress Cataloging-in-Publication Data
Risk management handbook for healthcare professionals /
    edited by Joseph S. Sanfilippo and Clayton L. Robinson
        p.; cm.
    Includes bibliographical references and index.
    ISBN 1-84214-069-8 (alk. paper)
        1. Physicians--Malpractice--Handbooks, manuals, etc. 2. Risk management--
    Handbooks, manuals, etc. 3. Medical care--Law and legislation--Handbooks,
    manuals, etc. I. Sanfilippo, J. S. (Joseph S.) II. Robinson, Clayton (Clayton L. N.)
        [DNLM: 1. Malpractice. 2. Risk Management. W 44.1 R595 2001]
    RA1056.5 R55 2001
    344.73'04121--dc21   2001021282

First published 2002

Typeset by Siva Math Setters, Chennai, India
Printed and bound by Bookcraft (Bath) Ltd., Midsomer Norton, UK

Contents

List of contributors

Paulette Freeman Adams, EdD, RN
University of Louisville
School of Nursing
Louisville, KY 40292
USA

John T. Ballantine, JD
Ogden, Newell & Welch
500 West Jefferson St, Suite 1700
Citizens Plaza
Louisville, KY 40202
USA

Leonard Berlin, MD, FACR
Rush North Shore Medical Center
Department of Radiology
9600 Gross Point Road
Skokie, IL 60076
USA

James Brungo, DPM
1946 Caribou Drive
Allison Park, PA 15104
USA

Jeffrey M. Bumpous, MD
Department of Otolaryngology
University of Louisville
601 S. Floyd Street, Suite 700
Louisville, KY 40202
USA

David A. Casey, MD
Department of Psychiatry
University of Louisville
Health Sciences Center
500 S. Preston St., Bldg A

Louisville, KY 40292
USA

William Cheadle, MD
Department of Surgery
University of Louisville
Louisville, KY 40292
USA

Ira J.K. Cohen, MD
980 Beaver Grade Road
Coraopolis, PA 15108
USA

Patrick J. DeMeo, MD
Departments of Orthopedics
    and Sports Medicine
Allegheny General Hospital
320 East North Avenue
Pittsburgh, PA 15212
USA

Sir John Dewhurst, FRCOG, FRCS
University of London
Queen Charlotte's and Chelsea
    Hospital
London
England

Leah J. Dickstein, MD
Office for Faculty and Student
    Advocacy
University of Louisville
School of Medicine
500 South Preston Street, Suite 214
Louisville, KY 40292
USA

Gary P. Duechle, JD
Medical Protective
10401 Linn Station Rd., Suite 132
Louisville, KY 40223
USA

David B. Gazak, JD, PhD
Darby & Gazak, P.S.C.
Attorneys at Law
2000 Citizens Plaza
500 W. Jefferson Street
Louisville, KY 40202
USA

Linda H. Gleis, MD
Department of Rehabilitation
    Medicine
University of Louisville
School of Medicine
Louisville, KY 40202
USA

Robert M. Hamilton, MD
PhyAmerica Physician Services
2828 Croasdaile Drive
Durham, NC 27705
USA

**Marianne Hopkins Hutti,
    DNS, WHNP-C**
Women's Health Nurse
    Practitioner Program
University of Louisville
School of Nursing
Louisville, KY 40292
USA

Joseph Joyce, MD
Department of Emergency
    Medicine
Allegheny General Hospital
320 East North Avenue

Pittsburgh, PA 15202
USA

Keith T. Kanel, MD, FACP
Division of General Internal
    Medicine
Allegheny General Hospital
320 East North Avenue
Pittsburgh, PA 15212
USA

Arthur H. Keeney, MD (Deceased)
Department of Opthalmology
University of Louisville

Karen Keith, JD
Weber & Rose
2700 Aegon Center
400 West Market Street
Louisville, KY 40202
USA

Jason P. Lockette, MD
Department of Otolaryngology
University of Louisville
School of Medicine
Louisville, KY 40202
USA

Linda F. Lucas, MD
Department of Anesthesiology
University of Louisville
School of Medicine
Louisville, KY 40292
USA

Robert K. Luntz, MD
Beth Israel Medical Center
Philips Ambulatory Care
10 Union Square East
New York, NY 10003
USA

Shafquat Meraj, MD
Department of Urology
Beth Israel Medical Center
10 Union Square East
New York, NY 10003
USA

Craig A. Mueller, DC
Mueller Chiropractic
1015 Dupont Road
Louisville, KY 40207
USA

David Muram, MD
Eli Lilly and Company
Lilly Corporate Center
639 S. Delaware Street
Indianapolis, Indiana 46285
USA

Harris M. Nagler, MD
Beth Israel Medical Center
Philips Ambulatory Care
10 Union Square East
New York, NY 10003
USA

Greg C. Nunnally, DMD
Nunnally & Watson PSC
3935 Dupont Circle
Louisville, KY 40207
USA

Dennis M. O'Connor, MD
Department of Pathology
University of Louisville
School of Medicine
Louisville, KY 40292
USA

Gerald W. Pifer, MD
Department of Orthopedics

Allegheny General Hospital
320 East North Avenue
Pittsburgh, PA 15212
USA

Tracy S. Prewitt, JD
O'Bryan, Brown & Toner
1500 Starks Building
455 South 4th Avenue
Louisville, KY 40202
USA

Lynn K. Rikhoff, JD
Jenkins Pisacano Robinson & Bailey
269 West Main Street, Suite 100
Lexington, KY 40507
USA

Clayton L. Robinson, JD
Jenkins Pisacano Robinson & Bailey
269 West Main Street, Suite 100
Lexington, KY 40507
USA

Joseph S. Sanfilippo, MD, MBA
Department of Obstetrics,
    Gynecology & Reproductive
    Sciences
University of Pittsburgh
School of Medicine
Magee-Womens Hospital
300 Halket Street
Pittsburgh, PA 15213
USA

Jan Schneider, MD
46 Thayer Lane
P.O. Box 1044
South Orleans, MA 02662
USA

Peter A. Schwartz, MD
The Reading Hospital
  and Medical Center
Department of Obstetrics
  and Gynecology
6th and Spruce Streets
Box 16052
Reading, PA 19612-6052
USA

Ronald L. Scott, JD
Health Law and
  Policy Institute
University of Houston Law Center
4800 Calhoun Road
Houston, TX 77204-6381
USA

Steven R. Smith, JD
California Western School of Law
225 Cedar Street
San Diego, CA 92101
USA

Nicholas G. Sotereanos, MD
Division of Adult Reconstructive
  Surgery
Allegheny General Hospital
320 East North Avenue
Pittsburgh, PA 15212
USA

George J. Taylor, MD
Medical University of
  South Carolina
21½ Pitt Street
Charleston, SC 29401
USA

Alfred L. Thompson, MD
University of Louisville
School of Medicine

Louisville, KY 40202
USA

Gerald D. Verdi, DDS, MD
Aesthetic Plastic Surgery Institute
444 South First Street
Louisville, KY 40202
USA

Gary M. Weiss, JD
O'Bryan, Brown & Toner
455 South 4th Avenue
Suite 1500, Starks Building
Louisville, KY 40202
USA

Robert White, PhD, MD
Department of
  Neurosurgery
Metro Cleveland University
  Hospital
Metro Health Medical
  Center
2500 Metro Health Drive
Cleveland, OH 44109
USA

Gerald D. Wilkie, MS, RPh
Norton Hospital
200 East Chestnut St
Louisville, KY 40202
USA

Stephen P. Wright, MD
Kosair Children's Hospital
P.O. Box 35070
Louisville, KY 40232-5070
USA

Preface

Do the terms: *voir dire, res ipsa loquitor, respondeat superior, supersedeas bond* sound foreign and unfamiliar? These are terms encountered everyday by physicians facing malpractice suits. This handbook has been written to help physicians understand the dialogue of the law, and to assist them should they ever have a malpractice claim filed against them. *The Risk Management Handbook* was inspired by questions asked by friends in the medical profession, former residents, and my own observations related to medicolegal issues facing clinicians today. What do you do when the phone rings and a concerned, distraught physician is on the other end of the line asking if you would serve as a medical expert in a lawsuit filed against him or her. Once that call has been placed, you will no longer, in all probability, have the freedom to interact with that physician in any way. 'Speak to no one about the case except your attorney' is wise advice.

What about preparation for a deposition or trial? Do you know how to prepare and provide the best assistance to your counsel? The statistics are frightening, for example, 73% of all obstetrician gynecologist can be expected to be sued 2.3 times. Within certain specialities up to 27% of residents will be sued.

You receive a letter from an attorney requesting medical records; you review them and then realize that the documentation 'isn't the whole story'. The temptation is to alter the records, thinking that in doing so, you will provide a more complete portrayal of what really happened. Now you may make the case indefensible as well as committing a crime by altering the medical record. Perhaps your day in court has arrived. It's the opportunity to convey your side of the story, how can you do this most effectively? The importance of maintaining your composure, being able to communicate appropriately, and keeping eye contact with the jury all come into play. This Handbook is designed to aid you in preventing litigation in the first place, it will also serve as a guide should you ever have to face a malpractice trial. For example, what's your role in jury selection. Your participation in the *voir dire* (questioning of prospective jurors) is particularly important. We often do not realize all of the factors that go into determining successful litigation.

How do you handle the anxiety you are about to go through, the effect on your family, your attitude to patients as each being a potential litigator? What sources do you have to assist you? Will this affect your career by limiting your practice in some way? Whether you are a medical student, resident physician, or allied health professional this Handbook is designed for you. It will provide you with the following list of 'D's'; delivery of care, diagnosis, disposition, documentation. Perhaps the phrase 'Document what you do and do what you document' will prove to be a helpful motto. Avoiding the 'anxiety of the law' for all in the medical profession is one objective of this book.

Each chapter is organized to provide you with:

The most common areas of litigation,
How to avoid such,
Advice for those in the midst of litigation.

Would it be in your best interest to hire your own attorney or should you use the one assigned to your case by your malpractice insurance carrier? Should you settle the case or get an independent opinion if your carrier plans to settle? You may not realize that a settled case will go to the National Data Bank for all to see. What about informed refusal, what liability do you have? Does your employment contract require you to notify your employer within 24 hours of being informed of litigation. Can you suggest to your attorney a number of individuals who might best serve as experts in your defense? Do you work at your patient communication skills? Do you know the pertinent literature revolving around the case at hand, what about major textbooks, what do they state? The Handbook provides you with direction in these areas.

The bottom line is that this book is designed to prevent litigation and keep you out of the courtroom. However, should you find yourself in a situation that requires the aid of counsel, this book will assist you in how to survive the current legal climate.

Dedication

To every practitioner in all walks of medicine, this book provides an 'investment' in patient care, in being a patient advocate and in evolving as a good clinician and communicator. It is designed to 'pay big dividends' in patient satisfaction, quality of care and avoiding the courtroom.

J. S. S.
C. L. R.

Acknowledgements

The editors wish to acknowledge Scott Whonsetler, Esq, for his assistance in the planning of this book; Alex Rose, Esq, and Karen Keith, Esq, for their input and critique. We wish to show our gratitude to our families for their support during the endeavor, and our colleagues for their suggestions and direction. A special acknowledgment is provided to recognize the death of one of our authors, Dr Arthur Keeney, opthalmologist and former Dean at the University of Louisville. Dr Keeney was an outstanding clinician and leader in our profession. He shared his expertise and leadership skills with all who crossed his path. He will always be remembered as a role model in our profession.

Joseph S. Sanfilippo
Clayton L. Robinson

1

The medical chart: preventative documentation

Clayton L. Robinson, JD

No single piece of evidence is more important in the medical malpractice trial than the physician's own record. A concise, organized, well-written set of records is virtually unassailable at trial. Furthermore, since it is a contemporaneous recording of the physician's observations and conclusions, the medical chart carries a level of credibility with jurors. Statements made by patients and their families in a courtroom are almost always regarded with a certain skepticism as there is a motive for secondary gain by the time they testify. In contrast, the physician's records are created well before anyone suspects a lawsuit, and well before a lawyer gets involved and begins molding his witnesses' memories.

Unfortunately, that sacred set of documents which many times is the difference between winning and losing a malpractice case can often be used against a physician. The difference between a medical chart that is useful in defending a case and a medical chart that casts the physician in a poor light is a function of four variables:

(1) Time spent in the creation of the record;
(2) Attention to detail;
(3) Ability to organize and record one's thoughts clearly;
(4) Completion of the record in a timely manner.

Accordingly, the basic guidelines for the preparation of medical records are as follows.

TREAT THE MEDICAL RECORD AS A LEGAL DOCUMENT:

The medical chart does not exist for the purpose of editorializing one's personal thoughts, but as an accurate documentation of a skilled professional's observations and clinical conclusions. To that end, you should avoid editorializing about a particular situation. I recall a case where a surgeon performed a procedure on the wrong part of a patient's body. Instead of admitting his error and advising his patient, he instead noted the error in his chart, further noting that he saw no need to tell her since she was 'probably crazy anyway'. Recording this observation in the chart was not helpful to the defense.

In another case, a suit was brought against a psychiatrist. The psychiatrist regularly treated a patient who subsequently committed suicide and the deceased patient's estate sued for malpractice. The office notes made during the doctor's last visit with the now deceased patient contained a rather detailed sketch of a turkey. Although I like turkeys, and Thanksgiving is a wonderful holiday, I could not help envisioning the opposing attorney cross-examining my client with that turkey sketch (now of course, enlarged to 48 × 60 inches and dry mounted).

These are extreme, and perhaps ludicrous examples, but they do illustrate a point. Assume that every mark you make will one day be placed in front of a jury considering whether your care was professional and appropriate.

MAKE TIMELY ENTRIES INTO THE MEDICAL RECORD

Many physicians carry a dictaphone while seeing patients, and actually dictate the chart entry in the presence of the patient. Making this a consistent practice is obviously strong defensive medicine. First, it is very difficult for the patient to later disagree with a chart entry that was dictated in his presence. If an inaccuracy is noted, surely the patient would bring this to the physician's attention at the time. Second, for clinical purposes, if a physician misstates or misconstrues a fact, it gives the patient the opportunity to point out the mistake to the physician.

It is also important to make chart entries in a timely manner. If an operative report is not dictated until a month after the surgery and the patient has had complications, the opposing counsel will suggest that the report was drafted by the surgeon for self-protection. Prompt completion of office and hospital chart notes is essential.

ALWAYS CHART SIGNIFICANT FINDINGS

Having cross-examined literally hundreds of professional expert witnesses who testify against physicians, I believe that the mantra 'if it was not charted, it was not done' is the song of the intellectually bankrupt. No physician or lawyer with any intellectual integrity believes all observations and all care is charted. Having said that, however, when an abnormal finding is observed, or a finding which is significant to ruling in or ruling out a diagnosis, that finding should be noted. Failure to do so leaves a physician relying upon memory rather than a contemporaneous document. Take the time necessary to chart a significant finding, write legibly, sign and ideally add a radiopager number.

CHART TELEPHONE CALLS

The method by which telephone calls are noted in the medical chart is often inconsistent. Frequently if a telephone call is charted at all it is on a scrap piece of paper or sticker then placed in the file. Equal care should be taken when charting telephone calls as when charting office visits. When the patient is present in the office, the physician can depend upon his own observations and diagnostic acumen. If a decision is being made by telephone to issue a prescription or to advise a patient regarding the need to come to the office for an examination, the necessity for cogent documentation is even greater. If things go wrong and a lawsuit follows, you can be sure that the patient's testimony will be that 'things were going to hell in a hand basket' and, although this was reported to the physician's office over the phone, nothing was done. Accordingly, it is advisable to document thoroughly the contents of all telephone calls, no matter how unimportant or innocuous they may seem.

AVOID CHANGES OR ALTERATIONS TO THE CHART

After a lawsuit is filed, particular attention should be given to maintaining the original chart in its original condition without additions, alterations or changes. The original chart should be secured in a safe place. Under no circumstances should the original chart be released from the office, unless it is for the purpose of introducing the original as an exhibit in court or unless its release is ordered by a judge.

KEEP DOCUMENTS PERTAINING TO LITIGATION SEPARATE FROM THE PATIENT'S CLINICAL RECORD

Once litigation is under way you will probably receive a variety of documents and correspondence from your attorney. I strongly recommend keeping a separate file for correspondence and documents pertaining to the lawsuit. Placing correspondence from your attorney or your malpractice carrier into your patient's chart is perilous. Clerical staff may not realize that letters from your attorney are not to be copied and sent out from the chart. Likewise, letters you send to your attorney should not be made part of the patient's original chart. Maintain a separate file for all legal correspondence and all communication between yourself, your attorney and your malpractice carrier. These documents should not become part of the patient's chart and should not be discussed with anyone other than your personal representatives.

2

The disgruntled patient: dealing with requests for records, threats of litigation and phone calls from lawyers

Clayton L. Robinson, JD

Invariably, all physicians at one point or another will receive a patient request for release of their medical records. The record request may come from a current or former patient, or perhaps from a lawyer. All requests for records are not identical; however, certain guidelines are universally applicable.

DO NOT ALTER YOUR MEDICAL CHART

Record alterations have rendered many defensible cases indefensible. Altering records raises the specter of conspiracy. Most jurors will suspect that a physician who changes his record, has done so to cover a mistake. The opposing attorney will argue that alteration shows consciousness of guilt. Even if the changes are minor, altered records make the physician's care difficult to defend. Moreover, alterations in medical records may give rise to a claim for punitive damages against a physician*.

WHEN IN DOUBT ABOUT PRODUCING RECORDS CONTACT YOUR ATTORNEY OR MALPRACTICE CARRIER

Certain items, including results of human immunodeficiency virus (HIV) testing may not be appropriate to produce even pursuant to a records

---

*Punitive damages or exemplary damages are defined as monetary damages designed to punish a civil party in order to deter misconduct. Punitive damages generally are not covered by liability insurance and, if awarded, must be paid by the defendant physician from his or her own personal assets.

release from the patient. Specific laws exist that likewise limit the ability of a physician to release records of psychiatric diagnosis, care and treatment. If you are not certain what ought to be released in response to a records request, contact your attorney or malpractice carrier for guidance.

DO NOT ATTEMPT TO CONTACT THE PATIENT OR THEIR ATTORNEY

In the event that you receive a letter from a patient or an attorney advising that the records are sought to investigate potential malpractice, the first inclination is to make personal contact with either the patient or their representative to 'explain what happened'. This almost never works and usually makes matters worse. In cases where the physician contacts the patient in an attempt to dissuade them from filing a malpractice action, the physician's statements are generally interpreted by the patient as an admission of liability. Statements by a physician who becomes a defendant in a lawsuit are admissible in court. Consequently, any statements you make to a patient in an attempt to dissuade them from contacting a lawyer or filing litigation may be used against you at trial. Similarly, any statements you make to the patient's attorney may be utilized in cross-examination. In reality, if an unhappy patient has contacted an attorney and is inclined to file a lawsuit, very little you say in a telephone conversation or letter is going to dissuade them from that course of action. The best course of action is to notify your malpractice carrier and/or your attorney and copy all your records.

ALWAYS SEND COPIES, NEVER ORIGINALS

Generally, requests for records made to a physician are for copies. Unless ordered to do so by a judge, I never permit my clients to release their original X-rays, videos, photographs or records. Copies can be made quickly and inexpensively. Ultimately, the original record may be the only evidence standing between the physician and a huge malpractice award. Copies certainly should be released to the patient or their representative with the appropriate authorization, but the originals should never be relinquished unless ordered by a court.

DO NOT KEEP MEDICAL RECORDS FROM YOUR OWN ATTORNEY

Once it becomes clear that a claim will be asserted against you it will be necessary for you to meet with your attorney. In advance of that meeting, your attorney will request a complete copy of your office chart. The operative word here is 'complete'. Many times I have met a client only to discover that a significant portion of the chart has not been copied and sent to me. Generally, the clerical staff in the doctor's office decide that a particular page, entry, note or billing statement was unnecessary to copy because they did not think I needed that. With all due respect to the staff, they are not in a position to know what may or may not be relevant in complex medical malpractice litigation. When your attorney requests a complete copy of all records, X-rays, photographs, etc., it is important to ascertain that each and every item is provided.

DO NOT ATTEMPT TO NEGOTIATE A
SETTLEMENT WITH A DISSATISFIED PATIENT

The threat of a lawsuit from a patient is perhaps one of the most unnerving events in the practice of medicine. All conscientious physicians depend upon a close physician–patient relationship to fulfill their responsibilities thoroughly and competently. The breakdown of that relationship to the point where the patient threatens a lawsuit not only undermines the physician's relationship with the patient, it causes the physician to regard future patients as potential courtroom enemies as opposed to a patient in need of healing.

When threatened with a lawsuit the physician should remain calm and not become argumentative. In practice, this is very difficult. However, it is counterproductive to argue a patient out of a medical malpractice lawsuit. Another mistake that I have seen physicians make from time to time is an attempt to 'negotiate the matter' with the patient. What the physician may regard as an attempt at resolution, the disgruntled patient will surely perceive as bribery. Although rules of evidence in most jurisdictions preclude reference at trial to any attempt by the parties to settle or resolve their claims, I have encountered some courts that have ruled that a physician's attempt to offer money to a disgruntled patient is admissible. In one case where a patient had suffered an intraoperative complication, the physician came to the patient's hospital room after admission and gave her money. In this particular case the patient's hospitalization precluded her from working, which caused great difficulty for her family as she was the sole source of income for her children. The physician wanted to provide her with cash to care for her children. This gesture was admirable and well intentioned. Unfortunately, at trial the gesture was characterized as a bribery attempt. If you wish to have a case resolved prior to the formal filing of a lawsuit, it is best to seek the assistance of your malpractice carrier or your attorney. An unsuccessful attempt by your attorney or your carrier to settle a claim or lawsuit will not be admissible at trial and will not be characterized in front of a jury as a bribe. Efforts by a physician to settle a case will generally not impress a jury as a gesture of magnanimity, but rather as an admission of guilt.

BE CAREFUL WHEN DISCUSSING UNTOWARD EVENTS AND COMPLICATIONS

Once the patient has shown an inclination to make a claim against you, be cautious in your future contact with that patient. It is not uncommon for a patient contemplating litigation to return to the physician's office with a concealed tape-recorder. As unusual as this sounds, I have encountered a substantial number of personal injury litigants who surreptitiously record conversations with their physicians. This has occurred so frequently that I now routinely request that the opposing counsel produce any audiotapes of conversations with my client. When speaking to a patient and explaining an untoward situation choose your words carefully. Even if you are not recorded, any statement you make is admissable in court if you are sued (it is not hearsay).

Another challenge is presented when a patient's attorney contacts the physician to 'discuss the case.' This generally occurs before a lawsuit has been filed. Many jurisdictions have ethical requirements which require the attorney to advise if you may be a potential party to a lawsuit. It would be naive, however, to believe that every attorney follows that directive. If you are contacted by an attorney and you suspect that it may pertain to a claim against you or another physician, contact your own attorney to ascertain what the ground rules will be prior to any interview. Your attorney may also be able to ascertain whether there is the possibility of your direct involvement in the action as a party. Often an attorney will contact the treating physician simply to gain a greater understanding of the physician's involvement in the treatment of a patient and an insight into the nature of the medical condition involved. It is often difficult to separate that type of innocuous situation from one which may be adversarial. A 10-minute telephone conversation with your attorney may enable you to differentiate between situations where you do or do not need to have an attorney present.

3

Informed consent and informed refusal

Steven R. Smith, JD

Informed consent is a process for implementing one of the most important values of our society and a basic principle of medical ethics: personal autonomy. The doctrine of consent is intended to ensure that people have an opportunity to decide for themselves what will happen to their bodies. The 'consent' part of the formulation is that there should be no 'touching' of a person without permission. The 'informed' part refers to the information that patients should receive in order to make a sensible decision.

Patients do not have the technical medical knowledge that allows them to make complicated medical decisions without information, and they must depend on practitioners for that information. It is, therefore, the obligation of the practitioner not only to obtain consent, but to provide sufficient information on which treatment decisions can be based. Patients may then take this information and apply their own individual values, hopes and fears to come to medical decisions that best fit their needs.

The first part of the chapter offers three basic suggestions to guide the practitioner in meeting informed consent obligations; it then discusses legal principles regarding informed consent; and finally discusses the legal consequences of not providing informed consent.

The second segment considers the concept of 'informed refusal'. It describes the duties of practitioners to provide information to the patient even when the patient is refusing recommended medical tests or treatment.

INFORMED CONSENT

Practical suggestions

There are three practical suggestions that can guide practitioners in everyday practice. While understanding the legal rules is helpful, practitioners will generally do the right thing if they:

(1) Ensure that patients have given reasonable agreement to any touching (touching includes prescribing pharmaceuticals, and 'electronic' touching such as X-rays).

(2) Provide the information that *this* patient needs to make sensible decisions for himself or herself. This is the heart of 'informed' consent: giving sufficient information, so that the patient may decide whether or not to accept treatment and to consider the alternatives.

(3) Document the consent and the consent process.

Another practical consideration is that the consent process is an excellent opportunity for patients to participate in their own treatment by being directly involved in management decisions. Such participation has been shown to improve outcomes, so apart from the legal requirements, practitioners should use the consent process as an opportunity to improve communication with patients, align patients' expectations to reality and encourage their participation in their own care.

Legal principles involving informed consent

When must informed consent be obtained?

On a technical level, consent must be given before there is any form of touching (directly or indirectly) of a patient. Consent to the most basic touch of an examination may undoubtedly be inferred from a patient appearing for diagnosis or treatment. Many institutions and practitioners, as a way of documenting consent, provide for a blanket consent to be signed when the patient is first seen. Such basic consent is undoubtedly effective for the usual, essentially noninvasive diagnostic procedures and treatment, but it is not an unlimited consent to all procedures.

The obligation of informed consent applies not just to treatment or surgery, it also applies to risky or invasive diagnostic procedures, and to the prescription of pharmaceuticals.

What general kinds of information must be given to patients?

As procedures become more physically intrusive, risky, experimental or non-standard, the level of information that patients should be given increases. While no special consent would be required to take a blood pressure, for example, an angiogram would require more specific consent. Within this general rule, there are four kinds of information that are commonly identified as being required:

(1) A description of the procedure proposed.
(2) An analysis of the significant risks and benefits of the proposed procedure.
(3) A discussion of alternatives to the procedure, if there are any.
(4) If the recommended procedure is rejected, then a disclosure of the risks of *not* accepting the proposed procedures or alternative.

The first of these seldom gives rise to disputes. The last raises issues of 'informed refusal' that are considered below. It is the second, and to some degree the third, in which most of the legal disputes have arisen, and it is on those that we will concentrate in the remainder of this section.

These are, of course, the minimum that must be disclosed. The practitioner is perfectly free to go beyond the minimum legal requirements.

What risks must be disclosed?

The starting point should always be, 'What information does this patient need to make a sensible decision, given the patient's situation (education and ability to understand medical concepts), goals, values and needs?' The general rule is that 'material' risks must be disclosed. That is, risks that would likely play a significant role in deciding whether to undergo the procedure. As a rule of thumb, the more severe a risk is, for example, death or permanent disability, the more an even small likelihood that it will occur should be revealed. On the other hand, less catastrophic risks, say a rash that lasts an hour, may not need to be disclosed.

What alternative procedures should be discussed?

If there are reasonable alternative procedures that might be considered, those should be discussed with the patient. In the case of prostate cancer, for example, it may be necessary for the practitioner to discuss various surgical alternatives, as well as radiation and possible chemotherapy.

This is not to say that practitioners cannot inform patients of their recommendations; indeed, they should do so. Beyond that, practitioners can be advocates for one approach or another, and can discuss the patient's decision, pointing out potential errors in understanding.

Should the consent be tailored to the individual patient,
or the same for all patients?

For years there has been a debate over whether the legal standard should provide information that is important to the typical 'reasonable' patient, or information that is important to this patient, given his or her individual goals, fears, etc. The better therapeutic view seems to be that the information should be tailored to the needs of the individual patient. For example, a small chance that a procedure could result in the loss of some manual dexterity might be of passing interest to a psychiatrist, but would be of much greater interest to a surgeon or professional pianist. Thus, it is better to tailor the discussion to the needs of the patient. One weakness of preprinted forms (discussed in documentation below) is that it is more difficult to tailor the forms to the patient.

A related question that arises is whether the physician is obligated to tell patients about risks they already know, or that a reasonable person would already know. While a number of courts have adopted the common sense approach that such information is generally not legally required to be repeated to the patient, it is dangerous to assume that the patient already knows the important risks of, for example, anesthesia. Physicians may overestimate the degree to which the public or an individual patient already knows risks and benefits. It is good practice to avoid assumptions of knowledge.

Does informed consent apply to prescribing drugs?

Informed consent rules apply to prescription drugs. In the past, this issue has not come up frequently, but in general, physicians are expected to ensure that patients understand the basic information described above and give instruction for the use of medicines. Increasingly, such information is provided by pharmacists, but physicians have the obligation to ensure that the patient has access to basic information about prescription drugs.

Are there exceptions to the informed consent requirement?

There are two generally recognized exceptions to the informed consent requirements. These are narrow exceptions and apply only in extraordinary circumstances. Practitioners should, therefore, use them only with caution and with full documentation in the medical records.

The first exception occurs when there is a medical emergency and there is no way of obtaining informed consent or refusal from the patient or next of kin. A common example is the patient who is brought to the emergency room unconscious and without family. In this situation, the law makes the reasonable assumption that most people would like treatment to proceed as necessary. This exception does not arise every time there is an emergency, but only when the emergency is combined with the inability to seek consent. At the same time, medical emergencies may not allow time for a formal, time-consuming consent process. Therefore, there are less rigid informed consent requirements in all medical emergencies in which time is of the essence.

The second exception occurs when a patient is highly subject to suggestion and the mere disclosure of a risk is likely to be enough to cause serious harm to the patient. This exception certainly cannot be used when the fact is that the patient knew of a risk which would cause him/her to refuse the treatment. It is a very limited exception, and is seldom justified. Where a practitioner relies on this, detailed documentation in the medical record is suggested.

Is there a particular procedure that should be used in obtaining informed consent?

There is no single, legally prescribed procedure for obtaining informed consent, and the appropriate procedure will depend on the circumstances. For example, the process that can be used in an emergency will be quite different than an elective procedure that may be scheduled weeks in advance.

When there are serious risks involved and time permits, there is a good argument to be made for a two-step process in which information is first given to the patient orally and in writing, then a follow-up meeting is held to discuss any questions and concerns. In some circumstances it may be wise to include one or more members of the patient's family in the discussions.

Are there special rules for special groups or procedures?

Some groups present special issues of informed consent. Children and incompetent adults, for example, cannot legally consent to most medical treatments. Their parents or guardians have that authority. There are certain exceptions in some US states for drug and STD treatment, emancipated minors and contraception, but those laws vary considerably among the states.

Many states have special informed consent rules related to abortion and permanent sterilization. There are also very strict informed consent requirements for experimental procedures, and the consent form for human subjects must be approved by the Institutional Review Board. In addition, procedures that deviate from standard practice (that is, generally accepted medical practice) should be accompanied by especially thorough informed consent.

In all of the instances in which there are special rules concerning consent, it is essential that the practitioner understands the rules and is prepared to document that the legal requirements of consent have been met.

Documentation of informed consent

Many institutions and practitioners prefer that the documentation of informed consent is via a form signed by the patient. Not uncommonly, where procedures are particularly invasive or risky, institutions have detailed consent forms that include a statement of the basic four elements described above (the procedure, risks and benefits, alternatives and the risk of no treatment). Written, signed consent forms are also usually favored by lawyers.

Such signed consent forms are, however, not generally required by the law. Rather, they provide some level of certainty that the consent was obtained should a dispute arise later. Some institutions have successfully eschewed the signed written consent form in favor of detailed medical record notations by the physician.

If there are not written, signed consent forms, practitioners must take special caution to ensure that there is very high quality documentation in the medical record. Such documentation should include the date and time of the informed consent discussion, a notation of the nature of the discussion and a statement that following the discussion and the opportunity to ask questions, the patient gave consent.

In a few instances, the law requires a signed, written consent. Examples include experimental studies and abortion. In some states, by statute a signed consent provides additional legal protection against claims that the consent was not adequate.

Liability for the failure of informed consent

The failure of informed consent may lead to liability for battery (generally no consent at all) or negligence (inadequate information). When such lawsuits occur, these are usually successful only where there is a gross lack of information to the patient, misconduct by the doctor or negligent treatment. In truth, there is very little risk of liability for lack of informed consent if the practitioner provides even the most basic information about the procedure.

State variations

The law governing informed consent is determined by the states; thus, the rules vary from state-to-state. The situation has been complicated by the fact that a number of state statutes have been adopted that define informed consent. These statutes have commonly been undertaken as 'malpractice reform', but have often confused rather than clarified the obligation of physicians. While the legal principles outlined in this chapter apply generally, it is important that practitioners understand the peculiarities of the states in which they practice. Ideally, practitioners will discuss these issues with an attorney who specializes in health law. It is wise to have an ongoing relationship with such an attorney, with periodic 'legal checkups' to ensure that practice is consistent with current legal principles.

INFORMED REFUSAL

An element of informed consent that is too often ignored is 'informed refusal'. This refers to the obligations that a practitioner has when a patient declines recommended procedures, whether treatment or diagnostic.

Informed refusal is, in some respects, a natural part of informed consent. If patients have the right to consent to treatment, then they must also have the right to refuse it. There are many reasons patients may reject procedures recommended by a physician. The procedure may violate religious or other deeply held beliefs; the patient's goals, fears and values may cause him or her to weigh the risks or benefits of a procedure differently than the physician; or the patient may not correctly understand the risks of failing to accept the recommendation. It is particularly this last group that informed refusal is intended to address.

Informed refusal arises from the fourth element of informed consent described in the informed consent section of this chapter. That is, part of informed consent that courts have recognized is the obligation to tell the patient the consequences of refusing the proposed treatment or alternatives. This obligation arises when the patient's refusal is such to put his or her health or life at some risk.

In some cases it is obvious that a patient's refusal of treatment requires attention and discussion. For example, a patient who says he/she will not accept the surgical removal of a possible melanoma may not appreciate fully the risks, and those risks must be explained.

In other cases, it may seem unlikely that the patient is not already aware of the risks, but even then the practitioner should emphasize, perhaps vividly, the risks. For example, in one case a woman refused a physician's recommendation that she have a Pap smear performed. The physician did not explain the risk that cancer could be detected at an early stage through the procedure. The woman later died of cancer that probably could have been detected at a curable stage if the Pap smear had been done as recommended. The court that considered this case held that the physician could be subject to liability for negligence. The court felt that the physician had breached a duty of care to the patient by failing to explain and emphasize the risk that the woman was running.

Documentation of informed refusal is important, but too often neglected. When a patient declines necessary treatment, it is wise practice to make a detailed note in the medical record. That note should not only describe the circumstances of the patient's refusal, but also specify the risks of refusal that the physician described. Where the risk is severe and the decision seems particularly unreasonable, the physician may want to send the patient a written document emphasizing the risk.

It is unusual for physicians to have patients sign 'informed refusal' forms. There are circumstances, however, where it is done. Patients who sign themselves out of a hospital against medical advice, of course, are often asked to sign forms that are essentially informed refusal forms.

As with informed consent generally, the process of obtaining informed refusal can serve a therapeutic function. It is an opportunity for the physician to open discussion of the reasons for refusal, and to consider unreasonable fears that the informed consent process may have engendered.

In some instances the nature of a patient's refusal may cause the physician to doubt the patient's competency. An incompetent patient can neither consent nor decline treatment, so if a patient is dangerously refusing treatment, the physician may need to consult with family members and the physician's attorney regarding the possibility of legal action to seek court-ordered treatment.

This discussion is not intended to suggest in any way that patients do not have a legal right to refuse treatment, even life-saving treatment. Competent patients do. For example, in most states a patient may refuse blood transfusions (e.g. for religious reasons) even though that will jeopardize the patient's life. Rather, it is essential that such refusal be informed, that the patient understand the consequences of the refusal.

CONCLUSION: A MATTER OF ATTITUDE

Informed consent and refusal are legal doctrines, but an exclusive focus on the legal standards is a mistake. The more important reason to be concerned about informed consent is that it is an important opportunity to expand the communication with patients and to help them become involved in making informed decisions about their own care. In turn this helps implement one of the most basic values of the medical profession and our society, patient autonomy.

BIBLIOGRAPHY

1. Byrne JA. *Informed Consent.* New York: McGraw-Hill, 1996
2. Grisso T, Applebaum PS. *Assessing Competence to Consent to Treatment: A Guide for Physicians and Other Health Professionals.* Oxford: Oxford University Press, 1997
3. Mazur DJ. *Medical Risk and the Right to an Informed Consent in Clinical Care and Clinical Research.* Tampa, FL: American College of Physician Executives, 1998
4. Switankowsky IS. *A New Paradigm for Informed Consent.* Lanham, MD: University Press of America, 1998
5. Tomes JP. *Informed Consent: A Guide for the Healthcare Professional.* Chicago: Healthcare Financial Management Association, 1993
6. Wear S. *Informed Consent: Patient Autonomy and Clinician Beneficence in Health Care.* Washington, DC: Georgetown University Press, 1998

4

Adult primary care

Keith T. Kanel, MD, FACP

Primary care refers to the community-based frontline medical services focused on the diagnosis of new problems, management of chronic medical conditions, preventative care and health maintenance. The bulk of these services are provided by specialists in internal medicine and family practice. Despite disparate training, the two specialties enjoy enormous overlap, and in most health-care systems practice side by side. General practitioners are the shrinking group of physicians whose training did not include board-sponsored residencies. Certified Registered Nurse Practitioners are advanced practice nurses with special skills in primary care, increasingly evident in physician practices and as providers in underserved areas.

THE PRIMARY CARE PHYSICIAN (PCP) MODEL

Throughout the 1970s, primary care was loosely defined as basic medical services offered by community practitioners. Physicians were reimbursed on a fee-for-service basis, and patients had nearly unlimited choice. Most selected generalists on the basis of convenience and familiarity, but were permitted to pursue second or specialist opinions freely. Duty was established only consequent to the first meeting.

As the physician work-force evolved towards advanced specialty care, the delivery of basic medical services became fragmented. The costs of specialists caring for basic problems, duplicated services, underutilized preventative care and unrestrained access to expensive new procedures prompted payors to look towards alternatives. Managed care promised to change this dynamic. In health maintenance organizations (HMOs), generalists were recast as 'gatekeepers', positioned as obligatory first-contacts for all health services. Access to specialty care required authorization by the gatekeeper. Patients and physicians retained free choice, but the expense of deviating from the least costly pathways was shifted back to the generalist (by decreasing capitation payments) or the patient (through out-of-pocket surcharges, or copayments).

From a risk management perspective, managed care has important implications. Patients, often with strong preconceptions of what they consider to be appropriate care, may view the mandatory involvement of a generalist as an obstacle. Consequently, the term 'gatekeeper' has been largely abandoned for the more innocuous 'primary care physician', or PCP. Patients may also be suspicious of prepaid plans which internally define a standard of care, and of physicians who are rewarded by limiting access to specialists. Although they have alternatives to managed care, the often prohibitive cost of going outside employer- or government-sponsored programs leaves some patients feeling trapped. Combined with the charged atmosphere created by illness in patients and families, these systems of managed health-care delivery may breed resentment.

In most primary care practices, only a portion of patients are in managed care plans. Nonetheless, physicians have been forced to retool their office systems to be competitive in this environment. The indirect effects of managed care should not be underestimated.

RISK MANAGEMENT AND PRIMARY CARE

One-quarter of all malpractice claims are filed against primary care doctors, more than any other specialty (Table 1). This information was drawn from the Physician Insurers Association of America[1], which compiles

Table 1   Malpractice claims in major medical specialties, cumulative data from 1 January 1985 to 31 December 1998. Data from reference 1, with permission

Specialty	Closed claims (n)
Adult primary care*	36 308
Obstetrics and gynecology	20 725
General surgery	16 195
Orthopedic surgery	14 979
Radiology	7 758
Plastic surgery	5 703
Anesthesiology	5 640
Pediatrics	4 558
Ophthalmology	4 322
Cardiovascular and thoracic surgery	4 021
Urological surgery	3 648
Neurosurgery	3 531

*Combined data from internal medicine (19 274) and family and general practice (17 034)

claims data from 21 physician-owned medical malpractice companies nation-wide (covering over 95 000 private practice physicians). The large number of claims reflects both the prevalence of primary care and increasing legal exposure.

Why patients file claims

Reasonable patients understand that medical care does not come with guarantees. Indeed, most who suffer bad outcomes do not file lawsuits[2]. Claims arise when patients are disappointed and frustrated that their treatment outcome fell well short of expectations. Incompetent care may be justifiably identified in this way. More often, competent care is faulted when patients had unrealistic expectations.

The human element cannot be underestimated. A malpractice claim is an expression of anger, and often stems from flawed doctor–patient relationships and communications. PCPs who effectively prepare their patients for suboptimal outcomes through effective communication are far less likely to be sued[2,3]. Other issues that irritate patients – administrative errors, rudeness of support staff, denials of unreasonable requests for tests and referrals – promote litigious behavior.

Malpractice issues against primary care physicians

Focus areas in primary care risk management are borne out by analyzing the nature of claims (Table 2). 'Error in diagnosis' is the most frequent allegation, reflecting traditional roles in the frontline evaluation of new medical problems, and in implementing screening of asymptomatic adults. Issues related to ongoing management of chronic medical problems breed charges of 'failure to supervise or monitor care', 'medication error' and 'failure/delay in referral or consultation'. Injury from 'improper

Table 2 Plaintiff claims of malpractice in adult primary care, cumulative data from 1 January 1985 to 31 December 1998. Data from reference 1, with permission

Nature of claim	n
Error in diagnosis	12 401
No medical misadventure	8 299
Improper performance of procedure	5 357
Failure to supervise or monitor care	3 439
Medication error	3 082
Procedure performed when not indicated or contraindicated	1 163
Failure/delay in referral or consultation	1 142

performance of procedure' relates to the physician's direct action, be it an interview or surgical operation.

Goals of risk management in primary care

The prime goal of risk management is to protect patients, to ensure that practitioners are competent and patient facilities are safe. A second goal is to minimize damage to physicians and practices from marginal or unwarranted lawsuits. Even frivolous claims extract a significant toll both emotionally and economically. The collection and analysis of claims data against PCPs help to identify weaknesses in their delivery systems, in the hope of offering a better service.

Outcomes of claims

Few malpractice claims ever go to trial. Table 3 gives the outcome of claims and suits filed through one Pennsylvania malpractice carrier. Over 90% of matters were settled out of court, most without loss payment. Of those that did proceed to trial, only one in five closed verdicts resulted in loss payment. Even without payment, the costs of litigation are fairly high. The average expenses for defending against a claim ranged up to $US40 000. Indemnity awards against internists in 1998 averaged $US262 511, with one of the largest payments of $US2 900 000[1]. All settled cases with payment over $US10 000 are reported to the National Practitioner Data Bank, a fact which may influence how PCPs are profiled in the future.

ERROR IN DIAGNOSIS

Patients newly diagnosed with significant medical conditions will almost always question whether the diagnosis should not have been made earlier, presuming that the treatment would be easier or the outcome better. 'Error in diagnosis' and 'delay in diagnosis' constitute 30% of claims

Table 3 Outcomes of claims and suits filed against primary care physicians. Data from Pennsylvania Medical Society Liability Insurance Company (PMSLIC): results of 3613 claims filed against internal medicine, family practice and general practice physicians from 1 January 1978 to 30 June 1998, with permission

Settled out of court, no loss payment	67%
Settled out of court, with loss payment	24%
Verdict, no loss payment	7%
Verdict, with loss payment	2%

Table 4 Ranked causes of 'error in diagnosis' claims in primary care, cumulative data from 1 January 1985 to 31 December 1998. Data from reference 1, with permission

Internal medicine

(1) Malignant neoplasms of the bronchus and lungs

(2) Acute myocardial infarction

(3) Malignant neoplasms of the colon and rectum

(4) Malignant neoplasms of the female breast

(5) Pulmonary embolism

General and family medicine

(1) Acute myocardial infarction

(2) Malignant neoplasms of the female breast

(3) Appendicitis

(4) Malignant neoplasms of the bronchus and lungs

(5) Malignant neoplasms of the colon and rectal region

against PCPs[1]. Such claims are widespread; in all medical specialties except anesthesia, they rank in the top five malpractice issues. The presenting medical conditions that most often lead to litigation in primary care are listed in Table 4.

Why diagnostic errors occur

Competent physicians will usually not miss obvious diagnoses, such as myocardial infarction in a middle-aged man with crushing substernal chest pain, or breast cancer in a postmenopausal woman with a new palpable mass. Diagnostic errors occur with atypical presentations, and in unlikely patients. One study of litigation in delayed diagnosis of cancer noted that plaintiffs presented *15 years younger* than patients with like tumors in the general population[4]. In unusual presentations, PCPs (and patients) may be so unconvinced that they elect to follow the complaint through an observation period. Occasionally, patients will be lost to follow-up, or perceive obstacles in coming back to the office (cancelled appointments, fear of hearing bad news, insurance problems, etc.). Abnormal test results can be lost or misfiled. An ensuing claim may then contend that the delay allowed the disease to progress to incurability, a conclusion not always scientifically correct[5,6].

Recommended adult screening standards may serve as valuable backups in preventing delayed diagnoses of certain diseases such as colon and breast cancer. However, this may create an added legal hazard for PCPs who do not rigorously follow those guidelines, either by disagreeing with them or through inadequate tracking. Unfortunately, universal screening standards do not exist for several high-claims diseases, such as coronary artery disease and lung cancer.

The 'big three': acute myocardial infarction, lung cancer and female breast cancer

The three diseases resulting in the most malpractice activity against PCPs are, in ranked order: acute myocardial infarction, lung cancer and female breast cancer (Table 4). They are not only statistically common, but they also result in sudden, profound and often irreversible changes in the lives of patients.

Acute myocardial infarction

Diagnostic delays of cancer are measured in months; for acute myocardial infarction (AMI), hours count. The standard of care for compelling chest pain is to refer to an emergency department, as thrombolytic therapy administered within 12 hours of onset may improve morbidity and mortality in acute coronary ischemia[7]. Less clear is how the PCP should handle out-of-hours telephone complaints of 'shortness of breath', 'shoulder pain', 'heartburn', 'nausea', etc. in patients at risk for heart problems. The PCP must decide whether to send the patient to the emergency department, or risk waiting until the office opens the next day. Adding pressure to the situation are insurance plans that adjust capitation downwards for 'inappropriate' emergency room referrals. Important points are:

(1) A pre-hospital electrocardiogram (ECG) is far more predictive of AMI than verbal symptoms[8], and should be obtained with any non-trivial chest complaint.

(2) The absence of chest pain does not preclude AMI; three-quarters of patients admitted with true coronary symptoms did not report that complaint[9].

(3) A history of a normal nuclear stress test significantly lessens the likelihood of a coronary event for no more than 24 months[10].

(4) Coronary chest pain in women is different. Women tend to wait longer before presenting and have more subtle ECG changes; nonetheless, their inpatient mortality is up to twice that of men[11].

Lung cancer

Lung cancer is currently the most prevalent and lethal of all cancers in the USA[12]. In women, it is 50% more common than breast cancer. Unfortunately, there are very few clues that permit diagnosis at a surgically curable stage, such as hemoptysis, dyspnea, chronic cough or persistent pneumonia. Moreover, there is no standard for chest X-ray population screening, even among smokers (although critics have raised concerns of methodological flaws in the studies cited in the 'no screen' approach[13]). Successful litigation against tobacco companies may draw attention to lung cancer as a risk management issue. Suggestions include:

(1) Persistent hemoptysis should never be ascribed to 'just bronchitis' in heavy smokers, even with normal chest X-rays[14,15]. PCPs should strongly consider sending patients for bronchoscopy.

(2) All smokers should be counseled on smoking cessation, and the encounter carefully documented in the record.

(3) Screening remains controversial. Some note that selective screening chest radiographs are indeed effective, and lead to a two- to three-fold increase in cure rate[16]. PCPs must also remain up to date with emerging screening strategies. New studies suggest cost-effectiveness of routine low-dose chest computerized tomography in heavy smokers[17].

Female breast cancer

All specialties combined, delayed diagnosis of breast cancer is among the top causes of malpractice litigation, and results in the largest indemnity payments. The most common reason for delay is that the examining physician was unconvinced by the clinical findings[5]. Some authors have pointed to the unfamiliarity of physicians with the atypical presentations of breast cancer (such as asymmetrical breast thickening, skin changes, nipple scaling and persistent discharge), and have successfully implemented PCP education programs[5,18]. The second most common reason is an over-reliance on diagnostic mammography in bringing the evaluation of breast complaints to a close. Up to one-third of claimants' mammograms in delayed diagnosis cases are normal[6], consistent with the false-negative rate of the test. It is notable that 50% of claims were initiated by women under the age of 40, although the incidence of the disease in this group is only 7%[5]. To limit risk:

(1) Any asymmetrical abnormality noted on examination or by the patient should always be taken seriously. PCPs often obtain a diagnostic mammogram and/or ultrasound scan, but a referral to a breast surgeon should be considered even if results from those studies are negative.

(2) Non-specific mammographic findings are often scheduled for a repeat view, generally after a few months. Although this is scientifically reasonable based on the biology of breast cancer[5,6], patients uncomfortable with this strategy should be given the option of specialty referral. When observation of a finding is planned, the PCP should maintain a 'tickler' file to ensure follow-up.

(3) Communication is essential. Screening mammography is variably ordered by either gynecologists or PCPs. Many mammography centers issue reports to both parties at the patient's request. Ultimately, it is the patient who must be informed. The Mammography Quality Standards Act of 1998 ensures that all patients receive a written notice, including steps to take for positive findings.

'NO MEDICAL MISADVENTURE'

'No medical misadventure' relates to claims filed against PCPs not alleging direct *clinical* negligence, but rather an ethical, legal or administrative lapse. Approximately 80% of claims are deemed frivolous, as when a referring PCP is enjoined as an 'innocent bystander' in a suit against a surgeon. The remainder include: vicarious liability (7% of all claims against PCPs), improper conduct by the physician (2%), consent issues (2%), billing and collection (2%), problems with records (1%) and breach of confidentiality (1%)[1].

Vicarious liability ('imputed negligence')

PCPs will often work together to maximize efficiency, setting up rotations of overnight and weekend 'call', covering each other's urgent office visits, and designating 'rounders' or hospitalists who handle in-patient care. Generally, such activities are limited to the partners in a group practice. At times, different groups may work together, not uncommon in integrated health systems or academic centers. It is not known whether adverse medical events increase when generalists participate in such arrangements; concerns have been documented when complex cross-coverage models have been used in residency programs[19].

These relationships carry vicarious liability, in which case the physician may be responsible for the negligent acts of a stand-in. Trust, common standards of excellence and highly effective communication are critical. Physicians should consequently not enter into such relationships without complete confidence. It should be noted that a PCP cannot be held responsible for malpractice of a consultant, only a surrogate. Misadventure by a nurse practitioner or physician assistant, however, does create liability for the supervising physician.

Lack of informed consent

Informed consent is the patient's permission to proceed with a treatment plan following a formal discussion of the desired outcome, alternatives and risks. This discussion, including an assessment of the patient's understanding, should be documented in the chart. Although state statutes vary, written informed consent is usually required only for surgical procedures, chemotherapy, radiation therapy, blood transfusion and experimental treatment. Many states also require written consent for human immunodeficiency virus (HIV)-related testing.

A study of informed consent discussions in primary care found them often to be abbreviated and incomplete, especially when several issues are covered in the course of a 15-minute 'return' office visit[20]. Creative use of pamphlets, videotapes and other materials may be useful. Efforts to improve informed consent should be viewed not simply as a risk management issue, but also as a way to improve patient satisfaction and outcome.

Breach of confidentiality

Any information obtained in the context of the doctor–patient relationship should be deemed confidential. The fact that a patient is in a PCP practice should not be divulged, even in casual conversation. Records should not be released to any agency without a written authorization (a 'consent to disclosure') signed by the patient for each request. Improper handling of medical records is the leading malpractice issue related to confidentiality.

PCPs must understand the concept of 'privilege'. This asserts that a certain portion of records may be withheld from release, particularly if it recounts personal communications or might harm ongoing treatment[21]. State laws are specific on this point, and should be reviewed. Similarly, records related to mental health, substance abuse and HIV care should not be released without special permission. Findings of other physicians in the patient's chart should be included in any request for records.

Table 5   Action prompting malpractice claims against primary care physicians, cumulative data from 1 January 1985 to 31 December 1998. Data from reference 1, with permission

Service	Internal medicine	Family and general practice
Interview, evaluation or consultation	8556	6572
Prescription of medication	3213	2708
Physical examination	1729	1263
Injections and vaccinations	969	558
No care rendered	830	733
Procedures involving cardiac and circulatory function	775	—*
Radiological procedures	565	578
Diagnostic procedures of the large intestine	446	—*
Operative procedures on skin	—*	434
Orthopedic procedures	—*	246

*Procedure not listed among ten most prevalent procedures for this specialty

IMPROPER PERFORMANCE

Injury related to 'improper performance' of medical procedures is one of the most traditional malpractice charges, and the top risk management issue in virtually all of the surgical specialties. In primary care, the 'procedures' most often cited in claims are the medical interview (48%), the writing of prescriptions (19%) and the physical examination (9%) (Table 5). Examples of improper performance might include failure to: take a complete past medical history, enquire about allergies, examine a painful body part or ask about drug reactions.

PCPs often worry about the malpractice risk of minimally invasive office procedures, e.g. flexible sigmoidoscopy, skin biopsy, exercise treadmill testing and uncontrasted radiographic studies. Only 12% of improper performance claims are related to these studies[1]. Nonetheless, PCPs who plan to offer them should be prepared to furnish evidence of competency, either certification from a training course, or a letter of tutelage from a specialist.

FAILURE TO SUPERVISE OR MONITOR CARE

The standard of care for many chronic conditions involves checking specific markers at fixed intervals, for example monthly prothrombin times in warfarin therapy, or quarterly glycosylated hemoglobin levels in diabetes mellitus. Standards are often delineated in clinical practice guidelines (see below). Other diseases demand regular re-evaluations dependent upon stability. The PCP is responsible for establishing follow-up for each patient, judging the ability to comply and pursuing appointments not kept. Computerized scheduling systems and front-office follow-up protocols are useful.

FAILURE/DELAY IN CONSULTATION OR REFERRAL

PCPs must be keenly aware of their own personal limitations in managing cases, and issue out-patient referrals and in-patient consultations to specialists appropriately. This is particularly pertinent in diseases where a rapidly changing standard of care has resulted in demonstrable differences in generalist and subspecialist care, such as acute myocardial infarction, stroke and asthma[22]. Differences may relate more to an individual PCP's clinical experience than a limitation of the field[23]. Informal 'curbside consultations' with specialists are common, but are insufficient substitutes[24].

FUTURE ISSUES

New models of managed care

The effects of HMOs are not always welcome. Competitive pricing may lead to unexpected changes in preferred drug formularies, out-patient therapies and specialist panels. Even the doctor–patient relationship can be disrupted; an Ohio study found that 25% of patients were forced to select new PCPs over a 2-year period due to changes in their employer-based insurance plans[25]. HMOs may also ask PCPs to shoulder too much of the responsibility of cost control. A recent survey of 7000 PCPs showed that one in four felt the scope of care they were expected to offer was inappropriate[26].

Some managed care organizations have consequently begun moving away from the rigid 'gatekeeper' model to more flexible 'point-of-service' plans. Further redesign of primary care with PCPs as 'co-ordinators' rather than 'gatekeepers' may improve satisfaction and quality[27], and reduce some of the tension that had been added to the doctor–patient relationship.

Will clinical practice guidelines be the new standard of care?

Key in medical negligence claims is the allegation that the standard of acceptable care has been breached. The 'standard of care' is viewed as that which a 'reasonable physician' would do in similar circumstances, and must take into account the present state of medical knowledge, local resources, patient preferences, etc. In litigation, the standard is ultimately established by expert testimony in court.

Clinical practice guidelines (CPGs) are documents that attempt to define 'best practice' parameters for important medical issues. They are fairly recent additions to the medical literature, usually assembled by expert panels who distill precedent, research, outcome data and opinion into a cogent set of recommendations. Some of the more widely used guidelines in primary care are given in Table 6. One study of guidelines between 1985 and 1997 found 279 documents in the medical literature[28]. Because of the rapid rate at which they are appearing, the Federal Agency for Health Care Policy and Research has established a website (www.guideline.gov), anticipating a library of over 3500 documents during the next 5 years.

Will CPGs be accepted as legal standards of care? At this time it appears unlikely. Guidelines played a significant role in fewer that 7% of malpractice cases as of 1995[29]. Concerns have been raised regarding oversimplification of complex clinical issues in attempts to keep documents concise and palatable[28]. Important barriers have also been identified which hinder the adoption of cursory recommendations by practitioners[30]. CPGs should be regarded as tools to help physicians provide better care, tempered by sensible discretion. From a legal standpoint, it is expected that they may be viewed as 'evidence of accepted and customary care, but they cannot be introduced as a substitute for expert testimony'[31].

Non-physician primary care providers

Certified Registered Nurse Practitioners (CRNPs) are increasingly being recognized as primary care providers, particularly by Medicare. These individuals hold at minimum an Associate's degree in nursing, and have completed 1–2 years of training in an accredited CRNP program. In most primary care settings they practice alongside physicians; however, in 22 states they may see patients independently, and have prescriptive authority in 46 states.

Will risk management issues in CRNP practices differ from those of physicians? Data are limited. In a New York City study, an independent CRNP practice demonstrated short-term outcomes in the management of stable chronic diseases that were comparable to those in surrounding physician practices[32]. Effectiveness in caring for unstable patients or in the performance of procedures was not examined. As misadventures of the CRNP may create a liability issue for the supervising physician, the roles of these extenders must be expanded cautiously.

Table 6 Commonly used clinical practice guidelines in primary care

Disease	Guideline	Issuing Organization	Date of last update
Hypertension	Sixth report of the Joint National Committee on Prevention, Detection, Evaluation, and Treatment of High Blood pressure (*Hypertension* 1994;23:275–85)	National Institutes of Health	1997
Hypercholesterolemia	Second report of the Expert Panel on Detection, Evaluation, and Treatment of High Blood Cholesterol in Adults (*Circulation* 1994;89:1333–445)	National Institutes of Health	1998
Diabetes	Report of the Expert Committee on the Diagnosis and Classification of Diabetes Mellitus (*Diabetes Care* 1999;22(Suppl 1):S5–19)	American Diabetes Association	1998
Heart failure	Guidelines for the evaluation and management of heart failure: report of the American College of Cardiology/American Heart Association Task Force on Practice Guidelines (*J Am Coll Cardiol* 1995;26:1376–98)	American College of Cardiology/American Heart Association	1995
Pneumonia	Community-acquired pneumonia in adults: guidelines for management (*Clin Infect Dis* 1998;26:811–38)	Infectious Diseases Society of America	1998
Myocardial infarction	1999 update: ACC/AHA guidelines for the management of patients with acute myocardial infarction (*J Am Coll Cardiol* 1999;34:890–911)	American College of Cardiology/American Heart Association	1999

3. Levinson W, Roter D, Mullooly JP, *et al.* Physician–patient communication: the relationship with malpractice claims among primary-care physicians and surgeons. *J Am Med Assoc* 1997;227:558–9

4. Kern KA. Medicolegal analysis of the delayed diagnosis of cancer in 338 cases in the United States. *Arch Surg* 1994;129:397–403

5. Osuch JR, Bonham VL. The timely diagnosis of breast cancer: principles of risk management for primary care providers and surgeons. *Cancer* 1994;74(Suppl 1): 271–8

6. Tartter PI, Pace D, Frost JD, Bernstein JL. Delay in diagnosis of breast cancer. *Ann Surg* 1999;229:91–6

7. American College of Cardiology/American Heart Association. 1999 Update: ACC/AHA guidelines for the management of patients with acute myocardial infarction. *J Am Coll Cardiol* 1999;34:890–911

8. Grijseels WM, Deckers JW, Hoest AW, *et al.* Implementation of a pre-hospital decision rule in general practice; triage of patients with suspected myocardial infarction. *Eur Heart J* 1996;17:89–95

9. Burt CW. Summary statistics for acute cardiac ischemia and chest pain visits to United States EDs, 1995–1996. *Am J Emerg Med* 1999;17:552–9

10. Gal R, Gunasekera J, Massardo T, *et al.* Long-term prognostic value of a normal dipyridamole thallium-201 perfusion scan. *Clin Cardiol* 1991;14:971–4

11. Vaccarino V, Parsons L, Every NR, *et al.* Sex-based differences in early mortality after myocardial infarction. *N Engl J Med* 1999;341:217–25

12. Landis SH, Murray T, Solden S, *et al.* Cancer statistics, 1999. *CA Cancer J Clin* 1999;49:8–31

13. Smith IE. Screening for lung cancer: time to think positive. *Lancet* 1999;354:86

14. O'Neil KM, Lazarus AA. Hemoptysis. Indications for bronchoscopy. *Arch Intern Med* 1991;151:171–4

15. Santiago S, Tobias J, Williams AJ. A reappraisal of the causes of hemoptysis. *Arch Intern Med* 1991;151:2449–51

16. Strauss GM. Screening for lung cancer. *Surg Oncol Clin North Am* 1999;8:747–74

17. Henschke CI, McCauley DI, Yankelevitz DF, *et al.* Early lung cancer action project: overall design and findings from baseline screening. *Lancet* 1999;354:99–105

18. Bartlett EE, Holman KI. Reducing malpractice risk and increasing quality in managed care. *Manage Care Interface* 1998;11:68–72

19. Petersen LA, Brenan TA, O'Neil AC, *et al.* Does housestaff discontinuity of care increase the risk for preventable adverse events? *Ann Intern Med* 1994;121:866–72

20. Braddock CH, Edwards KA, Hasenberg NM, *et al.* Informed decision making in outpatient practice: time to get back to basics. *J Am Med Assoc* 1999;282:2313–20

21. Griffith RA, Schneider DC. Safeguarding the confidentiality of medical and mental health records. *Med Staff Counsel* 1991;5:31–7

22. Harrold LR, Field TS, Gurwitz JH. Knowledge, patterns of care and outcomes of care for generalists and specialists. *J Gen Intern Med* 1999;14:499–511

23. Kitahata MM, Koepsell TD, Deyo RA, *et al.* Physicians' experience with the acquired immunodeficiency syndrome as a factor in patients' survival. *N Engl J Med* 1996; 334:701–6

24. Kuo D, Gifford DR, Stein MD. Curbside consultation practices and attitudes among primary care physicians and medical subspecialists. *J Am Med Assoc* 1998;280:905-9

25. Flocke SA, Stange KC, Zyzanski SJ. The impact of insurance type and forced discontinuity on the delivery of primary care. *J Fam Pract* 1997;45:129-35

26. St Peter RF, Reed MC, Kemper P, Blumenthal D. Changes in the scope of care provided by primary care physicians. *N Engl J Med* 1999;341:1980-5

27. Bodenheimer T, Lo B, Casalino L. Primary care physicians should be coordinators, not gatekeepers. *J Am Med Assoc* 1999;281:2045-9

28. Shaneyfelt TM, Mayo-Smith MF, Rothwangl J. Are guidelines following guidelines? *J Am Med Assoc* 1999;281:1900-5

29. Hyams AL, Brandenburg JA, Lipsitz SR, *et al*. Practice guidelines and malpractice litigation: a two way street. *Ann Intern Med* 1995;122:450-5

30. Cabana MD, Rand CS, Powe NR, *et al*. Why don't physicians follow clinical guidelines? *J Am Med Assoc* 1999;282:1458-65

31. Hurwitz B. Legal and political considerations of clinical practice guidelines. *Br Med J* 1999;318:661-4

32. Mundinger MO, Kane RL, Lenz ER, *et al*. Primary care outcomes in patients treated by nurse practitioners or physicians: a randomized trial. *J Am Med Assoc* 2000; 283:59-68

33. Brown JB, Boles M, Mullooly JP, Levinson W. Effect of clinician communication skills training on patient satisfaction: a randomized, controlled trial. *Ann Intern Med* 1999;131:822-9

34. Radecki SE, Neville RE, Girard RA. Telephone patient management by primary care physicians. *Med Care* 1989;27:817

35. Rich EC, Kralewski J, Feldman R, *et al*. Variations in the management of primary care: effect on cost in an HMO network. *Arch Intern Med* 1998;158:2363-71

36. Adamson TE, Tschann JM, Gullion DS, *et al*. Physician communication skills: a complex relationship. *West J Med* 1989;159:356-60

37. Bursztajn HJ, Brodsky A. A new resource for managing malpractice risks in managed care. *Arch Intern Med* 1996;156:2057-63

5

Pediatrics

Stephen P. Wright, MD

While usually thought of as a low-risk specialty, pediatrics is not without its own liability. Indeed, all primary care physicians are seeing an increasing trend of lawsuits as well as increases in rates of medical malpractice claims that are exceeding those of specialists. While payments in excess of $US100 000 constitute 32% of all claims paid, they also represent 83% of total indemnity[1]. Pediatrics ranked eighth in a list of specialties liable for payments of $US100 000 or more compiled by the Physician Insurers Association of America (PIAA). However, if one looks at average indemnities, pediatrics ranks second. Numerous factors may be responsible for this disturbing trend (Table 1).

WHAT IS THE SCOPE OF PEDIATRIC CLAIMS?

Most claims in pediatrics allege a significant departure from standard of care. This commonly encompasses errors or delays in diagnosis and improper prescriptions, consultations or evaluations. The most common diagnoses include: appendicitis, cerebral palsy, and other types of 'brain damage' and meningitis. Not surprisingly, 95% of claims arise from events occurring in hospitals (70%) and physician offices (25%)[1].

The increased penetration of managed care (i.e. capitation) inherently changes the doctor–patient relationship. Under capitation, the physician is rewarded in monetary terms for withholding diagnostic procedures and/or

Table 1 Factors responsible for increasing malpractice risk

Managed care
Gatekeeper concept
Erosion of doctor–patient relationship
Heightened expectations
Informed consent errors
Poor communication

treatment. The fewer tests that are ordered, the fewer prescriptions written, the fewer patients hospitalized, the more that goes into the kitty. This changed relationship, *per se*, makes the physician more vulnerable if an adverse outcome results.

WHAT SHOULD PEDIATRICIANS DO TO PROTECT THEMSELVES?[2]

First of all, you should practice quality medicine (Table 2). While capitation results in vulnerability from underutilization of resources, fee-for-service physicians can become greedy and do too much just to pad their pocket-book. Neither approach is honest, honorable or ethical. You will reduce your liability under any type of medical-care delivery system if decisions are based on sound medical principles.

Second, be selective about the managed care plans you join. While most physicians closely scrutinize contracts for reimbursement issues, many forget about other hidden pitfalls. Is it physician- as well as patient-friendly? Is the plan willing to resolve complaints in a friendly and timely manner? What happens and who is liable if the plan denies services and a patient injury results? You may be, if you do not protest loudly enough in support of sound medical judgement. In a 1986 California Appellate Court decision (Wickling *vs.* California), the Court ruled that 'the physician who complies without protest with limitations imposed by a third party payor, when his medical judgment dictates otherwise, cannot avoid ultimate responsibility for his patients' care'.

Many malpractice carriers deny coverage in a gatekeeper format. Study contracts closely for gatekeeper responsibilities and avoid them if at all possible. Always check with your malpractice carrier before signing any type of agreement.

Table 2 General prophylactic principles

Practice quality pediatrics
Base decisions on sound medical principles
Avoid gatekeeper responsibilities
Have your attorney and carrier review all contracts
Beware of hold-harmless clauses
Avoid medication errors
Be alert to non-medical risks
Do not alter patient records
Communicate, communicate, communicate
Document, document, document

Getting into a plan is one thing, getting out is another. Be particularly attentive to the exit procedures of any plan you join. Since you have a professional obligation to all patients in your practice, be particularly careful in notifying patients of your intention to withdraw from their plans. You must continue their treatment and give them a reasonable period of time to find another physician. Usually, a certified, return-receipt-requested letter sent a month in advance should be sufficient.

Also, be aware of hold-harmless clauses. Many carriers specifically exclude coverage. Under these circumstances you agree to assume all liability and cost in malpractice cases against you. Also, some plans require you to hold them harmless from *their* denial of benefit decisions.

MEDICATION ERRORS

Errors in prescribing or administering medications are another frequent and expensive category of claims[3]. This is unfortunate since most prescribing errors are preventable. They do not generally have an obscure cause. Table 3 lists the top five medication errors that represent nearly half of all errors in this category.

Prescription of incorrect doses is the leading cause of lawsuits that involve medication errors. Overdosing and underdosing can both be a problem. Obviously, when prescribing unfamiliar or infrequently prescribed drugs, be certain to consult appropriate references for correct dosing, indications and drug interactions.

Most pediatric drug errors involve antibiotics, steroids, non-steroidal anti-inflammatories and anticonvulsants. Be certain that your patients are not allergic to any prescribed drugs. It might be wise to specifically mention the above general categories. Also, document allergies in a highly visible and consistent place in the patient's chart.

Be attentive to patient complaints especially if a patient is on long-term medication. It could just be that the complaint is a harbinger of some unrecognized side-effect of the medication.

Take pains to inform the patient about the risk involved with the medications they will be taking. Many pharmaceutical companies have preprinted

Table 3 Top five medication errors

Incorrect dosage
Medication inappropriate for diagnosis
Failure to recognize or monitor side-effects
Failure to communicate properly and obtain informed consent
Failure to monitor drug levels

hand-outs available. Also consider developing your own hand-outs, either within your own office or in consultation with your local pharmacist.

Your best protection is to write down in the chart the dose prescribed, and the fact that you asked about allergies, that you discussed side-effects and alternatives, and that the patient received a copy of your written instructions. In addition, use a medication flow-sheet. This can give you a 'quick look' at the patient's medical history and can tip you off about problems, such as inappropriate refills or possible drug interactions.

NON-MEDICAL CAUSES

There are a number of non-medical reasons that can lead you into the litigation abyss. Your own life-style can serve as a catalyst. Flaunting expensive cars, houses, clothing and vacations can lead to jealousy, ill-will and an 'I'm-going-to-get-a-piece-of-success' mentality. Do not give any attorney or potential plaintiff (i.e. your patients) a reason to covet your home.

Also, look out for office hazards: loose carpet or tiling, a projecting counter top, a door that closes too harshly (watch those little fingers). Stay alert for hazards and, when identified, take care of them promptly. Encourage your office staff to do the same. Crawl around on the floor to see possible hazards from your patients' perspective. Periodically, review your liability contracts to be certain you have enough and the appropriate coverage for this type of liability[5].

EMPLOYEE ERRORS

Employee errors are one other type of office hazard that can make you vulnerable to damages[6]. Selection of qualified employees goes without saying. Screen for professional as well as personal qualities. Very few patients/ parents question the professional credentials of their physician or their physician's staff. They assume that you are qualified. Offensive, curt, rude or uncaring behavior will often get you into more trouble than lack of professional qualifications. Hire professionals who possess good 'people' skills and who can empathize with your families. This means that you need employees who have walked in your patients' shoes. In other words, hire people who are parents if at all possible. Their own experience will enable them to understand your patients' problems more readily. Also, heed the warnings listed in Table 4.

Your own 'people' skills can also be an important buffer against litigious patients. Being a medically or technically sound doctor is just not good enough. What can you do to improve along these lines? First of all, do not be in a hurry or at least do not appear to be. Sit down beside the examining table to take your history or discuss the current problem. Just the act of sitting will make your time with the patient *seem* longer. Call the patient by name and call the parents by name; this helps to personalize their visit. Make notes in the margins of the chart to remind you of personal tidbits. Referring to these on subsequent visits will make you look like a genius with a memory of an elephant. Do not panic when a parent pulls out a list. Patients whose questions are answered are much more satisfied and compliant with your care. Call parents at home to check on their child or baby. They will be impressed by your interest.

Just as 'location, location, location' is the key to a successful business, *'communication, communication, communication'* is the corner-stone of a successful liability strategy. Many lawsuits are generated as a result of poor communication, and many lawsuits are lost for the same reason.

How should you communicate? First of all, talk to, not down to, your patients and their parents. You would be surprised how many physicians do not actually tell their patients much at all. Make a point to let them know the following:

(1) What is wrong with their child;

(2) What you recommend they do to solve the problem;

(3) How long it should be before they see improvement if they follow your suggestions;

(4) What to do if improvement does not occur within the anticipated time-frame.

Written instructions are another important source of communication. Develop written patient-information hand-outs that cover the gamut of problems you are likely to encounter. Include both common and uncommon conditions: you can be sued just as easily dealing with either.

Consider the use of videos to supplement the education of your patients. This is an easy way to deliver valuable information in a relatively low-cost,

Table 4 Non-clinical caveats

Do not employ heavy-handed collection procedures
Do not allow clinical staff to administer medication without your approval
Require your signature to be on all test results before filing in charts
Document all patient contacts
Require your approval for all prescriptions and/or prescription refills
Do not allow untrained or unqualified personnel to give medical advice

time-saving manner. Subjects covered by videos can range from preventative care to developmental issues to procedural issues to disease issues. Professionally made videos should be screened for content to make sure that you agree with what is being said. Videos made by the American Academy of Pediatrics or other specialty society are another good source. Consider making your own. Patients would rather see and hear from you than from some unknown actor. They will appreciate the information and, besides, videos can serve as a good time-filler if you are running a little behind. The more that patients understand the risks and complications of their illness, treatment or procedure, the less likely they are to sue if a bad outcome results.

Remember, too, that communication is a two-way street. Do not lecture to the patient and then walk out of the room. Give the parent the opportunity to ask questions and express opinions. They will feel more a part of the decision-making process. 'Ownership' will result in less tendency to sue.

Unfortunately, communication by itself is not enough. It is equally important that you document what you have communicated, and that the patient or parent understands that communication. Remember, in a court of law, if you did not write it down, it did not happen. Also, remember to document a patient's refusal to follow your sound medical advice, and that you have advised the patient or the parent of the risks of refusal. Follow this documentation with a registered, return-receipt-requested letter that also warns of the potential risk[8].

WHAT SHOULD YOU DO IF YOU ARE SUED OR THREATENED WITH A LAWSUIT?[9-11]

First of all, do not panic. Bad outcomes are not always a result of bad care. If you have delivered standard care, communicated properly and documented appropriately, your liability will be minimal.

Whatever happens, *do not, ever, alter a patient record*. Doing so will only doom your defense to failure. You will not make a positive impression on the judge or jury. 'Doctoring' a record will at least cause them to ask 'if he did nothing wrong, why did he alter the record?' What is worse, courts have ruled that alteration of medical records shows an abject disregard for the law, and actual malice. *Just say 'no' if you get the urge to 'improve' a patient's record*.

Second, if sued, notify your malpractice carrier promptly. Some contracts require timely and early notification, so a delay could jeopardize your coverage. Also, consider retaining your own attorney to review the case rather than relying on the one provided by your malpractice carrier. Conflicts of interest can arise between you, other codefendants and the malpractice carrier. Write a letter to the involved parties (attorney, carrier and hospital) asking about any potential conflict of interest. This will force them to address the issue and make better decisions on your behalf, as well as give you some ammunition should problems arise in this area later.

Third, talk and correspond to no one other than your attorney about the case, and by all means co-operate with your attorney. Remember, you are not a litigation expert, the attorney is. You will not be on your own turf when the battle is fought, but on extremely unfamiliar ground where others will be in control. Become as familiar as you can with the legal system, be thoroughly involved in all aspects of your case, and learn all that you can regarding the medical issues. Research the literature, know your opponents and show respect for the system, the judge, the jurors and, yes, even your accusers. Give answers in plain English and educate the jurors, but do not talk down to them. Remember the 'three Bs': be professional, be clear and be yourself.

SUMMARY

The threat of malpractice accusation hangs over all clinicians. However, the simple measures outlined above, if employed consistently, will minimize risks. If you are sued, do not give up and 'jump ship'. Your life is not over. Learn to play the game, and in all likelihood you will prevail. If you do lose a case, remember, you will be joining the ranks of many excellent physicians. Also, remember to *'communicate, communicate, communicate'*, and *'document, document, document'*.

REFERENCES

1. Holoweika M. What are your greatest malpractice risks? *Med Econ* 3 August 1992: 141–59
2. Karp D. Avoiding managed care's liability risks. *Med Econ* 25 April 1994:68–72
3. Crane M. The medication errors that get doctors sued. *Med Econ* 22 November 1993:36–41
4. Porter W. Big houses can bring big trouble for doctors. *Med Econ* 4 May 1992:74–6
5. Horsley J. The liability most doctors overlook. *Med Econ* 27 September 1993:86–91
6. Karp D. Are these malpractice bombs ticking in your office? *Med Econ* 17 August 1992:128–35
7. Vander Veer J Jr. Pleasing patients: it's the little things that count. *Med Econ* 24 June 1996:177–80

8. Azevedo D. The courts warn: make sure you're telling patients enough. *Med Econ* 6 July 1992:55–70

9. Fisher D. How to win a malpractice suit. *Med Econ* 14 October 1996:52–60

10. Burg B. Malpractice – doctors' six fatal mistakes. *Med Econ* 12 February 1996: 226–36

11. Griffith J. Why defensible malpractice cases have to be settled. *Med Econ* 10 July 1995:153–8

6

Child sexual abuse

David Muram, MD

INTRODUCTION

Child sexual abuse is defined as:

'Contact or interaction between a child and an adult, when the child is being used for the sexual stimulation of that adult or another person. Sexual abuse may also be committed by another minor, when that person is either significantly older than the victim, or when the abuser is in a position of power or control over that child.'

The National Center on Child Abuse and Neglect (NCCAN) estimates the number of child-victims to be more than 200 000 per year. Most states now have laws that require physicians to report to a child protective agency all children suspected to be victims of abuse.

THE MEDICAL EVALUATION

History

As many victims of abuse may not exhibit physical findings typical of abuse, the history is a key piece of information needed to establish the diagnosis of sexual abuse. The questions must be open-ended and not leading. For example, it is preferable to ask a question such as 'Why are you here?' than 'Who hurt you?' The information should be recorded carefully using the victim's own words and not changed into adult terminology. An outline of the information needed is detailed in Table 1. Although a detailed history is desirable, the patient should not be made to repeat the story over and over again. In order to overcome deficiencies that arise from the limited verbal skills of the young victims, other interviewing techniques, such as play-interviews and anatomically detailed dolls, have been developed, but these techniques should be used only by expert interviewers. Sometimes it

Table 1 Obtaining a history from child victims of sexual abuse

General
Provide a comfortable environment
Language and technique should be developmentally appropriate
Allow sufficient time to avoid any coercive nature of the interview
Establish rapport with the child

Questioning
Initial questions should be non-directive to elicit spontaneous responses
Leading questions should be avoided; if used, responses to these questions should be
    carefully evaluated
Non-verbal tools, e.g. anatomically detailed dolls, drawings, may be used to assist the
    child in communication
Anatomically detailed dolls should be used primarily for the identification of body
    parts and clarification of previous statements
Psychological testing is not required for the purpose of proving sexual assault
At some point, the child should be questioned directly about the abusive relationship

is impossible to obtain a history from the child, and the physician is compelled to accept an account of the incident from relatives, police-officers, neighbors and other children. Throughout the encounter with the child, the physician should be aware of signs and symptoms commonly associated with child abuse, e.g. night terrors, change in sleeping habits, clinging behavior. The examiner should note the child's composure, behavior and mental state, as well as the child's interaction with her parents and other persons (Table 2).

The physical examination

Most children can be fully evaluated in an office setting. Young children (≤ 5 years) may become apprehensive when placed on the examination table, and placing them on the mother's lap may reduce their anxiety. The mother is asked to support the child's legs, permitting an unimpaired view of the genital area. Older children are asked to lie on the examination table, but the use of stirrups is generally not necessary. The patient is asked to flex her knees and abduct her legs, and support them by placing her hands on the dorsal aspects of the lower thighs. Following a general physical examination, the examiner exposes the vulva and vestibule by exerting light lateral and downward pressure on each side of the perineum. When exposure of the vaginal walls is necessary, the labia may be grasped between the examiner's thumb and forefinger and pulled forward, downward and sideways. The valsalva maneuver and the knee–chest position can be used in some patients to visualize better the lower vaginal walls.

Table 2 Non-specific symptoms seen in child victims of sexual abuse

Behavioral
Anxiety, fearfulness
Sleep disturbances
Withdrawal
Somatic complaints
Increased sex play
Inappropriate sexual behavior
School problems
Acting-out behaviors
Self-destructive behaviors
Depression, low self-esteem
Physical
Unexplained vaginal injuries
Unexplained vaginal bleeding
Bruising, bites, scratches
Pregnancy
Sexually transmitted diseases
Recurrent vaginal infections
Pain in the anal or genital area
Recurrent atypical abdominal pain

The use of magnifying devices to enhance anogenital findings is well accepted. The colposcope now appears to be the instrument of choice for the examination of child victims of sexual abuse. Colposcopy allows a detailed magnified inspection of the vulva to search for physical signs of abuse which may have escaped detection by unaided examination.

With most children the physical findings are less dramatic, or absent altogether. Some forms of abuse do not cause injury, and an examination is not expected to detect any physical evidence of abuse. Even when injured, many of these children may not be seen for weeks, months or even years after the incident occurred. However, when an acute injury is present, an examination under general anesthesia may be required for evaluation and repair.

Abnormal physical findings

The physical findings in most children are subtle or absent altogether. Some forms of abuse do not cause injury and an examination is not expected to detect any physical evidence of abuse. It has been shown that even in girls where sexual abuse has been documented, the medical evaluation fails to document specific findings in 50% of victims. There are no well-defined criteria or accepted terminology by which to classify physical

Table 3   The medical evaluation: classification of abnormal findings

Category		Abnormalities
Category 1	normal examination	no abnormalities detected
		variations of normal
Category 2	non-specific abnormalities	redness, irritation, abrasions
		friability of the posterior fourchette
		labial adhesions, hymeneal tags,
		hymeneal bumps and clefts
		non-specific infections
		bruising of the external genitalia
Category 3	suggestive of abuse	hymeneal–vaginal tear
		hymeneal–perineal tear
		sexually transmitted disease
		bite marks on the genitalia
Category 4	definitive abnormalities	presence of sperm
		pregnancy in an adolescent

findings of sexual abuse. Regardless of the classification one may use, all findings may be classified into one of four categories listed in Table 3.

Anal abuse is a common form of sexual assault against children, especially in male victims. Many victims of anal assault do not sustain significant physical injuries because the anal sphincter and anal canal are capable of dilatation. Penetration, even by an adult male penis, may occur without significant injury. Many victims are brought for an examination weeks, months or even years after the abuse occurred. By then, the injuries often have healed completely, and the physical examination reveals few, if any, abnormalities. Anal findings, when present, are not specific for abuse, and are sometimes dismissed by physicians as being associated with common bowel disorders, for example constipation or diarrhea.

Collection of evidence

While the primary objective of the physical examination is to attend to the medical needs of the victim, the examination has a secondary purpose as well, to collect samples which can later be used as evidence. Specimens for the proper medical management of the patient should be collected in the case of every victim. Furthermore, if the assault occurred within 72 hours of the examination, samples for the forensic laboratory should be collected and handled separately. A description of the specimens required is listed in Table 4. The specimens collected for forensic purposes must be noted in the record with a description of the location from which they were obtained and any associated findings, for example saliva collected from the patient's

Table 4   The forensic evaluation: specimens to be collected

General
Outer- and underclothing if worn during or immediately following the assault
Fingernail scraping
Dried and moist secretions and foreign material observed on the patient's body
Use Wood's lamp to detect semen
Oral cavity
Swabs for semen (2) if within 6 hours of the assault
Culture for GC and other STDs
Saliva, for reference
Genital area
Dried and moist secretions and foreign material
Comb pubic hair; collect all loose hair and foreign material
Vaginal swabs (3)
Wet mount
Dry mount slides (2)
Culture for GC and other STDs
Anus
Dried and moist secretions and foreign material
Rectal swabs (2)
Dry mount slides (2)
Culture for GC and other STDs
Blood
Blood type
RPR
Pregnancy text (blood or urine)
Alcohol/toxicology (blood or urine)
Urine
Urinalysis
Blood or urine
Pregnancy test
Alcohol/toxicology
Other
Saliva: use clean gauze or filter paper
Head hair: cut and remove sample
Pubic hair: cut and remove sample

GC, *N. gonorrhea*; STD, sexually transmitted disease; RPR, rapid plasma reagin

neck near a bite mark. All items collected must be individually packaged and clearly labelled, the containers and envelopes sealed and signed by the examiner.

TREATMENT

The following objectives must be addressed when treating a child who is a victim of sexual abuse:

(1) Repair of injuries and treatment of venereal diseases;

(2) Protection against further abuse;

(3) Psychological support for the victim and his/her family.

Repair of injuries

Superficial injuries (bruises, edema, local irritation) resolve within a few days and require no special treatment. Meticulous perineal hygiene is important in the prevention of secondary infections. Sitz-baths should be utilized to remove secretions and contaminants. In some patients with extensive skin abrasions, broad-spectrum antibiotics should be given as prophylaxis. In most patients, vulvar hematomas do not require special treatment. Small hematomas can usually be controlled by pressure with an ice-pack, and even massive swelling of the vulva usually subsides promptly when cold-packs and external pressure are applied. Bite wounds should be irrigated copiously, and necrotic tissue cautiously debrided. Anti-tetanus immunization should be provided if the child is not already immunized. Broad-spectrum antibiotics should be used in a therapeutic rather than prophylactic manner.

Injuries of the vagina or rectum may present surgical difficulties because of the small caliber of the organs involved. Special instruments are required, as well as proper exposure and assistance. Many vaginal lacerations are superficial, limited to the mucosal and submucosal tissues. Such tears are repaired with fine suture material after complete hemostasis is secured.

Treatment of venereal disease

If the child is asymptomatic, prophylactic antibiotic therapy is not necessary. Instead, treatment should be deferred until the results of cultures and serological tests for syphilis become available so that optimal therapy can be instituted. If vulvovaginitis is clinically suspected on the initial visit, appropriate antibiotic therapy is given. A repeat Venereal Disease Related Laboratory (VDRL) test is required 6 weeks later to detect seroconversion. Human immunodeficiency virus (HIV) testing should be offered in appropriate cases.

It is imperative that the child's safety is assured. Can the child be safely sent home? Sometimes it is advisable to provide temporary placement until this question can be confidently answered. All patients who are suspected to be victims of child sexual abuse should be referred to child protective services for further evaluation.

THE PHYSICIAN AS AN EXPERT WITNESS

Physicians, by virtue of their education, are often admitted as expert witnesses. They must communicate effectively with the judge and jury. Although the physician must remain scientifically correct, he or she should use simple language and terminology, so that the lay jury may understand his testimony. They are not permitted to narrate their answers, cannot explain ambiguous answers, and are frequently interrupted by objections from the lawyers and by comments from the judge.

To be considered credible, an expert must appear intelligent, unbiased and neutral. To be effective, the expert must overcome the skeptic's view that an expert will offer a biased opinion that favors the party who hired the expert witness. The expert must testify regarding the facts of the case, and may not offer an opinion on the issue of guilt, which should be determined by the judge or jury.

Preparing for trial

The following is an outline of the pre-trial preparation:

(1) Review the facts of the case. Review your records, laboratory data and references you plan to quote.

(2) Establish the purpose of your testimony. What is it that the attorney is trying to prove? What are the key issues that can be resolved with your opinion?

(3) What is the best way to present the opinion? Suggest and practice a set of actual questions and answers to be asked at trial.

(4) What are the problem areas? Review weak points or flaws. Discuss problem areas and plan your responses.

(5) If asked, you should talk to the opposing attorney. Otherwise, you will be accused of bias. Be polite and open, but nothing should be volunteered. If requested, share literature you plan to use in your testimony. Do not attempt to convince the lawyer that his or her client is 'wrong'.

The trial

Arrive just before your testimony, or arrange for a private room to wait your turn. Witnesses are usually excluded from the courtroom, and you do not want to wait in the hall. This is a position of vulnerability because you do not know anyone, but everyone is aware of who you are. Do not accept any materials handed to you by an opposing attorney. If you do, you may be cross-examined on that material and it may be introduced into the evidence, even if it is totally without merit.

You should listen carefully to all questions and look at the person asking the question when answering. It is important to look at the jury when the question asks for something to be explained to the jury. Remain calm and in control. Do not become angry during cross-examination. Charts, diagrams and 'chalk talks' are effective because they create the image that the expert is the teacher and everyone else is the student. You may state your opinion on direct examination. Describe your qualifications and experience, and explain how you reached your conclusions.

Please understand that the opposing counsel wants you to appear biased, dishonest, stupid and ignorant. He or she may want you to appear as a literature reviewer only, with no real knowledge or experience. He or she may try to maneuver you into being inconsistent or foolishly consistent.

Listen to the questions carefully. Some questions cannot be answered in the form in which they are asked. Do not answer a question you do not fully understand. If a lawyer raises an objection to a question, do not answer it until you are instructed to do so.

You may also be confronted with a statement you have made in the past that is inconsistent with your current testimony. You may have given a preliminary opinion, and, based upon a more complete analysis, your opinion changes. The opposing counsel may try to use the change to force you into admitting fallibility or even lying. Should that happen, you may explain the reason for the difference between the previous statement and your current testimony. You need to remember that, in the courtroom, truth is the absence of deceit. Therefore, as long as you believe that your testimony is true, then you are telling the truth.

The outcome of the trial should not become a personal matter for the physician. The verdict is decided by a jury, and the jury may have to consider all the facts and not only your testimony. You should accept the verdict regardless of your personal opinion.

REFERENCES

1. Adams JA, Harper K, Knudson S, et al. Examination findings in legally confirmed child sexual abuse: it's normal to be normal. Pediatrics 1994;94:310–17
2. Adams JA, Wells R. Normal versus abnormal genital findings in children: how well do examiners agree? Child Abuse Negl 1993;17:663–75
3. Berenson A, Heger A, Andrews S. Appearance of the hymen in newborns. Pediatrics 1991;87:458–65

4. Berenson AB, Heger AH, Hayes JM, *et al*. Appearance of the hymen in prepubertal girls. *Pediatrics* 1992;89:387–94
5. Berenson AB. Appearance of the hymen at birth and one year of age: a longitudinal study. *Pediatrics* 1993;91:820–5
6. Berenson AB. A longitudinal study of hymenal morphology in the first 3 years of life. *Pediatrics* 1995;95:490–6
7. Blake J. Gynecologic examination of the teenager and young child. *Obstet Gynecol Clin North Am* 1992;19:27–38
8. Boat BW, Everson MD. Exploration of anatomical dolls by nonreferred preschool-aged children: comparisons by age, gender, race, and socioeconomic status. *Child Abuse Negl* 1994;18:139–53
9. Bond GR, Dowd MD, Landsman I, *et al*. Unintentional perineal injury in prepubescent girls: a multicenter, prospective report of 56 girls. *Pediatrics* 1995;95:628–31
10. Cappelleri JC, Eckenrode J, Powers JL. The epidemiology of child abuse: findings from the Second National Incidence and Prevalence Study of Child Abuse and Neglect. *Am J Public Health* 1993;83:1622–4
11. de Villiers FP. The doctor as witness in child abuse cases. *South Afr Med J* 1992; 81:520–3
12. Devlin BK, Reynolds E. Child abuse. How to recognize it, how to intervene. *Am J Nurs* 1994;94:26–31
13. Emans SJ, Woods E, Flagg N. Genital findings in sexually abused, symptomatic and asymptomatic, girls. *Pediatrics* 1987;79:778–85
14. Emans SJ, Paradise JE. Sample sexual assault data sheet [Letter]. *Pediatrics* 1989;83:1073–4
15. Enos WF, Conrath TB, Byer JC. Forensic evaluation of the sexually abused child. *Pediatrics* 1986;78:385–98
16. Finkelhor D. The international epidemiology of child sexual abuse. *Child Abuse Negl* 1994;18:409–17
17. Gallagher P. Medical examination of children thought to have been sexually abused. *Med Sci Law* 1993;33:203–6
18. Gellert GA, Berkowitz CD, Gellert MJ, *et al*. Testing the sexually abused child for the HIV antibody: issues for the social worker. *Soc Work* 1993;38:389–94
19. Gellert G, Berkowitz CD. Pediatric acquired immunodeficiency syndrome: testing as a barrier to recognizing the role of child sexual abuse. *Arch Pediatr Adolesc Med* 1994;148:766–8
20. Gibbons M, Vincent EC. Childhood sexual abuse [Review]. *Am Fam Physician* 1994;49:125–36
21. Hobbs CJ, Wynne JM. Buggery in childhood – a common syndrome of child abuse. *Lancet* 1986;2:792–6
22. Jenny C, Kuhns ML, Arakawa F. Hymens in newborn female infants. *Pediatrics* 1987;80:399–400
23. Kerns DL, Terman DL, Larson CS. The role of physicians in reporting and evaluating child sexual abuse cases. *Future Child* 1994;4:119–34
24. Levitt CJ. Medical evaluation of the sexually abused child [Review]. *Primary Care* 1993;20:343–54

25. Levitt EE, Pinnell CM. Some additional light on the childhood sexual abuse–psychopathology axis. *Int J Clin Exp Hypn* 1995;43:145–62

26. McCann J, Simon M, Voris J, *et al.* Perianal findings in prepubertal children selected for nonabuse: a descriptive study [see Comments]. *Child Abuse Negl* 1989;13:179–93

27. McCann J, Wells R, Simon M, *et al.* Genital findings in prepubertal girls selected for nonabuse: a descriptive study. *Pediatrics* 1990;86:428–39

28. McCann J. Use of the colposcope in childhood sexual abuse examinations [Review]. *Pediatr Clin North Am* 1990;37:863–80

29. McCann J, Voris J, Simon M, *et al.* Comparison of genital examination techniques in prepubertal girls [see Comments]. *Pediatrics* 1990;85:182–7

30. McCann J, Voris J, Simon M. Genital injuries resulting from sexual abuse: a longitudinal study. *Pediatrics* 1992;89:307–17

31. McCann J, Voris J. Perianal injuries resulting from sexual abuse: a longitudinal study. *Pediatrics* 1993;91:390–7

32. Muram D. Genital tract injuries in the prepubertal child. *Pediatr Ann* 1986; 15:616–20

33. Muram D. Child sexual abuse – genital tract findings in prepubertal girls. I. The unaided medical examination. *Am J Obstet Gynecol* 1989;160:328–33

34. Muram D. Anal and perianal abnormalities in prepubertal victims of sexual abuse. *Am J Obstet Gynecol* 1989;161:278–81

35. Muram D. Child sexual abuse: relationship between sexual acts and genital findings. *Child Abuse Negl* 1989;13:211–16

36. Paradise JE. Predictive accuracy and the diagnosis of sexual abuse: a big issue about a little tissue [Review]. *Child Abuse Negl* 1989;13:169–76

37. Pokorny SF. The genital examination of the infant through adolescence. *Curr Opin Obstet Gynecol* 1993;5:753–7

38. Pokorny SF. Configuration of the prepubertal hymen. *Am J Obstet Gynecol* 1987; 157:950–6

39. Ricci LR. Medical forensic photography of the sexually abused child. *Child Abuse Negl* 1988;12:305–10

40. Ricci LR. False allegations of sexual touching [Letter]. *Pediatrics* 1995;95:797–8

41. Roberts RE. The trials of an expert witness. *J R Soc Med* 1994;87:628–31

42. Sirotnak AP. Testing sexually abused children for sexually transmitted diseases: who to test, when to test, and why. *Pediatr Ann* 1994;23:370–4

43. Soderstrom RM. Colposcopic documentation. An objective approach to assessing sexual abuse of girls. *J Reprod Med* 1994;39:6–8

44. Winterton PM. The criminal justice system and the sexually abused child. Help or hindrance? [Letter]. *Med J Aust* 1995;162:504

45. Wissow LS. Child abuse and neglect. *N Engl J Med* 1995;332:1425–31

46. Wynne JM. Injuries to the genitalia in female children. *South Afr Med J* 1980; 57:47–50

7

General surgery

William Cheadle, MD

Medical malpractice litigation remains a formidable problem for all of medicine, including most of the subspecialties. In general surgery, the risk remains high. Most surgeons spend 10–15% of their income on medical malpractice insurance. Although the individual cost to physicians is impressive, even more important is the overall cost to society in the form of defensive medicine. Clearly extra laboratory and radiological tests, as well as additional consultations, are often sought to make sure that one is not potentially missing a diagnosis of a particular disease, given the set of symptoms. This practice of defensive medicine is a huge expense eventually borne by society, and is specifically practiced because of fear of litigation. Although the vast majority of suits are either settled or defense verdicts when brought to trial, the fear of being a victim of legal entanglement is real. Certainly the practice of medicine has become exceedingly complex, and the standard set in the USA is so high that the public expects near-perfect results. Indeed, the result of medical care at this time is far more important to the general public than the physician–patient relationship. Indeed, lawsuits are brought about by poor results more often than poor rapport with patients. However, it is important to establish a good patient rapport, and to stick with a patient and their family throughout an adverse result until it is brought to a conclusion. It is of the utmost importance to be straightforward and honest with both the patient and their family about complications that occur, and to explain exactly why they occurred and how they are being addressed at present. It is also important that the staff at both the hospital and the individual practitioner's office are courteous and professional at all times. Often, suits are brought about when patients or their families hear unprofessional comments about patients from individual staff. In addition, it is important for us as physicians to spend time in answering all the questions that are asked. In general surgery, as well as any surgical subspecialty, one should also take time before an invasive procedure to inform fully the patient and their families of the indications, risks and benefits of the procedure. Time spent up front tends to enlist trust on their part, as well as minimize the time that needs to be spent thereafter if all turns out properly. If a complication occurs, at least then the family understands that this was a possibility, and that the physician has thought about it or even made provision for such a problem in advance.

The most common medical–legal problems in general surgery include delayed diagnosis of cancer, and technical errors that occur at the time of operation. Over the past 5 years, clearly alleged delay in diagnosis of breast cancer and technical errors during laparoscopic cholecystectomy have been the most common bases for lawsuits. In addition, failure to diagnose and treat ischemic peripheral extremities, resulting in what appears to be premature amputation to the patient and family, have also been a common source of litigation. Indeed, in the trauma setting, decisions on whether to revascularize or try to salvage an extremity versus early amputation are often difficult. It is obviously important to attempt salvage if possible, but prolonged attempts at salvage can jeopardize the life of a patient. If an extremity is beyond salvage based on the clinical setting, it is often better to let the patient and family realize that, and therefore delay amputation for a few hours or even a day or two to let them come to terms with the fact that the extremity is indeed non-salvageable, as opposed to an immediate amputation upon arrival at the hospital.

Breast cancer and its delay in diagnosis is probably the most widely discussed malpractice claim against general surgeons in the lay press. Clearly with this disease it is imperative to have good physician–patient rapport and a compassionate office staff. It is extremely important that each patient and their complaints be taken seriously. There is nothing worse than trivializing a complaint, only to find out that the patient actually has cancer a few months after being seen. Even if this is unrelated to the initial visit, rapport is of the utmost significance in this area. It is important to take time to listen to the patient and to perform a thorough physical examination, ultrasound and mammography if warranted. Probably the best thing one can do if unsure about a breast mass is to re-examine the patient 1 or 2 months later. The advent of stereotactic biopsy, which requires a smaller incision, has made biopsy of indeterminate lesions even more commonplace. Comparing the practice in the USA to that in Great Britain, there are approximately 10–15 biopsies of benign lesions for every malignant one in the USA, whereas in Great Britain there is a three to one biopsy ratio in favor of malignancy. Probably this difference is directly related to the practice of defensive medicine; biopsy, when there is no sampling error, is certainly definitive. It is important to try to read the patient's mind and figure out what they expect to be done. For the most part, as general surgeons we are seeing the patients to give a second opinion when they are referred from either their primary care physician or gynecologist. The patient should be asked what their other physician has told them about this particular problem and what their expectations are. If one physician suggests biopsy and the second does not, that already puts the second-opinion physician in a situation with a certain degree of risk should cancer be diagnosed. If it appears that the patient and the family are unhappy with your recommendations, it is quite helpful to obtain a further opinion from one's partners or from other physicians outside the group. This is rarely necessary, but valuable in certain circumstances. Many times, more than one lesion in one breast, or multiple lesions in both breasts are present. It is important to document and discuss each lesion. The increased use of ultrasound in the office is helpful in this respect. The patient should be asked prior to biopsy which breast the lesion is in and where it is. Occasionally, a palpable lesion will change or even disappear between the office visit and the scheduled biopsy time. For those women with multiple lesions in both breasts in which only one lesion is suspicious, it is important to reconfirm which one it is. In this situation, close collaboration with the radiologist performing the needle localization is vital to pinpoint the lesion. Another problem that the clinician faces is proper radiological interpretation of the film which was followed by suggestion for biopsy. Some radiologists are quite liberal about this, and if the surgeon does not feel that a biopsy is indicated, a second opinion from another radiologist who is particularly qualified in reading mammograms would be appropriate.

The advent of the application of laparoscopy to general surgery has brought about a huge number of lawsuits in the area of injured common bile ducts. Between 1990 and 1992 there was a wholesale switch from open cholecystectomy to laparoscopic cholecystectomy, taught completely outside the walls of residency programs. Again, it is important to be honest with the patient and their family about what has happened, and aggressive reoperation should be instituted as soon as the diagnosis has been made if this is warranted. There are many different types of bile duct injuries that occur during laparoscopic cholecystectomy. Many can be repaired by the original surgeon. Such patients should be referred to a tertiary center if local expertise is not available. Often, patients are more upset about the delay in referral than they are about the original injury itself. It is important to study the biliary tree if patients are not progressing well after laparoscopic cholecystectomy.

ONCE A LAWSUIT IS FILED

Once notified by the plaintiff's attorney that the patient either has filed a lawsuit or is potentially doing so, the physician should seek legal counsel. At no time should the physician answer any questions from the plaintiff's attorney outside a deposition setting. In many cases the plaintiff's attorney is simply trying to find evidence suggestive of medical malpractice as opposed to formally filing a suit. If a physician has had a suit formally filed, there are many things that a physician can do to help him- or herself. The first is to cooperate fully with one's own attorney and to take the suit seriously. You can be sure that the plaintiff's attorney will take it very seriously and to trivialize it is inappropriate. Obviously prior documentation is important, and it may take the form of the office record or the patient's chart. Not only is it important to document facts such as symptoms, physical findings, and laboratory and radiological tests, but it is also quite helpful to document the physician's line of thinking at a given time. The physician will be expected to give a discovery deposition that will be led primarily by the plaintiff's attorney. It is exceedingly important that the physician involved is thoroughly familiar with the patient's care as determined by all of the available records. Often, a plaintiff's attorney will try to make a big issue out of a small piece of a medical record. The physician must be able to interpret this correctly. The plaintiff's attorney will also try to surprise the physician if possible, and thorough preparation in reading not only the office records and medical charts, but also some of the medical literature about the disease and its complications is necessary. It is also important for the physician not to appear defensive during the deposition, nor during the trial for that matter. The key to this, obviously, is having an answer prepared for any possible question that the plaintiff's attorney might ask. The discovery deposition usually provides for most such questions. It is certainly possible to think through somewhat different answers that might be more appropriate to the jury after the discovery deposition has been given. The plaintiff's attorney will often cite discrepancies, but it is important for the physician to be firm in his opinion about why he acted as he did, having thought this through more fully. The physician involved ought to be present at the discovery deposition of other experts, in particular the plaintiff's experts. The physician should also be present throughout the entire trial, and spend plenty of time upon the stand explaining fully to the jury why he or she has taken these particular actions. I think that the longer a physician is on the witness stand, the more comfortable he or she becomes. It is important for the physician to sell himself to the jury as much as he would to a patient or their family. If the jury believes that the physician acted appropriately and believes in his honesty and integrity, then it is all the more difficult for the plaintiff's attorney to convince the jury that a deviation from standard of care has taken place. In the main, I believe that most juries, made up of people who are lay public, tend to side with the physician if he or she is believable and is really telling the truth. It is important, therefore, not to appear arrogant and unapproachable, but down-to-earth and able to explain the rationale behind decision-making at the level of the jury. It has been my impression that jury members fall into one of two categories. The first group are those who are a little more elderly, perhaps retired, and have a genuine interest in the legal system and appropriate justice. The second group are those who generally are younger, often eager to get away from their jobs to do something different, and may not be so well informed or even pay proper attention during the trial. The physician and the experts should try to figure out which category individual jury members fall into. For those who seem to be aware and attentive, it is important to make eye contact with them several times, and perhaps direct an answer towards one or two jury members, as opposed to looking all over the court room. This is an effective communication technique to enlist confidence in the person on the witness stand. Obviously, the most difficult portion of the trial is the cross-examination by the plaintiff's attorney. This is highly variable and can be very direct, stark, argumentative and often downright derogatory. The physician must not allow him- or herself to get into an argument with the plaintiff's attorney. On the other hand, it is very important to take time to think about the individual questions that are asked, and to take time to explain the rationale behind one's answer to the jury. 'Yes' or 'no' answers should be avoided as much as possible without an explanation of why to the jury. If it appears that the plaintiff's attorney is painting a picture inconsistent with what one has been testifying towards, one's testimony should be augmented to convey a clear notion to the jury of what was going on in the physician's mind during the time the patient was being cared for.

Although it is difficult, the physician must try not to take the nature or the outcome of the suit personally. There are literally hundreds of thousands of active suits across the country. Indeed, most physicians have been named in a suit during their career. Although settlement of such a suit is attractive from a time standpoint, fighting a suit in court is often worthwhile, particularly if the suit is inappropriate.

8

Psychiatry

David A. Casey, MD

In terms of their specialty, psychiatrists have a relatively low risk of facing a legal suit for malpractice. However, as the nature of psychiatric practice has rapidly evolved over the past decade, this legal risk has escalated greatly. Historically, many psychiatrists have offered intensive, psychotherapy-based treatment, each to a relatively small group of patients. Such treatments are often of long duration, with strong doctor–patient relationships. This practice style contributes to a low risk of lawsuits. In recent years practice has evolved into short-term therapies, usually involving medication management. Each psychiatrist tends to see a much larger group of patients, typically with less frequent and in-depth interaction. Psychiatrists are also more likely to work with or supervise others (such as licensed clinical social workers) who provide psychotherapy. In these treatment relationships, the psychiatrist may be exposed to legal risk based on care provided by these other therapists. Today there is intense pressure to avoid or limit hospitalizations; sicker patients are treated in out-patient therapy. Many of these changes have resulted from the advent of managed care, which has had a tremendous impact on psychiatric practice. At the same time, courts have shown a willingness to hold psychiatrists responsible for acts of their patients, even acts committed long after treatment has ended.

Family physicians and other specialists provide a large measure of psychiatric care. The community standards by which they are judged may differ from those of psychiatrists. Nevertheless, careful attention to important principles of psychiatric risk management will serve these specialists as well.

Psychiatrists, as all physicians, have a 'fiduciary' duty to provide competent treatment for their patients. This duty begins as soon as a psychiatrist–patient relationship has been established. Therefore, attention is required to delineate the nature of therapeutic relationships. For instance, giving

Table 1 Confidentiality

Patients advised of limits of confidentiality at onset of therapeutic relationship
Managed care may require sharing clinical information

casual advise to friends or acquaintances outside the counseling room could be problematic, especially if a bad outcome ensues. When a psychiatrist works with another therapist, the nature of the relationship (e.g. consultative, contractual, employer–employee, supervisory) must be understood by both parties. As in therapeutic relationships, the boundaries must be clarified.

Patients in psychiatric treatment have a legal entitlement to confidentiality (Table 1). This is a crucial trust which can only be broken with the explicit consent of the patient (or their legal guardian), or under direct court order. Exceptions to this rule occur when the patient is a threat to themselves or others, or has committed reportable offences such as child abuse. In fact, the psychiatrist may be compelled to breach confidentiality in such circumstances. Patients should be advised of the limits of confidentiality at the outset of a therapeutic relationship. The exact nature of confidentiality and reporting requirements differ from state to state. Practitioners must familiarize themselves with the legal requirements for their particular jurisdiction. Many managed care programs require sharing of clinical information for certification of treatment. Generally, medical insurance recipients have waived their confidentiality rights in this circumstance.

Certain types of arrangements demand special attention, because they do not imply a true treatment relationship and will not be held confidential. For instance, workman's compensation, insurance or forensic evaluations will lead to the filing of a report with a third party. Patients must be made aware of the non-therapeutic, non-confidential nature of such an arrangement. Documentation of the nature of the consultation, as well as the patient's consent (or appropriate legal approval) is crucial. In essence, in these cases the psychiatrist is not working for the patient but for another party. For this reason, it is very difficult for a psychiatrist to serve as treating physician and simultaneously play another role, such as in a workman's compensation evaluation.

Certain types of situations are especially likely to be involved in psychiatric malpractice actions (Table 2). These include suicide or injury to self, homicide or injury to others, misdiagnosis and negligent treatment. Sexual relationships with patients or other forms of exploitations have been the

Table 2   Predisposed to malpractice actions

Suicide
Injury to self or others
Homicide
Misdiagnosis
Negligent treatment
Sexual exploitation

Table 3   Judgement regarding level of care

Careful assessment
Thoughtful reasoning
Thorough planning
Risk factor assessment
Complete documentation

focus of an increasing number of lawsuits. Each of these situations is briefly explored.

Patients who commit suicide or seriously injure themselves present a high risk of a psychiatric malpractice action. Typically, such cases will involve questions of whether there was an appropriate evaluation of the suicide risk (as well as careful documentation). Ensuring that patients at risk receive appropriate supervision or hospitalization is another important element. Patients who hurt or kill themselves while hospitalized present a particularly high risk of legal action. Protection of such patients is one of the major reasons for hospitalization; physicians and hospitals will be expected to meet a high standard. Suicidal thinking is an extremely common finding in psychiatric practice. Not all such patients warrant hospitalization, and in fact hospitalization itself is not entirely benign (stigmatization, possible loss of job, etc.). The psychiatrist must make a judgement about the appropriate level of care (Table 3). Such judgements require careful assessment, thoughtful reasoning, thorough planning and complete documentation. Risk factors must be assessed, such as level of depression, alcohol or substance abuse, psychosis, painful or life-threatening medical illness, previous attempt, explicit suicidal planning and access to a means of suicide. These must be weighed against the patient's level of environmental support, reasons for living, religious beliefs and so on. There is no 'cook-book' approach; instead, evaluation must be individualized. Frequently, family or other significant supporting individuals must be involved in treatment planning. Managed-care case managers frequently

Table 5   Tips to avoid malpractice

Sound clinical care
Establish strong therapeutic alliance
Appropriate consultation
Attention to confidentiality
Continuity of care
Documentation
Address patient calls and complaints
Never alter records

However, appending additional notes documenting circumstances and clinical reasoning is permissible if they are clearly dated and labeled. Generally, psychiatrists should work with unhappy patients to resolve disputes. However, once a malpractice suit is filed contact should usually cease.

9

Radiology

Leonard Berlin, MD, FACR

The specter of malpractice litigation has unrelentingly influenced every facet of radiological practice for more than three decades. This chapter begins by discussing the prevalence and nature of radiological malpractice by categorizing the various allegations of wrongdoing levied against physicians involved in radiology, and then identifying trends according to type. This will lead to a recognition of where medicolegal risks lie in radiology, so that risk management processes can be developed to minimize malpractice exposure and improve patient care.

The true prevalence of medical malpractice and malpractice claims among physicians is not known with certainty, but some recently published data give a good bird's eye view of the situation[1]. One study reviewed 31 000 hospital records and found adverse events in 3.2% of them; negligence was presumed to be responsible for one quarter of these. With regard to radiology specifically, 12% of radiologists in one study carried out over a 10-year period had been involved in malpractice litigation, whereas in another study carried out over a period of 20 years the equivalent figure was between 10 and 15%. Nationally, it has been estimated that more than 40% of practicing radiologists have been sued at least once in their career since 1987.

CATEGORIES OF LAWSUIT

Allegations of missed diagnoses have consistently been the most frequent cause of radiological malpractice litigation (Table 1) over the past 25 years. These now account for more than 70% of all malpractice lawsuits filed against radiologists. Litigation relating to missed bone abnormalities of all types, including fractures, dislocations, malignant lesions, inflammations and other non-specified conditions, accounted for the greatest percentage of cases until 1985, but rates then fell precipitously. Allegations of missed malignant lesions of the lung have remained at a high level, and for a short

Table 1   Most common causes of litigation

Missed breast cancers on mammography
Missed malignant lung lesions
Complications from radiological examination
  (angiography most commonly)
'Failure to order': non-radiologist (e.g. mammogram)

time in the early 1990s led the list of causes of radiological lawsuits. However, beginning in the mid-1990s and to date, allegedly missed breast cancers on mammograms took over as the most frequent cause of malpractice litigation involving radiologists.

The percentage of radiological malpractice cases alleging complications resulting from radiological examinations or procedures ranges from 12 to 20%. The largest subgroup of complications centers on angiographic procedures, accounting for about 40% of the total.

The number of malpractice suits classified as 'failure to order' constitutes a substantial proportion of radiological malpractice litigation. The incidence of these lawsuits has been rising, and the specific nature of the allegations has been changing. Lawsuits charging patient injury as a result of the failure to order mammograms are now common. This is not surprising, because enormous publicity has been generated by such organizations as the American Cancer Society, the American College of Obstetrics and Gynecology and the American College of Radiology, to promote mammographic examinations. Non-radiological physicians who fail to adhere to breast radiography screening guidelines have been placed in increasing medicolegal jeopardy, for it is the public's perception that any delay in either detection or treatment of breast cancer is life-threatening and tantamount to malpractice.

Malpractice litigation involving radiation oncology is relatively rare, accounting for only about 3% of the total cases filed. The complaints in radiation oncology lawsuits relate generally to complications of radiation treatment; several isolated cases claim either that radiation treatment was performed without appropriate indication or that it was withheld for inappropriate reasons.

'Slip-and-fall' is a term commonly used by risk managers, attorneys and insurance personnel to describe those lawsuits filed by patients claiming injury as a result of falling off examination tables, chairs or carts; slipping on floors; tripping over furniture; or being inadvertently struck by equipment or portions thereof. Although radiologists are not usually alleged to be negligent in these cases, nonetheless, the radiologists' professional liability insurance carriers bear the costs of defense and of any ensuing compensation. Slip-and-fall cases account for less than 5% of all radiology-related cases.

NEW TECHNOLOGIES

A distinctive characteristic of radiology is the constant introduction of new technology and equipment. Techniques such as computed tomography (CT) and magnetic resonance imaging (MRI) are developed in research laboratories, refined in universities, and then rapidly diffused for general use throughout the radiological community. Eventually, these technologies also find their way into the courts.

The lag time between the introduction of technology and the date of the first lawsuit alleging its negligent use is changing. For example, the first malpractice lawsuit in Chicago specifically including sonography among its allegations was filed in 1982, more than a decade after the introduction of sonography into medical practice in Chicago. CT was first introduced into the Chicago area in 1974, but not until 1982 did it first become the subject of a malpractice suit. MRI was first utilized in Chicago in 1983, but only 4 years passed before a lawsuit was instituted claiming that it was used inappropriately. The lag time is clearly getting shorter.

As the new millennium unfolds, we are witnessing further emerging radiological technology such as positron emission tomography, computed radiography, digitalization of images, transmission of radiological images through teleradiology, PACS (picture archival and communication systems), advances in CT such as helical scanning, refinements in sonography such as the use of contrast agents, and continuing innovations in MRI sequencing. While few or no malpractice lawsuits focusing on or alluding to these developments have yet been filed, there is little doubt that, because of faster dissemination of medical knowledge and greater sophistication among plaintiffs' attorneys, many cases involving these technologies will soon appear in the malpractice arena.

Radiological malpractice in the future will also be affected by several additional factors such as modifications in the certification process and institution of limited recertification by the American Board of Radiology and new standards published by the American College of Radiology, as well as clinical guidelines and parameters issued by other medical professional organizations, and economic considerations related primarily to the growth of managed care plans and capitation–payment–gatekeeping arrangements.

RADIOLOGICAL ERRORS

The frequency of perceptual 'misses' among radiologists has not changed appreciably in the past 50 years and is not likely to change in the foreseeable future. Radiographic misses, particularly when they involve breast, lung or colon cancer, frequently generate malpractice litigation. The missing of a lesion seen on radiographs which delays the timely diagnosis and possible cure of a malignancy that, as a result of the miss, results in severe harm or death to a patient, is a serious if not catastrophic event. Once an abnormality shown on a radiograph is pointed out and becomes so obvious that lay persons such as judges, jurors and other attorneys can see it, it is not easy to convince anyone that the radiologist who is trained and paid for seeing the lesion should be exonerated for missing it. It is no wonder that most of these cases are settled before trial with payment to the patient.

RISK MANAGEMENT: ERRORS

Risk management in radiology practice can lessen the likelihood of incurring a medical malpractice lawsuit while maximizing the chances for a successful defense if such a suit is filed, and, at the same time, enhance good patient care. The following pointers will help to achieve these three goals (Table 2).

A radiologist's accuracy can be no greater than the quality of radiographs presented for interpretation. Although technologists may physically perform the examinations, it is the radiologist that interprets the radiographs who is responsible for determining whether the examination is adequate, and it is the radiologist who bears the ultimate legal liability for an inadequate radiograph that fails to show an abnormality. Poor-quality radiographs will increase the likelihood of missing a lesion. Radiologists should insist that patient positioning and radiographic exposure are adequate before interpretation[2].

All radiological facilities should have written policies that describe the imaging views required and the technical factors to be used for all radiographic examinations.

Technique charts or routine phototimer settings may not always result in ideally exposed radiographs. In cases of overexposure, radiologists must use their best judgment to determine whether a radiograph can be properly interpreted with the use of a bright light. Similar judgment about whether an underexposed film or one on which the patient has been poorly positioned can be adequately interpreted must also be made by the radiologist. If radiologists decide that the radiographs are readable, I encourage

Table 2   Avoiding litigation

Role of technologist: proper patient positioning and radiographic exposure
Written policy regarding imaging views
Proper radiographic exposure: comment if over- or underexposed
If incomplete study interpretation is rendered, document reasons and follow-up
As appropriate, comment on patient's condition
Management of uninterpretable film
Ideally, relook at the film when reviewing with referring physician
Obtain clinical information and review previous films and reports
Consult when necessary
Think 'statistical probabilities', not all or nothing
Call referring physician for urgent or unexpected significant findings

them to use phrases such as 'Film is somewhat over- (or under-) exposed (or patient positioning is not optimal), but the radiological examination is still felt to be of reasonable diagnostic quality', as appropriate. By utilizing such phrases in a report at the time of image interpretation, radiologists can help to explain and even defend their judgment at some future time, should litigation ensue.

Occasionally, circumstances may prevent technologists from obtaining all required views in a particular radiological examination. Should radiologists determine that they can interpret such an incomplete study with reasonable accuracy, they may do so, but they should document in their report the reasons for deviating from established policy.

If the patient's physical condition prevents a technologist from completing radiography with all required views or with optimal exposure techniques, the radiologist should make every attempt to encourage the technologist and the patient to obtain a complete examination. If this is not possible, the radiologist should state in the report that the examination was incomplete because of the patient's condition, and should specify which views were not taken or what areas of anatomical interest were not sufficiently visualized. The report should also state that repeat or follow-up views need to be performed when the patient's condition permits.

If a radiologist believes that a radiograph cannot be properly interpreted because of poor exposure or positioning, an immediate repeat radiograph should be requested if the patient is available. If the patient is not available, the radiologist should render a report stating that the study cannot be interpreted, giving the reasons why, and stating that repeat radiographs have been requested. In such situations, the radiologist should attempt to recall the patient directly or, if that is not possible, contact the referring physician who can recall the patient. Documentation of the recall or attempted recall should be in the report.

Radiologists can diminish the likelihood of error by having available as much patient information as possible, and by taking enough time carefully to examine the patient's relevant previous radiographic studies in addition to current radiographs.

Radiologists reading the same radiograph at different times disagree with themselves as much as 20% of the time. Therefore, when asked by a referring physician 'What did you find on the radiological examination of my patient, Mr. Smith?', instead of answering, 'I've already read the film, and it's normal' a better answer would be 'I did read the film as normal, but let's look at it again together.' A second look by the radiologist with or without a referring physician or colleague will occasionally reveal a radiographic finding that was initially overlooked[3].

Although it seems obvious, it must still be emphasized that all radiologists must maintain basic ordinary knowledge of the kinds or radiological examinations they interpret. If a radiologist feels inadequate to interpret a particular study, the radiologist should defer it to, or at the very least confer with, an associate who is knowledgeable about the imaging technique[4].

It is unrealistic to expect, and the courts do not require, that every radiological examination be interpreted by the best-qualified radiologist. Costs and logistics of individual group practices govern distribution and availability of radiological resources. In certain group practices, some or all of the radiologists have undergone fellowship training and limit their practice to a specific subspecialty. When the primary subspecialist is unavailable and is being covered by a radiologist with less training or experience, care must be taken to ensure that the substitute possesses adequate knowledge. This precaution is vital after-hours when one radiologist may be on call for an entire group practice. Patients undergoing radiological examination after-hours are entitled to the same quality of care as those examined during normal working hours.

Radiologists should obtain as much clinical information as possible, review the patient's previous radiology studies and reports, and have radiology textbooks for their immediate reference before rendering radiographic interpretations[5].

Making instant or rapid diagnoses may be acceptable goals in film-reading conferences, but doing so in every-day radiology practice may cause radiologists to limit diagnostic possibilities and may increase the likelihood of error. Taking sufficient time during radiographic interpretation for deliberation and reflection is essential for good judgment.

Conscious attempts to increase the number of diagnostic possibilities will help to dispel the compulsion to reach a hasty conclusion. Although it is unrealistic to expect radiologists to list in writing a complete differential diagnosis in every radiography report, nonetheless, before concluding an interpretation, radiologists should ask themselves 'Is there any diagnosis other than the one I have made that can explain the radiological findings?'

Consultation with radiology colleagues and referring physicians before rendering final reports should be encouraged. Often, diagnostic possibilities not entertained by a single radiologist working in isolation will be raised as a result of such dialogs.

Diagnostic radiologists should think in terms of statistical probabilities rather than dogmatic or 'all or nothing' radiology rules. They must keep an open mind.

'If you do not think of it, you will not diagnose it' is a basic axiom in diagnostic radiology. One cannot emphasize too much the need for radiologists constantly to reinforce and expand their reservoir of radiology knowledge through reading current scientific literature and attending continuing medical education programs.

COMMUNICATION

Breakdown in communication between patient and doctor is a causative factor in as many as 80% of malpractice lawsuits[6]. Traditionally, radiologists believed that their duty to communicate results did not extend beyond dictating and signing their report. As a matter of courtesy and good medical practice, the radiologist might decide to telephone the patient's physician if the radiographic findings seem to warrant immediate treatment, but in the past this was not mandated, nor was there any requirement to document the process[7].

In more recent years, however, court decisions dealing with radiological communication have held that radiologists have definite legal duties to communicate radiological findings to referring physicians, and sometimes to patients themselves on a timely basis – in fact, immediately if the patient's care requires it. That the courts are expanding the communicative responsibilities of radiologists is illustrated in two court decisions.

An Ohio appellate court, dealing with the failure of a radiologist to communicate immediately the presence of a distal humeral fracture, noted that radiologists have direct obligations to patients even though the radiologists may never see the patient personally[8]:

'In some situations indirect service may provide justification for the absence of direct communication with the patient, but that does not in any way justify failure of communication with the primary care physician … We are unable to agree … that radiologists … who merely provide what they term "indirect medical care" may somehow categorically escape all liability once such a practitioner has made a correct analysis and has done no more than to relay this information through ordinary hospital channels. Once the physician–patient relationship has been found to exist … the professional responsibilities and duties exist despite the lack of proximity, or the remoteness of contact between the two as where a consulting physician is involved in the case in only a limited manner. Therefore, all physicians involved in a case share in the same duties and responsibilities of the primary care physician to the extent of their involvement.'

Emphasizing that radiologists cannot escape the duty to communicate immediately with the referring physician when they discover a radiological finding that requires immediate treatment, the Arkansas Supreme Court, in a case wherein a radiologist failed to report immediately to the referring physician that a chest radiograph showed that an endotracheal tube had become dislodged, stated[9]:

'Knowing that the tube was not in place, the [radiologist] nevertheless handled the situation as a matter of routine. While this routine was taking its course, [the patient] was in a life-threatening situation and indeed almost died. He deserved more than routine care under these circumstances … When a patient is in peril of his life, it does him little good if the [radiological physician] has discovered his condition unless the physician takes measures and informs the patient, or those responsible for his care, of that fact.'

In 1991, recognizing the importance of diagnostic radiology communication, the American College of Radiology issued its *Standard for Communication* and later revised it in September 1995 to state: 'If there are urgent or significant unexpected findings, radiologists should communicate directly with the referring physician … Documentation of actual or attempted direct communication is appropriate.' This *Standard* was further revised in 2000: 'In those situations in which the interpreting physician feels that immediate patient treatment is indicated (e.g. tension pneumothorax), the interpreting physician should communicate directly with the referring physician, other health-care provider, or an appropriate representative. If that individual cannot be reached, the interpreting physician should directly communicate the need for emergent care to the patient or responsible guardian, if possible … In those situations in which the interpreting physician feels that less urgent findings or significant unexpected findings are present, the interpreting physician or designee should directly communicate the findings to the referring physician, other health-care provider, or an appropriate representative'[10]. With regard to mammography, federal law has been passed that now requires all radiological facilities to notify all patients of the results of their examinations directly by US mail.

It is clear that timely and appropriate communication of radiological results to referring physicians has been recognized as essential by the courts, and codified by the American College of Radiology in its standards. All radiologists must familiarize themselves with and comply with these standards.

RISK MANAGEMENT: COMMUNICATION

The following risk management pointers will help radiologists deal appropriately with communication issues (Table 3).

If the radiologist has any reasonable belief that a radiological finding requires treatment of the patient before delivery of a written report in the mail or onto a patient's hospital chart, the radiologist should telephone the report to the referring physician immediately.

If the referring physician cannot be located, a verbal report may be left with the physician's nurse or associate, with the acknowledgment by that individual that he or she will assume the responsibility of notifying the referring physician or undertaking care of the patient himself or herself. If none of these individuals can be located, the radiologist should attempt to locate an alternative physician who is covering for the primary physician. In rare situations where the radiologist cannot locate the referring physician or his or her substitute and the radiologist feels that immediate treatment of the patient is necessary, the radiologist should contact the patient directly and inform the patient to come to a hospital emergency department for care[11].

While radiologists traditionally report results to the referring physician rather than to the patient directly (except for self-referred patients undergoing mammography), from a legal point of view, the radiologist's ultimate responsibility is to the patient. If the radiologist cannot transmit urgent reports to the patient's physicians, then he or she must transmit them to the patient directly.

Once a radiologist decides that a finding is important enough to require a telephone report, he or she must continue efforts to reach the referring

Table 3 Advice and challenges

Dilemma of the inability to reach the referring physician
Communicate directly with the patient
Facilities are required to give the patient a written report within 30 days of mammogram
Document all verbal communications: 'I called you'; 'No, you didn't'
Issue an addendum

physician or an acceptable alternative to complete the communication. Terminating attempts at communication because the referring physician is not easily available places the radiologist in greater medicolegal jeopardy than not having attempted to telephone in the first place.

Once verbal communication is completed, it should be documented. A medicolegal truism states: 'If it was not documented, it was not done.' A radiologist who, several years after an incident, says to a jury, 'I think I called the referring physician, but I can't remember for sure and have no documentation that I did', loses credibility. Nothing is worse in defending a medical malpractice lawsuit than having two physicians pointing fingers at each other, one saying, 'I called you', and the other saying, 'No, you didn't'. Documentation at the time an event takes place is credible evidence in a court of law[12].

Documentation of verbal communication should be placed in the radiology report if possible. If the verbal communication has not been completed until after the radiology report has been dictated and signed, then the radiologist should keep a log in the department and document all pertinent discussions as they occur. An acceptable alternative would be to issue an addendum report that documents the communication.

Names or addresses of referring physicians may be incorrect, transcription of the written report may be delayed until after the patient has been discharged from the hospital or from the care of the physician, reports may be lost in the mail or in a hospital delivery system, or ordering physicians may overlook reports. Radiologists should never assume that a written report will automatically reach its destination. Therefore, radiologists should make reasonable attempts to ensure that the names and addresses of patients and referring physicians are accurately printed on radiology reports. Radiologists should also periodically review departmental policy regarding distribution of radiology reports to ensure that efficient delivery is being accomplished.

Radiologists should verbally communicate any significant unexpected radiological finding to the ordering physician in addition to sending the written report through the postal service or hospital mail. Fax communication has not yet been established as an acceptable alternative.

Radiologists should reasonably attempt to foresee delays in transmission of routine reports and whether such delays would necessitate direct communication with referring physicians. For example, a long holiday weekend in which no mail is delivered, or a technical breakdown in dictation or transcription equipment, should prompt the radiologist to telephone reports that would otherwise travel through regular channels.

Radiologists should take special care in communicating abnormalities shown on radiographs that have been ordered as a matter of routine, such as a chest radiograph before surgery. Referring physicians are less likely to expect abnormalities on these routine examinations, and therefore may not seek results. Because these reports have a greater chance of getting lost in the system, significant abnormalities should be directly communicated by the radiologist.

If a radiologist cannot reach the referring physician by telephone, the radiologist may give a verbal report to the physician's designated deputy. If neither the physician nor the designee can be reached within a reasonable time, or if the physician or designee is unknown, the report should be communicated directly to the patient.

All verbal communication should be documented on the radiology report. If the verbal communication is not completed before the written report is issued, radiologists should consider issuing a written addendum to the report that documents completion of the communication. Alternatively, radiologists may keep a log in the radiology department that documents all pertinent discussions with referring physicians when the discussions occur.

It must be constantly kept in the minds of all radiologists that communication of the results of a radiological examination has become just as much the duty of radiologists as is the rendering of the radiographic interpretation[13].

CONSEQUENCES OF BEING SUED FOR MALPRACTICE

Although being sued for malpractice is the most common consequence of committing a medical error resulting in patient injury, it is not the only, nor even necessarily the most serious, after-effect. There are two sequelae that could be far more catastrophic to a radiologist's career: institution by a state licensing board of disciplinary proceedings that could result in the loss of a medical license, or the filing of criminal charges that could result in a jail sentence[14]. Other onerous sequelae include loss of malpractice insurance, issuance of a report to the National Practitioner Data Bank, and termination as a provider of radiological services by third-party payors such as Medicare, Medicaid or managed care organizations. The initiation of punitive actions against physicians that go far beyond conventional malpractice litigation is clearly on the rise. This phenomenon is undoubtedly fueled by the news media, which give considerable attention to, and tend to sensationalize, medical mishaps and physician error. Such publicity clearly fans the flames of the public's anxiety about errant physicians, and foments concern that medical malpractice is rampant and uncontrolled by professional and government agencies[15].

An example of why public perception of physician quality may be deteriorating is the national coverage of the death of a successful New York playwright several years ago owing to alleged physician and radiologist malpractice[16]. The 35-year-old writer and composer of a hit Broadway musical (Rent) died of a ruptured thoracic aneurysm after having been treated and released, without correct diagnosis, from two New York City hospitals. The state health commissioner publicly faulted doctors in both hospitals for not being thorough or aggressive enough in their efforts to find a reason for the patient's chest pain. 'Had the correct diagnosis been made, there's a possibility that effective treatment could have been rendered', she said. Health department officials 'were so incensed' with the two hospitals that they immediately imposed US$6000 and US$10 000 fines and sent the names of the doctors involved to the state Office of Professional Misconduct for investigation. The patient's chest radiographs that had initially been interpreted as normal were later 'deemed abnormal' by five health department consultants: the heart was 'slightly too large' and the aorta 'too long', according to a front-page newspaper account.

Others have voiced concern that insufficient disciplinary actions are being taken by state licensing boards against errant physicians. 'If we tolerated this kind of laxity with pilots, we would have a major plane crash every day; for doing things for which doctors are merely slapped on the wrist, pilots would be gone', says Sidney Wolfe of the Public Citizens Research Group. As a result, medical disciplinary activities are being stepped up in many US states[17].

Another adverse consequence of being accused of medical malpractice is the requirement that such events be reported to the National Practitioner Data Bank. Congress created the data bank in 1986, when it enacted the Health Care Quality Improvement Act. Designed to reduce malpractice, the act requires hospitals to report actions restricting physicians' privileges, malpractice insurance companies to report indemnification payments paid on behalf of physicians, and state licensing boards to report disciplinary actions taken. Because physician data bank records are available to hospitals, insurance companies and managed care organizations, some concern exists that an unfavorable National Practitioner Data Bank report may adversely impact upon a physician's career.

Charging physicians with criminal activity has historically involved allegations of insurance (including Medicare and Medicaid) fraud, sexual abuse of patients or illegal use of controlled substances, although criminal prosecution of physicians in these cases has remained rare. In the past several years, however, a spate of criminal prosecutions of physicians centering on charges of reckless endangerment of patients or gross negligence has occurred.

Summarizing the current status of criminal prosecution of physicians, one researcher explained that the law defines reckless endangerment as the 'conscious disregard of a known and substantial likelihood of injury to a patient'. Indeed, if the patient dies as a result of the injury, a charge of manslaughter may be initiated. Although responsible physicians have 'nothing to fear from the criminal law', admonishes the researcher, 'physicians who intentionally or recklessly disregard the patient's safety may properly face criminal prosecution'[18].

Allegations of malpractice may also impair a physician's ability to continue as a provider to patients in managed care organizations[19].

RISK MANAGEMENT POINTERS

The following pointers will assist radiologists in dealing with these ever-increasing disciplinary and data-collecting measures.

Radiologists should keep in mind that a national data bank that permanently documents adverse actions taken against them pertaining to malpractice indemnification, restriction or other penalties imposed by government agencies on their medical licenses or professional status, or suspension or revocation of hospital privileges, is in operation and that similar repositories either have been established or are being considered in many states. Although the degree to which an adverse entry in a data bank will impair a radiologist's career has not yet been determined, it nonetheless should be emphasized that the information contained in these data banks is available to hospitals, managed care organizations and insurance companies. Because a documented unfavorable professional event could exclude a radiologist from obtaining a managed care contract, privileges in

Table 4   Words of advice for those undergoing litigation

Pursue dismissal or a verdict of non-liability
Attend depositions of adversarial witnesses
Attend the trial
Resist: do not settle just because 'it's easier'
   or 'I don't have the energy or time to proceed to trial'
Periodically check one's own national data bank record

a hospital, malpractice insurance at standard cost or a state medical license, radiologists should be protective of their record and should make every effort to *keep it unblemished*.

Radiologists who are sued for malpractice should try to achieve dismissal of the lawsuit or a verdict of non-liability (Table 4). This is best done by co-operating fully with defense attorneys and assisting in uncovering medical facts that buttress, and seeking out expert witnesses who can support, their actions. Unless specifically advised to the contrary by their attorneys, radiologist defendants should attend depositions of adversarial witnesses and should attend the trial itself.

Settlement of a malpractice lawsuit, or acceptance of a compromise agreement arising from an investigation by a state licensing board or a hospital disciplinary committee, should be entered into with great caution and only if the radiologist believes, after consultation with an attorney, that no better alternative exists. Radiologists should never agree to a settlement or a compromise agreement because it is 'easier' or 'simpler' to do so, or because they 'do not have the energy or time to resist'. Radiologists should not be beguiled with flippant reassurances that such settlements guarantee no imputing of guilt. The opposite is usually true: a settlement voluntarily agreed to by a radiologist is generally considered by governmental agencies and insurance companies as an admission of wrongdoing to the same degree as a verdict or decision reached by fact-finding bodies such as a jury or a board. What might seem to be a 'not guilty' entry in a databank today may well assume significant importance and come back to haunt the radiologist tomorrow.

A radiologist who receives an enquiry from a hospital, insurance company, state licensing board or similar body that indicates it is contemplating or launching an investigation into the activities of the radiologist should answer promptly and fully and consider consulting an attorney. Often, early responses and even a personal appearance, if allowed, may satisfy an investigator and pre-empt a fully fledged and costly proceeding.

Because reporting errors often occur, radiologists should periodically check their own national data bank record to make sure it contains no inaccuracies.

REFERENCES

1. Berlin L, Berlin JW. Malpractice and radiologists in Cook County, IL: trends in 20 years of litigation. *Am J Roentgenol* 1995;165:781–8
2. Berlin L. Malpractice issues in radiology: the importance of proper radiographic positioning and technique. 1996;166:769–71
3. Berlin L. Perceptual errors. *Am J Roentgenol* 1996;167:587–90
4. Berlin L. Malpractice issues in radiology: possessing ordinary knowledge. *Am J Roentgenol* 1996;166:1027–9
5. Berlin L. Malpractice issues in radiology: errors in judgment. *Am J Roentgenol* 1996; 166:1259–61
6. Levinson W. Physician–patient communication: a key to malpractice prevention. *J Am Med Assoc* 1994;272:1619–20
7. Berlin L. Reporting the 'missed' radiologic diagnosis: medicolegal and ethical considerations. *Radiology* 1994;192:183–7
8. *Phillips* v. *Good Samaritan Hospital*, 416 NE2d 646, 1979 (Ohio App. 1979)
9. *Courfeau* v. *Dodd*, 773 SW2d 436 (Ark 1989)
10. *ACR Standard for Communication: Diagnostic Radiology*. Reston, VA: American College of Radiology, 1999
11. Berlin L. Malpractice issues in radiology: communication of the urgent finding. *Am J Roentgenol* 1996;166:513–15
12. Beckman HB, Markakis KM, Suchman AL, Frankel RM. The doctor–patient relationship and malpractice: lessons from plaintiff depositions. *Arch Intern Med* 1994; 154:1365–70
13. Kline TJ, Kline TS. Radiologists, communication, and resolution 5: a medicolegal issue. *Radiology* 1992;184:131–4
14. Brahams D. Doctors and manslaughter. *Lancet* 1993;341:1404
15. Gavzer B. When doctors are the problem: why some doctors may be hazardous to your health. *Parade* 14 April 1996:4–6
16. Rosenthal E. Two New York hospitals fined for lax treatment of 'Rent' playwright, who later died. *New York Times* 13 December 1996:A21
17. Law requiring self-policing falls short of intended response. *USA Today*, 11 September 1995:2
18. Annas GJ. Medicine, death and the criminal law. *N Engl J Med* 1995;333:527–30
19. Kertesz L. Horror stories aside, HMOs may be curbing malpractice. *Mod Healthcare* 5 August 1996:56

Table 1   Major categories* of complications. Adapted from reference 1, with permission

Complications	Percentage of claims
Death	35
Nerve damage	15
Brain damage	12
No obvious injury	5
Airway trauma	5
Eye damage	3
Emotional distress	3
Pneumothorax	3
Stroke	3

*Only the major categories of complications with an occurrence rate of 3% or greater are included

Table 2   Major categories* of damaging events. Adapted from reference 1, with permission

Damaging events	Percentage of claims
Respiratory system	37
Equipment problems	9
Cardiovascular system	6
Wrong drug or dose	4

*Only the major categories of damaging events with an occurrence rate of 3% or greater are included. In the respiratory system category only damaging events with an occurrence rate of 2% or greater are included

Table 3   Causes of malpractice claims filed against anesthesiologists

All cases	Adult non-obstetric	Obstetric	Pediatric
Death (35%)	death (39%)	maternal death (22%)	death (50%)
Nerve damage (15%)	nerve damage (16%)	newborn brain damage (20%)	brain damage (30%)
Brain damage (12%)	brain damage (13%)	headache (12%)	nerve damage (1%)
Minor injury (29%)	minor injury (4%)	minor injury (32%)*	minor injury (12%)

*Includes headache, pain during anesthesia, backache and emotional distress

NERVE INJURY

Nerve injury is a common patient injury related to anesthesia, and a major source of professional liability for anesthesiologists (Table 9, Figure 2). Although the mechanism of injury cannot be explicitly determined in the majority of cases, nerve injuries are often considered to be the result of positioning problems or needle injury. Some individuals may be more susceptible than others. For example, males more often filed claims for ulnar

Table 4 Payment data

	Pediatric	Adult	Obstetric	Nerve injury
Payment frequency				
Payment (%)	64	59	53	47
No payment (%)	26	33	38	53
Data missing (%)	10	8	9	0
Median payment ($US)	111 234	90 000	293 000	18 000
Payment range ($US)	—	15 000–6 million	675 000–5.4 million	188 000–2.1 million

Table 5 Relationship of complications to anesthetic technique

	Adult	Adult non-OB	Obstetric	Pediatric
General anesthesia (%)	70	76	33	89
Regional anesthesia (%)	24	20	75	3
Other (%)	—	—	< 2*	—
Missing data (%)	6	4	< 1	8

*Claims made because of lack of anesthesia availability; OB, obstetric

Table 6 Analysis of closed claims studies

Seventy-six per cent of all obstetric and 74% of all non-obstetric claims were considered to be related to anesthetic complications

Claims involving general anesthesia were more frequently associated with death, severe injuries and higher award payments than those involving regional anesthesia

Airway management was identified as the most critical event related to adverse outcomes

Seventy-two per cent of adverse outcomes due to respiratory events were considered to be preventable with better monitoring

Claims were filed more often by women (62%) than by men, except for nerve injuries, where claims were filed in equal proportions

Pediatric injuries were more severe than adult injuries, and more often related to respiratory events. Fifty per cent of pediatric patients died and 30% had brain damage, compared with 35% and 11% of adults, respectively

nerve damage (69%). Patients filing claims for nerve injury were generally healthy, as opposed to patients with other injuries such as respiratory events, who more commonly presented with pre-existing conditions which predisposed them to complications.

ANESTHESIA EQUIPMENT AND MONITORING

Anesthesia equipment problems are reported as 9% of damaging events leading to malpractice claims against anesthesiologists (Table 10). In OB

Table 7 Analysis of obstetric (OB) anethesia claims[7]

The overall payment rate for OB claims (53%) did not significantly differ from that for non-OB claims (59%)

Maternal convulsions represented the single most common cause of anesthetic-related morbidity/mortality in OB patients, most often due to intravascular local anesthetic injection. In most cases, bupivacaine was the anesthetic agent used. Eighty-three per cent of convulsions resulted in maternal and/or fetal neurological injury or death

Aspiration of gastric contents was a more common complication

Of the OB claims, 67% involved Cesarean section, 33% vaginal deliveries

Thirty-two per cent of claims involved relatively minor injuries, including headache, pain during anesthesia, backache and emotional distress

Headache was the third most common complication and resulted in payment in 56% of cases

Table 8 Distribution of claims for adverse respiratory events. Adapted from reference 2, with permission

Event	Percentage of respiratory claims	Percentage of total claims
Inadequate ventilation	38	13
Esophageal intubation	18	6
Difficult tracheal intubation	17	6
Airway obstruction	7	2
Bronchospasm	6	2
Aspiration	5	2
Premature tracheal extubation	4	1
Unintentional tracheal extubation	3	1
Inadequate FIO_2	2	1
Endobronchial intubation	1	< 1
Total	100	34

claims, 45% of equipment problems were related to severed epidural catheters, with the remainder due to ventilation equipment. Adverse outcomes related to gas delivery equipment, although rare (occurring in only 2% of claims between 1961 and 1994), resulted in injuries of high severity. Death or permanent brain damage resulted from almost all injuries. Equipment misuse was three times more common than equipment failure and included broken, disabled or ignored alarms and monitors.

Of all anesthesia claims, 78% of adverse events were judged to be preventable with the use or better use of monitoring, particularly pulse oximetry and capnography (Table 11). Ancillary personnel played a prominent role in initiating events. Although advances in technology and monitoring

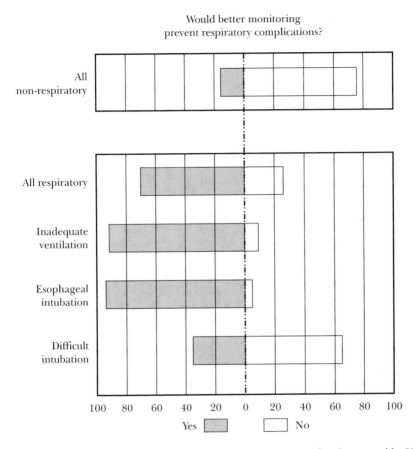

Would better monitoring
prevent respiratory complications?

Figure 1   Percentage of adverse outcomes that the reviewers considered preventable (Yes) or not preventable (No) with better monitoring in each of the major groups of respiration adverse events. The incidence of 'impossible to judge' was 1–3% in the respiratory groups and 9% in the non-respiratory group ($p < 0.05$, compared with non-respiratory claims). From reference 2, with permission

standards should improve outcomes related to anesthesia equipment, adverse outcomes related to anesthesia equipment have continued throughout the 1990s. Cost containment issues may also be a factor, since older equipment is more likely to be involved in anesthesia complications and product liability litigation.

STANDARD OF CARE AND ANESTHESIA LIABILITY

It is apparent that adherence to the standard of care alone is not adequate to prevent litigation. Payment has been reported in more than 40% of

Table 9   Claims for nerve injury. Adapted from reference 3, with permission

Nerve	Percentage of claims
Ulnar	34
Brachial plexus	23
Lumbosacral nerve root	16
Spinal cord	6
Sciatic	5
Median	4
Radial	3
Femoral	3
Multiple nerves*	2
Other nerves*	5
Total	100

*Includes phrenic, pudendal, perineal, seventh cranial nerve, long thoracic, optic nerves, and unspecified other nerves, each with a frequency of < 1%

Table 10   Adverse outcomes. Adapted from reference 4, with permission

Equipment group	Death (n)	Brain damage (n)	Awareness/ fright (n)	Recovery delayed (n)	Tracheostomy scar (n)	Pneumothorax (n)
Breathing circuit	10	10	1	5	1	1
Vaporizer	7	3	5	0	0	0
Ventilator	7	5	0	0	0	0
Supply tanks or lines	6	2	0	0	0	0
Anesthesia machine	3	0	1	0	1	0
Supplemental O$_2$ tubing	1	1	0	0	0	2
Total	34	21	7	5	2	3

Table 11   Monitors deemed useful in cases of preventable injuries or deaths. From reference 5, with permission

Monitors	Overall* (%)	Regional (%)	General (%)
Pulse oximetry	40	80	32
Capnometry	2	1	2
Pulse oximetry plus capnometry	51	16	58
Other	5	0	6
Not specified	2	1	2

*In five cases the type of anesthesia employed was not specified

claims when the anesthesia care was judged to be appropriate (Figure 3). In cases where anesthesia care was judged to be substandard, however, payments were made in more than 80% of cases. Although severity of injury alone does not appear to influence likelihood of payment, there is a

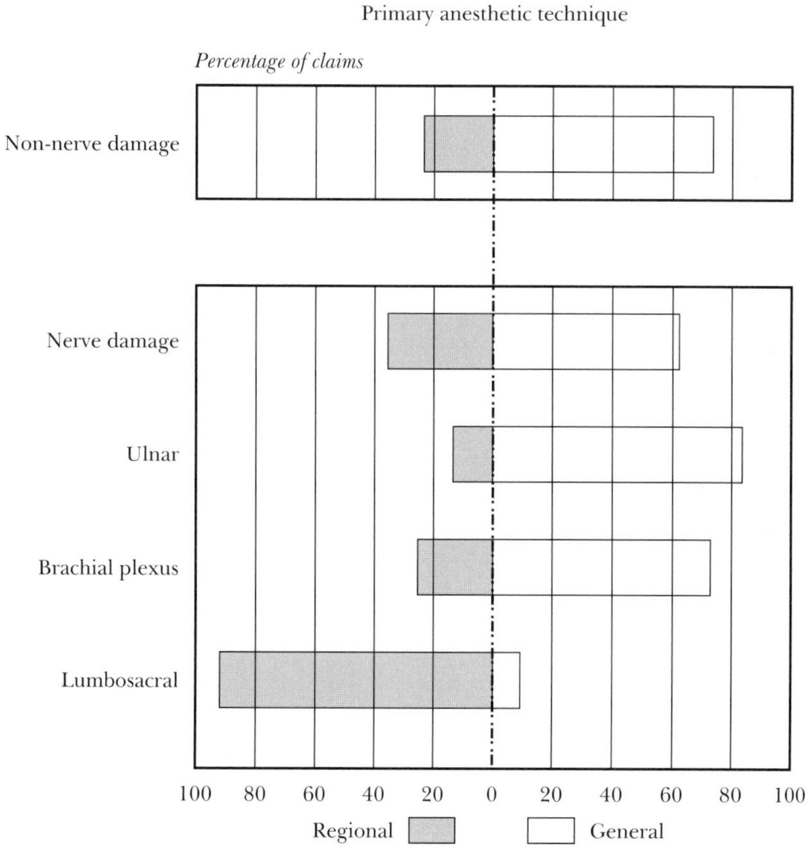

Figure 2 Incidence of regional and general anesthesia in each category of injury ($p < 0.01$ compared with non-nerve damage). From reference 3, with permission

close association between failure to provide care to the prevailing standard and severity of injury (Figure 4).

Published practice standards, guidelines and parameters are increasingly being used in malpractice litigation for inculpatory and exculpatory purposes[8]. A relevant practice parameter may be introduced as evidence of the standard of care under the common law provisions of most states, provided it meets certain criteria of reliability. Preliminary evaluation of the use of such guidelines in anesthesia, as published by the American Society of Anesthesiologists, indicates that adherence to simple and clearly defined practice standards and guidelines is generally beneficial in adjudication for physicians involved in litigation. Thirty-eight per cent of defense attorneys for physicians reported that guidelines had been important in more than one case during one year studied.

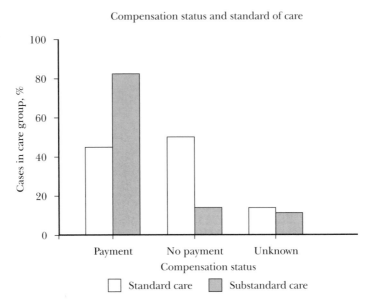

Figure 3 Incidence of compensation among patients who did or did not receive appropriate care (for whom appropriateness of care could be judged). There is a significant association between incidence of compensation and standard of care ($p \leq 0.1$). From reference 6, with permission

SUMMARY CHECKLIST TO AVOID/SURVIVE LITIGATION

Evaluate

(1) Carefully evaluate patients preoperatively. There is an association between pre-existing conditions and adverse outcomes and anesthesia claims, particularly in relation to respiratory events.

(2) Evaluate your preparedness and the preparedness of ancillary staff, including nurses and technicians, to deal with adverse events in your facility.

(3) Evaluate your facility, equipment and techniques to determine to what extent they may contribute to damaging events and what can be done to correct these issues.

(4) Evaluate your ability and willingness to establish a rapport with your patients and their families. Physicians who have not established favorable relationships are more likely to be sued, especially when their treatment does not significantly differ from the standard of care.

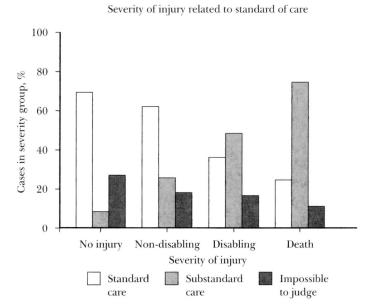

Figure 4   Incidence of standard and substandard care in each severity of injury group for 1004 lawsuits. There is a significant association between standard of care and severity of injury ($p \leq 0.1$). From reference 6, with permission

Educate

(1) Educate yourself and your staff as to the common causes of adverse events and appropriate measures for prevention and treatment.

(2) Include in your continuing education information concerning new techniques, equipment and monitoring devices. Be sure you understand and have practiced this information prior to an emergency.

(3) Educate your staff, especially nurses and technicians, in the use of anesthesia and respiratory equipment in both routine and emergency situations.

(4) Educate your patients concerning the plans and risks for their anesthetic care. Research indicates that patients are not unduly alarmed by careful explanations of risk. Such explanations may help you establish a valuable relationship with your patients and their families.

(5) Learn about your options for malpractice coverage in your area and in your specialty. Be aware of changing conditions in coverage and legal concepts.

Prepare

(1) Prepare yourself, your workstation and your staff for unexpected challenges and complications.

(2) Check out anesthesia machines and equipment in accordance with accepted guidelines.

(3) Have both routine and emergency equipment and supplies in good repair in a convenient location known and available to you and your staff.

(4) Prepare an emergency intubation cart located in a convenient location with emergency airway equipment including various stylets, laryngoscopy equipment, masks (such as laryngeal mask airways), fiberoptic laryngoscopes and bronchoscopes, and cricothyrotomy equipment. Your familiarity with the use of this equipment and the ability of your staff to assist you is even more important than the type of equipment you choose.

(5) Label medications and syringes and prepare them in reasonable quantities, doses and dilutions. Anticipate your needs and prepare accordingly.

(6) Have a separate box or other container for emergency airway supplies and equipment, as well as emergency drugs (code box), in a centralized, convenient location.

(7) Purchase liability coverage from a reliable carrier. Carefully investigate your options. Be aware of terms and limits of your policy and their implications in your practice.

Practice prudently

(1) Practice prudently in accordance with established standards for your specialty. The American Society of Anesthesiologists publishes practice parameters, standards and guidelines annually in the membership directory. Understand their application to your practice.

(2) Protect your patients from eye injury and nerve damage with appropriate padding and other protective measures.

(3) Keep careful records. Include preoperative checks, routine protective and monitoring measures, as well as emergency events and interventions.

(4) Involve yourself and other members of your department in facility quality-assurance and peer-review, including ongoing assessment and improvement projects.

(5) Participate in hospital committees regarding purchase and utilization of capital equipment, supplies and pharmaceuticals.

(6) Promptly report adverse outcomes to your insurance carrier and participate in the investigation of such events with your carrier and your hospital risk management department.

REFERENCES

1. Cheney FW, Posner KL, Caplan RA. Adverse respiratory events infrequently leading to malpractice suits. A closed claims analysis. *Anesthesiology* 1991;75:932–9

2. Caplan RA, Posner KL, Ward RJ, Cheney FW. Adverse respiratory events in anesthesia: a closed claims analysis. *Anesthesiology* 1990;72:828–33

3. Kroll DA, Caplan RA, Posner D, Ward RJ, Cheney FW. Nerve injury associated with anesthesia. *Anesthesiology* 1990;73:202–7

4. Caplan RA, Vistica MF, Posner KL, Cheney FW. Adverse anesthetic outcomes arising from gas delivery equipment: a closed claims analysis. *Anesthesiology* 1997;87:741–8

5. Tinker JH, Dull DL, Caplan RA, *et al*. Role of monitoring devices in prevention of anesthetic mishaps: a closed claims analysis. *Anesthesiology* 1989;71:541–6

6. Cheney FW, Posner KL, Caplan RA, Ward RJ. Standard of care and anesthesia liability. *J Am Med Assoc* 1989;261:1599–603

7. Chadwick HS, Posner KL, Caplan RA, *et al*. A comparison of obstetric and nonobstetric anesthesia malpractice claims. *Anesthesiology* 1991;74:242–9

8. Hyams AL, Brandenburg JA, Lipsitz SR, *et al*. Practice guidelines and malpractice litigation: a two-way street. *Ann Intern Med* 1995;122:450–5

11

Emergency medicine

Robert M. Hamilton, MD, and Joseph Joyce, MD

INTRODUCTION

Emergency department claims represent approximately 19% of total claims and 18% of total dollars paid in malpractice cases.

Emergency medicine faces many of the same legal challenges discussed in other chapters of this book. However, emergency medicine specialists evaluate patients from multiple specialty areas in unscheduled visits, often at odd hours, when hospital diagnostic and consulting services are not available. These difficulties, along with the sheer volume of patients presenting with diverse problems ranging from non-acute to critical, present special challenges to the emergency medicine specialist. Emergency departments across the USA see approximately 100 million patient visits per year and account for over 25% of all hospital admissions. The large number of patients seen and the high acuity provide fodder for those orchestrating malpractice lawsuits.

This chapter addresses common areas of litigation, provides suggestions for limiting risks in these areas and discusses 'dos' and 'don'ts' if litigation occurs.

A brief historical perspective on the medicolegal climate in the USA is helpful in assessing the current issues in emergency medicine, as well as projecting possible future directions.

In the 1960s medical malpractice insurance was relatively inexpensive. For a few hundred dollars, an occurrence-based policy could be obtained. Emergency departments were poorly organized and any physician, regardless of background, could work in the 'ER'.

As the 1970s progressed, a boom in malpractice suits led to tort reforms and serious professional liability concerns. As the number of suits increased, so did the awards leading to sky-rocketing insurance rates. During this time, especially the later 1970s, the specialty of emergency medicine began to emerge and be recognized. Specific postgraduate training programs began, and physicians began to focus on the special issues unique to emergency medicine. Risk management also developed, as physicians with special expertise in emergency medicine began studying the issues. Through analysis of emergency medicine it was recognized that specific claims to dollar losses were related to a small number of clinical problems.

During the 1980s, the American College of Emergency Physicians (ACEP) reformed the insurance committee and later the liability committee into the medical–legal committee, to deal with malpractice and other legal concerns. Hospitals began to require increasing professional liability coverage from emergency physicians. Malpractice insurance became more difficult to obtain. Insurance premiums increased dramatically, and many insurers stopped insuring physicians altogether. It was predicted that the late 1980s and the 1990s would see soaring malpractice costs. However, this has not occurred, and insurance rates have been relatively stable and constant since the mid 1980s. In emergency medicine there has been a dramatic improvement in record-keeping, general administration and quality assurance–risk management. These have certainly helped to improve experience in the area of professional liability.

Part of the malpractice problem revolves around the assumption that good care leads to good outcomes and bad care leads to bad outcomes. Even physicians tend to believe this, and studies have shown that physician-reviewer judgments varied by 30% towards malpractice if a bad outcome was known.

The good news, if any, is that the number of emergency medicine malpractice claims closed without indemnity payment has ranged from 61 to 75% in various studies. This is supported in a recent study of claims in Massachusetts: the percentage of cases closed without indemnity payment has increased, comparing the period pre-1988 with the period since 1988.

COMMON AREAS OF LITIGATION IN EMERGENCY MEDICINE

The majority of risk in emergency medicine is concentrated in several clinical areas (Table 1). Specific circumstances predisposing to increased risk are conveyed in Table 2.

Chest pain

Research has shown that even with adherence to rigid protocols, 4–5% of myocardial infarctions (MIs) or unstable angina will be discharged from the emergency department. Missed MI represents the largest single dollar loss

Table 1   Most common areas of litigation

Non-traumatic chest pain in adults
Extremity trauma/fractures
Wound care
Febrile infants/children
Abdominal pain

Table 2   Pearls: increased malpractice risk

Patients who return for unscheduled second or third emergency department visits
Intoxicated, psychotic, mentally retarded patients or patients under the influence of drugs
Very old or very young patients
'Sign-out' patients: change of shift
Illiterate patients
Discharged patients with abdominal pain of unclear etiology, and loose follow-up plans
Pregnant patients with pain and no proof of intrauterine pregnancy
Abnormal vital signs not repeated or explained, or incomplete vital signs
Failure to look at medicine list, allergies or patient medical instruction when prescribing new medications
Verbal orders for medications
Patients who leave against medical advice, without signing
Medical screening examinations for health maintenance organization patients
Following consultant's advice (by phone or in department) when it conflicts with your plan
Failing to explain risks in detail when obtaining informed consent
Physicians pointing fingers at other care-givers
Patient family complaints
Incomplete medical records
Lack of communication
'Moonlighters' with limited emergency medicine experience

in emergency medicine malpractice suits. With 4.5 million chest-pain visits to emergency departments annually and approximately half of those admitted, a discharge error rate of 4–5% results in 22 000 patients being sent home inappropriately. The causes are many, including the uncertainties of the cardiogram and inexact history/physical findings.

Up to one-third of patients have premonitory symptoms prior to onset of their MI. These symptoms may exist for a month beforehand, and may be dismissed by the patient and physician alike. It is important to realize that ischemia, even without infarction, can cause fatal arrhythmias. It is therefore important to treat unstable angina as if it were a MI. These patients need to be admitted and monitored. Ideally they should have nitrates, aspirin, beta-blockers and heparin administered; if there is no contraindication, the $2\beta,3\alpha$-glycoprotein inhibitors should be considered in patients with S–T elevations or depressions.

Cardiac enzyme testing, although helpful when positive, provides almost no help in anginal patients. In patients with MIs, often 6–9 hours elapse from pain onset prior to elevation in enzymes. Fortunately, the acceptance of the 23-hour admission and chest-pain centers in the emergency department have lessened the difficulty in monitoring patients who are in the low-risk category. Statistically, ischemic pain is rare in males less than 40 years and females less than 50 years of age. However, electrocardiograms (ECGs) are often recommended in patients with chest pain who are over 30. Cardiac risk factors are very important considerations in chest-pain evaluation and should be carefully documented.

Transfers of patients with chest pain are dangerous. Arrhythmias are common in the first few hours after an infarction and these patients should be considered unstable for transfer. Managed care may put undue pressure on the treating emergency physician; however, financial considerations should never compromise patient care. If transfer is necessary to a higher level of care, carefully document the risks and benefits and send the patient in a mobile intensive care unit with a Registered Nurse and a paramedic trained in advanced cardiac life support.

Extremity trauma

Up to 25% of all emergency medicine malpractice cases result from failure to diagnose a fracture. Limiting these missed fractures requires a sophisticated approach to the history/physical examination and X-ray interpretation.

Problems may occur owing to altered mental status from drugs and alcohol, psychiatric issues, distracting injuries and X-ray interpretations. Many fractures do not show up on X-ray and proper views must be obtained. If a car is involved in an accident and the front, left fender is damaged, it may not be visible from the right or back views. The same principle holds for fracture evaluation. In addition, some principal fractures are not expected to show up on initial X-rays. These include blow-out fractures of the orbit, navicular fractures, and stress fractures of the feet, legs and ribs.

If a fracture is suspected and the X-ray image appears negative, treat the patient as if they have a fracture, splint extremities and provide for non-weight-bearing crutch-walking. Follow up with bone scans, magnetic resonance imaging (MRI) or computed tomography (CT) scans as indicated. If a fracture is found, document the neurovascular function both before and after splinting.

In certain cases, X-rays are not indicated. It is particularly important in these patients to document absence of bony tenderness and absence of pain in the joint above and below the injury.

Document gait for injuries to the lower extremities. In patients who can easily walk, this will reassure family members. In those who cannot, the physician will need to rethink his/her diagnosis.

If further studies are needed, do not hesitate to call the radiologist. An arteriogram may be needed with certain injuries, especially in fracture dislocations of major joints such as the knee. Insist on proper X-ray views. These may not have been obtained because of patient pain. Films that are too light or dark or have movement artifact are inadequate.

Wound care

Many malpractice claims occur each year because of wound management issues. Approximately one-third of these cases are due to retained foreign bodies and one-third allege missed nerve and tendon injury.

Foreign bodies are often missed because they were not suspected by history, or the appropriate diagnostic test was not performed. Most glass and all metal show up on X-rays. Wooden foreign bodies rarely show up on radiographs, but imaging should be done and a meticulous examination should be performed. Documentation of exploration, wound cleansing and irrigation are extremely important in defending these claims.

Foreign bodies are more difficult to find and remove than one would think, even when located by X-ray. Such patients require early and close specialist follow-up. Informing the patient of the possibility of a retained foreign body may decrease the likelihood of filing suit if one is eventually found.

Although emergency medicine physicians are generally not expected to know how to repair tendons (except perhaps extensor) and nerves, they are expected to recognize injuries when structures are damaged. Patients will not often volunteer or recognize loss of sensation or function, and the physician must examine specifically for these injuries.

With a partial tear, a tendon may still appear to function well with minimal bleeding, but often will show impaired or painful motion against resistance. The wound should be explored for tendon damage while the affected parts are put through a range of motion. A tendon laceration that occurs while the affected joints are flexed or extended may not be visible with the extremity in a neutral position.

Nerve testing should include two-point discrimination for injuries on the hand or fingers, with special attention to the side of the finger distal to the side of the skin laceration. If such an injury is found, consultation with the follow-up specialist should be initiated.

The old adage 'document what you do and do what you document' is especially important in the area of wound management. Discharge instructions should indicate detailed wound care, signs of infection and follow-up recommendations.

Febrile infants and children

The febrile child may ultimately be diagnosed with bacteremia, pneumonia, abdominal infections and many other entities. Failure to diagnose meningitis represents one of the highest dollar-per-case categories of payment in emergency medicine. These cases represent approximately 15% of total payments in emergency medicine claims, but only about 2% of total claims filed in emergency medicine. The disability is great in these young patients, and often blame is placed on failure to diagnose and initiate early treatment.

Febrile infants that should arouse suspicion on the part of the treating physician are listed in Table 3. Two-thirds of cases of bacterial meningitis occur in children under the age of 18 months. This creates diagnostic difficulties. Stiff neck, Kernig's or Brudzinski's sign, headache and other signs or symptoms simply may not be present. A bulging fontanel is a late sign and should not be relied upon. Vomiting, lethargy and poor feeding, although non-specific, are characteristic of infants with meningitis.

Be careful of descriptions in the medical record that indicate lethargy, listlessness or toxicity. These descriptions, even if placed in the record by non-physician personnel, require extensive explanation if not present; if present, a lumbar puncture is required.

If you are not worried about meningitis, explain why in the chart. A record that paints a picture of a smiling child that interacts and looks around the room does not indicate a seriously ill child.

Table 3 Signs and symptoms of meningitis in children

High-pitched cry
Apnea
Bulging fontanel (late sign)
Headache: severe
Neck stiffness
Altered mental status/neurological examination
New-onset seizure
Petechial rash
Infant with poor feeding, unconsolable or irritable

Abdominal problems

Common abdominal syndromes in emergency medicine are often the result of failure to diagnose. These conditions include appendicitis, ectopic pregnancy, and ruptured spleen, liver or viscus.

Weeding out the many non-emergent, non-surgical causes of abdominal pain is time-consuming and often difficult. Less than 50% of abdominal pain eventually results in specific diagnosis, and often this does not occur during the emergency department visit. Many serious problems resemble minor problems such as a viral syndrome when in their early stages. Much like a car on an assembly line, it takes time to recognize eventually what the final product will be. At a certain time, enough information becomes available to make the diagnosis. Although reassuring patients is an important part of medicine, too much reassurance can be dangerous when the diagnosis is in doubt. The physician must be willing to say to all patients with seemingly minor abdominal pain that it may represent something more serious. Explicit instruction to return for increasing pain, fever, etc. should be given to ensure follow-up and avoid a false sense of security. Listed in Table 4 are several points that may help in dealing with abdominal-pain work-ups.

IF A CLAIM IS FILED

The day that the notice of a malpractice claim filing arrives is often the beginning of a prolonged ordeal. Many cases are not closed for 4 or more years after the filing of a claim. The physician needs to measure his/her response and conserve emotional energy for the long road ahead.

First and foremost, the physician should consult with a legal counsel. All requests for information should be placed through the medical records department or an attorney. Do not discuss related matters with others

Table 4 Abdominal pain assessment

Beware of patients who minimize their symptoms

Confirm positive/negative physical findings on sequential
examinations. Time waiting for laboratories can be a useful
buffer, allowing a re-examination

Not all patients have textbook symptoms: expect variation

Avoid discharging patients with a non-specific diagnosis
after giving narcotics. Pain requiring narcotics while
in the emergency department often requires
23 hours' observation

Submit a pregnancy test for all women of child-bearing
years even if they are taking birth-control pills or have
an intrauterine device or tubal ligation

A positive pregnancy test, with pain as the presenting symptom,
requires sonographic localization of the pregnancy

Avoid using pelvic inflammatory disease as the diagnosis
unless obviously present. Bleeding from a leaking ectopic
pregnancy can cause the same symptoms

Suspect ectopic pregnancy in all women with pain presenting
in the child-bearing years

Mentally retarded, psychotic or drug- and alcohol-intoxicated
patients are difficult to examine. When involved in trauma,
they require re-examinations and often prolonged observation.
Err on the side of safety

Document all pertinent negative historical and physical findings

Pain sensation and ethnic response to pain varies considerably.
Beware of the stoical patient involved in a major trauma

Fracture and muscular pain can be extremely distracting,
causing other significant injuries to be missed

Table 5 'Dos' and 'don'ts' when a claim is filed

When amending a chart, initial and date changes

Do not alter or 'lose' records

Complete records at the time of patient encounter, do not rely on
memory

Do not omit findings in the record

Keep extraneous, funny, derogatory or sarcastic material out of
charts

Chart telephone communication with patient/family

involved in the patient's case or, ideally, anyone at all. Silence is especially important if you are contacted directly by the plaintiff's attorney. Even if they promised, they will not list you as a defendant. The attorney's game is to divide and conquer. Getting health-care workers to point to colleagues and identify weaknesses in patient care goes a long way towards winning their case.

Your attorney will obtain external expert review of your record and care rendered. Try to maintain objectivity. No case is perfectly documented, and in retrospect we all could have done things a little better. Listen to your attorney and the external reviewer. If they believe that the case is not defendable, obtain a third independent review. Pursuing a weak case will ultimately result in high emotional and financial costs.

Table 5 lists some 'dos' and 'don'ts' if a case if filed. Alteration of records after a case is filed can have devastating results in front of a jury. Credibility is lost and even the uninvolved parts of the record will be questioned for validity. This is contrasted with amendments which are legitimate changes in a record. The original entry should have one line drawn through it and remain legible. The amended information should be initialled and dated, so that it is clear when the entry was made. Amendments should occur prior to notice of a claim. Prospective attention to your records will go far in preventing future suits.

It should be obvious that attention to systems, risk management, quality assurance and documentation issues will help to decrease risk. Understanding what are the high-risk clinical areas in emergency medicine will help the practitioner to focus extra attention on these patients.

REFERENCES

1. Bonner, S. Chest pain and reducing the legal risks. *ED Legal Lett, Am Health Consult* 1998;9(11):105–12
2. Curran, WJ. Legal history of emergency medicine from medieval common law to the AIDS epidemic. *Am J Emerg Med* 1997;15:658–70
3. Dunn JD, Mayer TA. Future legal issues in emergency medicine. *Emerg Med Clin North Am* 1993;11:933–51
4. Fish, E. *Preventing Emergency Medicine Malpractice*. Medical Economics Books, 1989
5. George, JE. The emergency department medical record. *Emerg Med Clin North Am* 1993;11:889–903
6. Karcz A, Korn R, Burke MC, *et al*. Malpractice claims against emergency physicians in Massachusetts 1975–1993. *Am J Emerg Med* 1996;14:341–5
7. Karcz A, Holbrook J, Burke MC, *et al*. Massachusetts emergency medicine, closed malpractice claims: 1998–1990. *Ann Emerg Med* 1993;22:553–9
8. Rusnak RA, Borer JM, Fastow JS. Misdiagnosis of acute appendicitis: common features discovered in cases after litigation. *Am J Emerg Med* 1994;12:397–402
9. Schutte, JE. *Preventing Medical Malpractice Suits*. Hogrefe and Huber, 1995

12

Obstetrics and gynecology

Jan Schneider, MD

The incursion of managed care into the practice of obstetrics and gynecology has recently replaced the medicolegal crisis as the greatest concern of practicing physicians. Even so, the relentless stream of litigation continues to cast a constant shadow over the specialty. The assault of litigation causes a great deal of expense, generates much emotion and influences virtually every doctor–patient interaction.

National data from a survey by the American College of Obstetricians and Gynecologists indicated that 73% of practicing obstetrician–gynecologists had been sued at least once (Table 1)[1]. The average physician reported 2–3 lawsuits. These data were based upon a 44% response rate; whether obstetricians who had been sued were more or less likely to complete such a questionnaire is not known. No matter what bias may have affected these data, they surely confirm that there is a high risk of litigation in obstetrics and gynecology. An additional, most chastening figure was that 27% of residents reported that they had been sued at least once as a result of events which occurred during their graduate education.

The survey also confirmed that the obstetric component of practice was the most likely to result in litigation with a 60%/40% split between obstetrics and gynecology. Particularly worrisome was that one-third of the obstetric claims (Table 2) were based on what was classified as a 'neurologically impaired baby'. These 'bad baby' cases are the big-ticket items which result in the greatest jury awards. Other sources indicate that the average settlement in such cases is more than $US600 000. Medicolegal settlements and jury awards of more than a million dollars represent just 3.6% of all cases, but cost more than half of all premium dollars.

Obstetrician–gynecologists represent approximately 5% of physicians in the USA. Yet this 5% generates 15% of all lawsuits which result in 36% of all payments made by medicolegal insurance companies. Not surprisingly, the specialty is under considerable scrutiny, and not much loved by the

Table 1 Obstetrics and gynecology

Seventy-three per cent of OB–GYNs sued at least once
Average number of claims per OB–GYN is 2.3
Twenty-seven per cent of residents sued at least once
Sixty per cent are OB claims and 40% are GYN claims
Fifteen per cent of all physician claims are in OB/GYN
Thirty-six per cent of all insurance payments are for OB/GYN

OB–GYN, obstetrician–gynecologist; OB/GYN, obstetrics/gynecology

Table 2 Obstetrics (OB) claims

Thirty-three per cent of OB claims for 'neurologically impaired baby', average settlement $US600 000
Three and a half per cent of all cases involve payments of > $US1 million

Table 3 Avoiding litigation

Defensive practice the rule of the day
Defensive practice improves quality of care
Maintain standards of care
Obtain proper informed consent using correct procedure: can it be proved?
Remember 'the retrospective' …
Proper legible documentation: what was done, when and why
Avoid angry or critical notes
Timely record entries
Incorrect entries: draw a line through initial and date, write correct entry below
Communication is key
Compassion often makes a difference
Risk management role

insurance carriers. The average annual premium paid by an obstetrician–gynecologist is approximately $US50 000. Thus, the 40 000 physicians in our specialty are responsible for a total expenditure of two billion dollars each year. As Everett Dierksen once said, this is 'real money'.

The key to a better world is obviously to avoid litigation (Table 3). The 'pollyanna' solution is to state that good competent practice will solve the problem. The reality is that the world is not perfect, that complications and bad outcomes happen in spite of the best of care, and that virtually any bad outcome will generate a lawsuit. A bad outcome alone may result in litigation, but is in itself not enough for the lawsuit to succeed.

The plaintiff's attorney must prove that there was failure to meet standards of care, that there was negligence, and that the physician failed to provide 'the required skill and knowledge ordinarily exercised by competent physicians'; the plaintiff must also show that such 'negligence' caused the specific injuries. The sad reality is that even when standards of care were fully met, this may at times be difficult to prove in a court of law. This is particularly true when the obstetrician did not take certain basic steps which are essential for the defense should a lawsuit occur. The plaintiff always has the wisdom of retrospect, and this can only be countered by sound defensive practice. Defensive practice not only saves the day should a lawsuit come: defensive practice also improves the quality of care.

The plaintiff's allegation of failure to meet standards of care may be considered at three levels. The worst is termed *res ipsa loquitur*: Latin for 'the thing speaks for itself'. This applies to situations where negligence is so obvious that the plaintiff is not required to produce an expert witness in the court room. Events such as a retained sponge or instrument, surgery on the wrong patient, the wrong operation or removal of the wrong organ are clear examples. Such cases tend to make the front page of the newspaper and cannot be defended. The issue is not whether money will exchange hands, but how much.

More challenging and often more chastening are situations where practice was less than ideal and a bad outcome occurred. Such clinical situations can often be viewed from several sides, and may contain elements which are defensible. Ugliness is ultimately in the eye of the beholder, and the beholder may be a jury. Examples include practice in violation of hospital rules, regulations or protocols, such as the giving of oxytocin without the obstetrician being in the hospital. Other examples are a delayed response to a patient with complications, such as bleeding, fever or shock, and trauma caused by the physician, such as the result of badly applied forceps, shoulder dystocia with neurological damage, or ureteric or bowel laceration at surgery.

The most difficult and emotionally troubling are situations where there was a bad outcome although care was fully within standards. To these situations the term 'maloccurrence' is often applied. The harsh reality of medicine is that bad things do happen to good people. Litigation, in such cases, gives plaintiffs the opportunity to pursue any of a wide array of imaginative allegations. As always, prevention is infinitely better than legal cure. Prevention is hinged upon defensive practice.

Defensive practice may be considered at three phases: before the event, after the event and, finally, even after a lawsuit is filed. Before the event, the first critical issue is to ensure full informed consent. It is a legal requirement that the patient be 'made aware of the nature and risks of a medical procedure or treatment, prior to agreeing to its performance'. This is not only a legal essential, but is a moral and medical requirement as well. There must be a 'meeting of the minds' between the physician and the patient before any procedure is performed. However, in retrospect, it may be difficult to prove that this was done. Every hospital has its own array of consent forms. Yet a lonely signature on such a form is usually not enough to convince a jury that a patient was fully counseled. It is a wise precaution for the physician to hand-write an entry on the form or in the chart, documenting the content of the counseling and the complications and options that were discussed with the patient. It is wise to ensure that any such entry is signed by both the physician and the patient. There is no jury that can deny that a patient was fully counseled if she signed her name to such a handwritten entry. These additional steps are time-consuming, but can save endless agony later should a tubal sterilization fail, or a postoperative complication happen, and the patient denies that she was ever warned that any such thing was possible.

Also before the event is defensive practice during the process of care. If there is a bad outcome at the end of the road, the plaintiff always has the advantage of retrospect. With the wisdom of hindsight, any of a series of decision points along the road can be highlighted as times when standards of care demanded that an alternative approach to therapy should have been pursued. The key to the later defense of such situations is timely and contemporary documentation. Documentation is the light that illuminates the forks in the road, and is the light that clarifies prospectively how decisions were made. It is the light which later will make it infinitely more difficult for a plaintiff to suggest that care was not given in a thoughtful way. It may be that in retrospect another clinical option might have been better, but, if it can be shown how, why and when decisions were made, these can be much more easily defended. It is particularly tragic in situations such as a long and complicated labor, when the nurse's notes confirm that the obstetrician was present for many hours, but there are no notations by the obstetrician to prove that full thought was given to each decision as it was made.

Documentation not only creates a paper trail of the care given, but surely also enhances the quality of care. Documentation is like consultation. When, in an acute clinical situation, one physician requests a second opinion from another, the very process of preparing to present the case often makes obvious what must be done. In a similar vein, the process of writing a note describing the clinical situation will frequently clarify the thinking and decision-making process. Documentation improves the quality of care.

Documentation must describe what was done, when it was done and why it was done. It must be accurate. This may seem obvious, yet ridiculous situations such as dictation error may cause great damage. A recent example in a shoulder-dystocia case was an entry stating 'suprafundal pressure' when 'suprapubic pressure' was meant. The simple one-word error made the lawsuit virtually indefensible. Entries must be factual. They must be not angry. There is nothing more damaging than an angry note in a record. Angry notes by a nurse, such as 'the doctor still has not answered his pager', can be devastating. Notes must be uncritical. Entries in the record which fault another health-care provider do not help the care of the patient and do not reflect the care that the patient received, and the only beneficiary is a plaintiff's attorney should the case come to litigation. Entries must be timely. Physicians often do not know what 'D.D.' represents on a discharge summary or operative note: the initials denote the date of dictation. It is particularly embarrassing if the date of dictation is after a complication was recognized, and even more embarrassing if it is beyond the date when the lawsuit was filed.

The record must be legible. It is particularly difficult to prove that appropriate care was rendered when notations made at the time cannot be read. Jokes about doctors' handwriting are clearly 'unfunny'. Equally unfunny are illegible signatures. It is a reflection of vanity for an individual physician to have a flamboyant and attractive signature which cannot be traced to the signatory at a later time. 'Everybody knows my signature', is simply not true. Writing a beeper number only is also not tenable. Beeper numbers cannot be traced years later. There is nothing more difficult than attempting to prove that appropriate physicians were present during a critical component of care, when signatures cannot reveal who was there. Any signature should have the name written in simple capital letters below.

Perhaps most important is that records must not be lost. This is particularly true of the fetomaternal monitor strip. Monitor strips have no further value to the patient (the fetus, now a child), but for medical–legal purposes they must be produced, should litigation happen. The monitor strips, particularly before the days of electronic recording, were bulky and difficult to store and were lost all too frequently. A defense attorney in Philadelphia said, 'Lost evidence is the defendant's passport to the land of disaster.' Indeed, if a monitor strip is lost, the implication is often that there was deliberate destruction.

One final essential is that entries must be unaltered. If an error is made (which happens not infrequently, such as an entry in the wrong chart, or on a wrong date), it is proper and easy to draw a line through the entry, initial and date the correction, and write the correct entry below. It is not tenable to erase or cover an entry so that it cannot be read, because in retrospect, this allows allegation of fraud. With the allegation of fraud comes the nightmare of claims for punitive damages.

Once a bad outcome occurs, the situation becomes emotionally charged and difficult for everyone concerned. Whenever there are complications, most physicians feel a burden of guilt with a great temptation to run and hide. That is not acceptable: as physicians, we must be there. The first priority is to repair any damage, whether there be a laceration in the bowel, a tied ureter, a gathered abscess or a compressing hematoma. The second priority must be to explain to the patient and her family what happened and how it happened. At the same time, the risk management team and perhaps the insurance company must also be informed, since it is highly likely they will hear more about the case. A difficult decision is whether any financial concession should be made when a complication occurs. There is a school of thought that implies that any 'writing off' of bills is a confession of less than optimal care. However, simple compassion may sometimes make all the difference in the world. If this includes some changes in billing, these may be very worthwhile.

A critical issue in a situation where there were complications is not to start pointing fingers and blaming others. Statements such as 'I left before this happened', or 'I consulted with the surgeon and it was the surgeon who said...', or 'If the pediatrician had performed more timely resuscitation', only add to the plaintiff's target and do no good. Misery does not love company.

Once the lawsuit is filed, a long and painful process begins (Table 4). The average time between the filing of a lawsuit and its disposition is currently 4.5 years. These become difficult times. Inevitably, the physician relives the events of the case, over and over again. Many physicians become clinically depressed, and counseling may be very helpful. Much time is devoted to what is termed 'Discovery'. This includes legal papers such as Interrogatories and Answers to which the physician becomes almost a bystander. It is essential that the obstetrician–gynecologist trusts his or her attorney during this process. Discovery usually includes the obtaining of depositions (Table 5). A deposition can be a long and arduous process. The physician must understand what this is all about. The physician must know that the deposition is taken under oath, and that the transcript is admissible in court. It is, therefore, critical that there be no contradictions between what is said at the deposition, and what is later said in court. Even more practical is the need to recognize that a deposition may last for hours.

Table 4 Recommendations when 'in litigation'

Average time between filing and disposition is 4.5 years
Fifty per cent of cases spontaneously resolve
Control emotions
Depression is inevitable
Consider counseling
Trust and follow attorney's advice
Know it is a legal, not medical, issue
Eighty per cent of trial cases are won by the defendant
Jury awards are often four times greater than settlements

Table 5 Deposition pointers

Deposition transcripts are admissible evidence in court
Avoid contradictions during the deposition
Watch the fatigue factor during deposition
Just answer the question (succinctly)
Allow your attorney to object before answering the question

Fatigue becomes a factor, and with fatigue, there is always a risk that a question at the end of the deposition will be answered somewhat differently than it was in the beginning. Theoretically, the same question cannot be asked more than once, but depositions are sometimes so long that the defense attorney may not object quickly enough or realize that a question is asked again. If a variant of the answer is given, it can be made to appear that there was dishonesty. Another problem is that physicians want to say too much. We are so eager to defend ourselves and to prove to everyone, including the plaintiff's attorney, that we are good doctors, that instead of answering the question, we tend to go on and on. The shorter the answer to any question, the better it is for defense. Finally, it is essential that in any situation such as a deposition, one has legal representation. Physicians have been virtually trapped into appearing at a deposition without representation, and their statements have ultimately been used against them.

In the average 4.5 years between the filing of a lawsuit and trial, approximately one-half of cases are dropped or dismissed, and one-third are settled. Only about 10% go to trial. Obviously, those most difficult to defend tend to be settled. It is not surprising, therefore, that almost 80% of those that do proceed to trial are won by the defense. However, it is a harsh fiscal reality that, when they are lost, jury awards tend to be four times greater than settlements for similar situations. The 20% that are lost generate both expense and, at times, damaging newspaper publicity.

Table 6 Witness pointers

Avoid anger
Be diplomatic and maintain decorum
Do not 'lose your cool'
Do not treat it as a joke
Address the jury

The courtroom is a frightening place, it is degrading, and the defendant physician will hear his or her care being criticized in the most demeaning manner. It is difficult to be phlegmatic under these circumstances. There are certain rules which may be helpful (Table 6). The first is to avoid becoming angry. There is an old adage 'Those whom the gods would destroy, they first make angry.' To lose one's cool in the witness stand can do great harm. A second rule is to maintain decorum. When on the witness stand, the defendant physician must remember to address the jury. Although the questions are asked by counsel, it is the jury that needs to hear the answer. A simple fact is that when the defense attorney asks the question, it is the defendant physician's *answer* that matters. Yet, when the plaintiff's attorney asks the question, it is usually the *question* that matters. The courtroom is a difficult, trying, emotionally charged environment. Tears tend to flow and the physician must recognize that this will be a difficult time. On the other hand, the defense will usually win because those cases where there is probability of loss are settled long before they get to trial.

Litigation is a major problem in our specialty. It is an expensive component of our practice. It is a most traumatic and trying time in one's career. But by adequate preparation and understanding the rules, the obstetrician–gynecologist can not only do much to avoid litigation, but also be ready to face it head-on and with confidence, should it come.

REFERENCE

1. American College of Obstetricians and Gynecologists. Overview of the 1996 Professional Liability Survey. *ACOG Clin Rev* 1998;3(2)

13

Physical medicine and rehabilitation

Linda H. Gleis, MD

Why would a physiatrist be sued? As a specialty, are we not trained in team-work, with the patient as the key member in the establishment of goals? Are we not trained to be holistic in our approach, focusing our efforts on the dimensions of goal achievement: physical, psychological, emotional and spiritual? Do we not include the family in this process, recognizing that the family is critical to successful outcomes? Do we not establish a longer-term relationship with our patients by the very nature of the functional problems that they face?

The fact is that, as a specialty, we are not likely to be sued. Our specialty lends itself to the development of a relationship with our patients that reduces the likelihood of being sued, i.e. a longer-term relationship that involves holistic patient care in connection with the family in the context of a supportive, informational, educational dialog. The likelihood of a physi-atrist being sued is lower than in other specialties classified by insurance carriers in similar risk categories, such as neurology, pediatrics, family practice and dermatology. Losses for physiatry were closer to those for very low-risk categories of psychiatry and pathology[1].

When, then, are we likely to be sued? The answer is: when one of the key elements in the development of the physician–patient relationship is com-promised, leading to patient dissatisfaction with the outcome. 'When faced with a bad outcome, patients and families are more likely to sue a physician if they feel that the physician was not caring and compassionate'[2].

When we talk to our patients, do they perceive that they have our atten-tion? What message does our body language send to reinforce our words? Do we signal that we are in a rush or impatient? Do we remember that this is a new experience for our patient even though it is routine for us? Do we remember that repetition is the key to learning? Do we ask our patients to share their concerns and questions about the proposed treatment plan and regularly discuss progress or obstacles to progress? Are we empathetic to

Table 1 Review of claims made nationally against physiatrists from January 1991 to December 1996 based on personal communication with Medical Protective Company, Claims Department, Fort Wayne, IN

Allegation	Average payment paid per case (US $)
Failure to prevent condition	52 500
Improper treatment	45 126
Improper administration	40 000
Failure to diagnose fracture	20 000
Improper positioning	11 250
Misdiagnosis	2 500

what the patient may not verbalize but fear, in terms of prognosis, impact on bodily functions, daily care activities, and the ability to provide for self and family? Ultimately, the patient recalls how the message was delivered more than the actual message itself.

Personal communication with the Claims Department of the Medical Protective Company of Fort Wayne, IN, has shown that they had only 13 paid cases involving physiatry for the years spanning January 1991 through December 1996. Table 1 delineates the nature of the condition and average payment per case. Conditions prompting the allegations included misdiagnosis of a cerebrovascular accident (CVA), failure to diagnose a fracture, failure to prevent conditions of a fall and a decubitus, improper treatment of a CVA and the spine, and improper administration of drugs.

As such, when a patient is first evaluated, a consistent approach helps to ensure thoroughness. I use the five 'Ds' in the delivery of care: diagnosis, diet, disposition, data and drugs, and I apply the broadest definition to these categories.

Diagnosis   Is the diagnosis established at the time of the patient referral consistent with my clinical knowledge and experience in this area? Have I carefully reviewed previous records to assess for other injuries that may not have been addressed at the time of the initial onset? Has my review of systems been thorough as to other areas of disease or injuries that may have been overlooked in the acute phase, especially in injuries that have led to altered consciousness or ability to perceive pain? Is my examination consistent with information obtained from the history and review of systems? Collectively, this allows for development of the medical diagnosis and the functional deficits that will need to be addressed during the rehabilitation process.

Diet   Patients with multisystem involvement are often in a negative nutritional and fluid balance, especially those with a diagnosis of traumatic brain injury, spinal cord injury or CVA. These conditions compromise oral intake and evacuation. What nutritional requirements need to be met based on the patient's current status? How will these nutrients need to be delivered? What are the likely complications when intake is altered, and how will these be monitored, especially with fluid balance and maintenance of hydration? Will other tests be needed to further assess nutritional/fluid advancement? How will elimination/evacuation be influenced based on intake? What programs will need to be established to ensure adequate output and prevent constipation or diarrhea? How will the patient's weight influence this process? The whole focus in this category is on maintaining balance between input and output while meeting the nutritional and/or special dietetic needs.

Disposition   Again, the patient with multisystem involvement may have a condition that impairs mobility, tolerance level and/or judgment. When writing orders and the prescription for therapeutic intervention, do I clearly identify precautions and establish the parameters so as to prevent further injury? Do I anticipate areas in which complications are likely to develop and specifically address these in daily care orders and monitoring? Do I outline activity level and parameters for advancement of activity? When patient judgment is compromised, have I addressed safety-related parameters?

Data   Often, other tests are needed to establish a diagnosis, monitor current status or anticipate possible complications. If this involves procedures, have I explained the proposed procedure, the reason why requested, what information will be gained and the possible risks? Are consultations needed to assist in special-needs care?

Drugs   At the time of the patient evaluation, there is often a list of medications that have been used during the patient's acute-care phase. These often number more than ten. What medications are being used at the time of referral or transfer that were not required prior to the patient's present illness or injury? Are any still needed and, if so, for how long? Do any require routine monitoring? Are any additional medications needed?

Finally, information is needed regarding the facility and/or therapist who will be providing the hands-on delivery of the therapeutic prescription. Often, this work is done by specially trained allied health-care professionals, but not under the supervision of a physician, and may be delegated to an individual with only basic knowledge in the field. 'The physiatrist will often bear, or at least share, responsibility together with a non-physician technician who injures the patient'[3]. What knowledge do I have regarding the skills of the therapist or outcome quality of the facility

Table 2   'Dos' and 'Don'ts': a brief guide for physicians recently named in a malpractice suit

---

DO notify your professional liability carrier immediately

DO keep in close touch with your case manager, who along with the defense
   attorney (if needed) will be your key contacts in resolving this case

DO talk to your family: let them know what is going on so that they can
   be a support to you

DO become intensely familiar with the case: reread the records, all of them,
   so that you can help your case-worker and attorney do the best job of supporting you

DO continue to treat your patients in the same way that you have been comfortable
   with. This is a difficult time for you, and the temptation may be to become
   distant from your patients for fear of doing something 'wrong'. Nothing could
   be worse: patients know when their doctor is not communicating or relating
   to them, and that is when they are more likely to be dissatisfied

DO think about the case in question: you will not be able to help thinking about
   it anyway. But when you do, look for the medical issues that may be helpful
   for the defense team to know about later. Become your own toughest critic
   on this case, and you will be your own biggest asset in its defense

DO keep in mind that very few lawsuits go to trial, and most of those that
   do are resolved in favor of the defending physician

DON'T contact the patient who filed the action against you, even if your most
   burning question is 'Why did you do this?'

DON'T alter the record in any way

DON'T take personally the accusatory language of the summons or complaint:
   lawyers have spent years perfecting the phrasing and tone of these
   documents to satisfy the requirements for filing a suit. They almost always
   come straight from a word-processor, and not from a patient's mouth

DON'T file a personal countersuit until you have talked to your case manager
   and defense attorney. By all means talk to your own lawyer if you want
   to: defense counsel is provided for you as it is needed

DON'T feel that you are alone or unique: over the past 10 years, nearly a quarter
   of a million malpractice suits have been filed in the USA, most of
   them against wonderful caring doctors

---

where the therapy is provided? What is the state of technology used? What
are the protocols for risk management? Is there physician oversight at the
facility? Is it accredited by the Commission on Accreditation of
Rehabilitation Facilities (CARF)?

In summary, physiatry as a specialty carries a very low risk for a malpractice suit, less so than other specialties assigned by insurance carriers
to the same risk category. This in part is secondary to the communication links fostered by the nature of the physiatric patient relationship.
Ultimately, however, it is the quality of the communication links that
determines whether or not litigation is initiated. If care is compassionate,
the likelihood of a suit is significantly reduced, even in the event of a

poor outcome. Compassion is demonstrated in both our verbal and our non-verbal communication, with documentation of this in the patient record by means of our written communication. The medical record is the best line of defense and, as such, should be legible, complete, accurate, and inclusive of phone and family contacts with documentation of correspondence, compliance/non-compliance, recommendations and follow-up. Ensure confidentiality is maintained. If there is a mishap, do not avoid the patient or family: explain what happened in terms the patient and family will understand and do so as soon as possible after the event occurrence.

In the event that an allegation is made and a suit is brought against you, the advice is the same. There is no difference in the recommended advice based on the nature of the specialty. Table 2 lists the 'dos' and 'don'ts' based on advice from the Kentucky Medical Insurance Company.

REFERENCES

1. Fellechner BL, Findley TW. Malpractice in physical medicine and rehabilitation: a review and analysis of existing data. *Am J Phys Med Rehab* 1991;70:124–8
2. Levinson W, Roter DL, Mullooly JP, *et al*. Physician–patient communication. *J Am Med Assoc* 1997;277:553–9
3. Louiselle DW, Williams H. *Medical Malpractice*. New York: Matthew Bender, 1991

14

Neurosurgery

Robert White, PhD, MD

MEDICAL MALPRACTICE AND THE NEUROSURGEON

Medical malpractice will continue to be a major professional issue as we move into the 21st century. There is no evidence that its pernicious involvement and its detrimental effect on American medicine will be significantly reduced or changed. Like all surgical specialties, neurosurgery suffers from this unfortunate professional disease. Today, neurosurgeons are paying between 50 and 250 thousand dollars or more per year for malpractice insurance coverage, and in some cases the situation has become so bad that a number of neurosurgeons have left medicine altogether, have moved their practices geographically, or are actually practicing without insurance coverage. Litigation in itself is almost an unspoken social disease. It is difficult to obtain solid statistics, particularly for neurosurgery, but it should be acknowledged that any neurosurgeon who has been in practice for a period in excess of 10 years and has carried out, and carries out, a major number of surgery cases regularly will have averaged at least two malpractice involvements. While this chapter has been designed for the surgical neurologist in practice, much of what is written here would seem appropriate for neurologists as well as those in other surgical specialties.

At least the threat of a malpractice suit constantly hangs over the practice of medicine today. If a neurosurgeon, or any physician, becomes involved in a malpractice litigation, then it often becomes a serious emotional issue for the doctor. It will follow the neurosurgeon through his days of practice and in may ways it may even affect his approach, for example his aggressiveness, as far as actual surgery is concerned. Such litigation is unfortunately a disturbing phenomenon, with many personal and professional facets. It is one that has far-reaching financial implications for the surgeon and the practice, as well as very serious personal psychological effects which can often lead to mental depression. Thus, even a potential threat of malpractice involvement represents a 'social virus' that continues to be destructive to neurosurgical practice in the USA. In actuality, we cannot measure the total professional losses, financial and scientific, nor the personal deficits, both financial and emotional, that accrue from medical malpractice litigation at the present time. But, in all probability, they are incalculable.

The practice of neurosurgery today is, in many ways, becoming more and more procedure-oriented. Literally every week and every month, new forms of biotechnology are introduced for use in an operating-room setting, for example instrumentation for stabilizing and fusing the spine, and guidance and navigational systems to ensure that the pathology is localized within either the brain or the spine for stereotaxic biopsy. Advanced technology is now available to assist the surgeon, not only in localizing the abnormal lesion but also in removing it more completely. The consequence of all of this is that neurosurgeons are operating on more and more difficult cases, and they are able to perform surgery on many patients that previously were simply not amenable to interventional techniques. All of these new diagnostic methods and operating technologies, as they are introduced into ordinary practice, will raise additional malpractice possibilities and lead inevitably to major opportunities for litigation and judgment.

Throughout recent decades, various published studies[1] have historically demonstrated that the primary anatomical area representing a 'virtual minefield' for medical malpractice litigation for the neurosurgeon has been the spine, particularly the lumbar and the cervical regions (Table 1). Despite advanced diagnostic methodology and surgical instrumentation, including new microscopic and endoscopic techniques to treat diseases of the spine and the nerve roots, there continues to be a significant amount of patient dissatisfaction with the surgical management outcomes. The neurosurgeon suffers here from the generally held public belief which is all pervasive in modern-day medicine – that the patient should expect perfection from their doctors. Under these unattainable circumstances, those undergoing surgical procedures on their spine would expect to be pain-free and be able to return to normal functioning.

Neurosurgery is practiced at a time when the entire population thinks in terms of litigation. Thus, the consequence of introducing new procedures and equipment, in spite of their superb design, but often hyped by advertising, only increases the patient's demand for excellent outcomes. Finally, the simple fact that we live in a litigious society, constantly questioning the neurosurgeon's competence, the operation itself and the results, contributes to the continual pernicious effect of the medical malpractice legal industry on neurosurgical practice.

Table 1   Sources of malpractice liability in neurosurgery. Modified from reference 1

Major anatomical categories
Spinal surgery
   lumbar (25%)
   cervical (17%)
   thoracic (5%)
Trauma
   spinal (12%)
   cranial (7%)
Cranial surgery (17%)

Specific circumstances
Unsatisfactory outcomes
   neurological deficit: disability, paralysis, pain
Complications
   infections, cerebrospinal fluid leakage, materials left in wound, postoperative
   hemorrhage, operation at wrong anatomical site, dislocation of bone plate or plug
   (spine), unstable (spine) wound breakdown, inappropriate postoperative management
   (e.g. drug therapy)
Misdiagnosis
   inadequate preoperative work-up, operation performed for incorrect reasons and/or
   increased disability
Delay in treatment
   death, increased neurological deficit

While the human spine represents the major anatomical area, as far as malpractice litigation is concerned, the cranium and its intracranial contents have not escaped. Here we find once again the same general issues of dissatisfaction with outcomes and lack of appreciation of expected complications. The fact that many of the procedures that the neurosurgeon must perform are in the intracranial anatomical area, and the results of which, under the best of circumstances, may be judged as unsatisfactory, obviously leads to these conclusions. In other words, the outcomes are simply not perfect nor were they designed to be. The operation may be life-saving, but the individual may be left with a major neurological deficit. This is certainly true for neurovascular surgery involving aneurysms and arterial–venous malformations (AVMs), where the patient may have been perfectly normal prior to surgery. This is also true for certain types of tumor surgery.

One of the major areas that poses difficulties in neurosurgical patient management, and continues to represent a fertile area for malpractice suits, has to do with infections of the central nervous system, particularly those in and around the brain. This would include the cases of brain abscesses, empyemas, meningitis and ventriculitis. These can be missed today through delay and not immediately employing imaging studies such as computed tomography (CT) and magnetic resonance imaging (MRI). Frequently, such individuals early on may not seem to be suffering from major intracranial infections, in spite of the fact that they may present with conditions representing infections involving their sinuses and bony structures of the skull (mastoid). Thus, they may simply not be studied appropriately or adequately, and the neurosurgeon in consultation may not insist upon an appropriate imaging study. Another area of concern is the non-appreciation of subarachnoid hemorrhage. This is an area of diagnosis which, ordinarily, the neurosurgeon should not miss, but can still be at fault by not undertaking surgical treatment soon enough. The patient may only have a headache and, on rare occasions, the appropriate studies do not indicate that there has been subarachnoid bleeding. Nevertheless, these individuals can bleed very soon for a second time, and this hemorrhage may be devastating. As a consequence, all of these areas relating to neuro-vascular disease remain fertile for litigation.

We should also remember that after the spine itself, central nervous system trauma, involving both the spine and the brain, represent a major area for malpractice suits. Certainly the spinal column and its contents once again provide a serious litigious anatomical region for neurosurgeons in terms of both conservative and creative management of spinal trauma. Here it is often argued that if nothing is done, then something (surgery) should have been done, and if the neurosurgeon has done something (operatively), then he or she should have done nothing. Of course the fact still remains that no matter whatever treatment is carried out, it may be judged inappropriate. The management of spinal fractures and spinal trauma, for example the non-diagnosis of osseous fractures and not providing proper immobilization and stability to the spine, remains a very difficult area for management simply because there are no absolute guidelines in this vital area, even today. Nevertheless, the neurosurgeon must simply continue to work within a potentially litigious area of management for a region of critical patient care for which appropriate guidelines representing agreed-upon standards of care have not been established. Tragically, these standards of care are often established at the time of litigation in the courtroom, based on what passes for the presumed level of practice at the time and geographical location. The national neurological organizations of today have not drawn up the appropriate standards of care for these conditions; perhaps this is just as well, since they may vary to some degree between various individual neurosurgeons and certainly in various areas of the country. Thus, the modern-day neurosurgeon within the framework of his/her practice is constantly at risk of malpractice litigation. One's situation may be no different from that of other surgical colleagues, but often the financial judgments in neurosurgical malpractice cases are extremely high because they can not only involve death, but also frequently result in paralysis of one form or another, or there may be the loss of some vital neurological function such as vision.

AVOIDANCE OF LITIGATION IN NEUROSURGERY

Many will correctly argue that to avoid medical litigation borders on the impossible in the course of a long career in neurosurgery. Certainly anyone who has performed a large number of neurosurgical interventions over a considerable period of time will have come to the attention of the malpractice profession and, of course, suffered the infamy of being sued by his or her patients. Still, there are some 'well-worn steps' that all of us can take to reduce significantly the numbers of patient malpractice liability encounters (Table 2).

The first, and by far the most important step, is to know your patient and their family. If you feel during your initial interviews in dealing with them that something is not right (often nothing more than an innate feeling of 'something wrong') in the relationship, then you are probably correct, and under such circumstances you should not become involved with that particular patient. On the other hand, under ordinary circumstances, it is extremely important to set up a meaningful and comfortable relationship with the patient and, if possible, with his or her spouse and family. It can not be stressed often enough that you have to become a 'friend' of your patient. He or she has to trust you, and they have to believe in what you are recommending to them. You, above all, have to be honest and straightforward in presenting the patient's problem, and the solution you are advising to improve or eliminate it. This 'bonding' that you must establish between yourself as the surgeon of record and your patient is the 'bedrock' of your association with each person who falls under your responsibility, and this delicate relationship must always be built on mutual trust and faith.

The second step (which is almost a corollary of the first) is to commit yourself to being absolutely sure that the patient you are going to manage, medically or surgically, fully understands the following:

(1) The reasons for either the surgery or the conservative treatment;
(2) The details of the operation itself as far as is appropriate (described in layman's terms);

Table 2   How to avoid litigation in neurosurgery

---

(1) Know your patient and family (PAF)

(2) Be sure the PAF fully understand all aspects of the procedure

(3) Be thoroughly trained, experienced and board-certified

(4) Maintenance of detailed and accurate records is absolutely essential

(5) Obtain an appointment at the university and belong to the appropriate medical and neurosurgical societies

(6) Speak in public on neurosurgical, neuroscience and health-care issues

(7) Always plan for litigation: 'think litigation' and be prepared, mentally and professionally

(8) If complications develop or the outcome seems less than satisfactory, begin to discuss these issues immediately and repeatedly with family and patient, and be sure to discuss them adequately and appropriately

(9) Be involved at your hospitals and clinics, politically and professionally

(10) Know your hospital staff and demand high performance from all your associates, e.g. nurses, consultants, anesthesiologists

---

(3) Alternative methods of treatment that might be considered but are not appropriate and why;

(4) A reasonable understanding of the expected outcome as well as the possible complications of the care, particularly if it will be invasive in nature.

Unfortunately, studies indicate that even under the best of circumstances, patients who have signed carefully prepared consent forms and have been 'educated' by both the surgeon and a special nurse frankly do not remember in any great detail what was said to them during these training interviews. For example, such published reports[2] have demonstrated that only 43% of the patients interviewed immediately after the educational session were able to retain the information. In 6 weeks that figure had dropped to 38.4%. Thus, it appears that no matter how carefully constructed and orchestrated, informational transfer periods involving the doctor and nurse with the patient appear to result in, at best, less than 50% retention of vital facts relating to their immediate future medical/surgical management.

The third point is that, as an expert in the special field of neurosurgery, you must maintain confidence in yourself as a surgical operator and as a practicing doctor fully capable of delivering the care your patients require, no matter how complex and controversial. Have faith in yourself. This will require attending appropriate courses devoted to new operative techniques, as well as review sessions in old techniques. These should include review and demonstration courses in which 'hands-on' opportunities are provided for individual surgeons. Thus, you must maintain clinical abilities and operative expertise, both surgically and medically, by attending review courses to update constantly your educational background. Also, if you practice within a group, or if there are other neurosurgeons within your hospital, it would be beneficial from time to time to have your patient care activities examined by your partners or associates in neurosurgery. It would be important to have one or more of these individuals to operate with you on your cases, and see whether or not your performance is really up to the mark. All of this should be done over and above recommendations of the standard hospital committees established for staff performance review.

Other important areas that are constantly recommended to assist the neurosurgeon in reducing the number of malpractice litigations are as follows.

Detailed and appropriate records must be maintained. Often the modern-day hospital and office record is incomplete, abbreviated and difficult to read. It is extremely important, if at all possible, that both your own office notes and your entries in the hospital records are dictated and placed into the record as typed manuscripts, including the details of the diagnosis, physical examination and indications for surgery (as complete as possible), as well as written documentation as to what was discussed with the patient and family, including the review of alternative methods. Additionally, since neurosurgeons are operating on older and older people, many of whom have major medical diseases and will be undergoing much more difficult procedures, their outcomes will be less assured in terms of patient neuro-surgical satisfaction. In all such cases it is mandatory to have appropri-ate consultations. For example, with heart disease, ask the cardiologist to examine these patients and assess their ability to undergo surgery. Their consultation notes and their medical recommendations for management both before, during and after surgery must be part of the record. There must be a clear statement on their part that the procedure can be per-formed with a reasonable degree of medical safety. Additionally, in turn, they should be available to assist in the management of these seriously ill patients following surgery, and appropriate notations and follow-ups by these consultants should be entered into the patient's record.

Daily, or twice per day, notes should be entered into the record by the neurosurgeon him- or herself if the patient is in the intensive care unit. Daily notes by the neurosurgeon of record should be made when these individuals are on the open ward. These can be brief but to the point. If at all possible, these notes should be dictated and incorporated into the patient's record with a copy available in the office. The appropriate data and *time* should always be placed on these records, never to be altered. Remember: date and time everything legibly. Also, make sure that what you write in any patient's record is always legible!

Since complications and less than adequate outcomes do occur with patients, these must be carefully documented in the hospital record. The issue of less than satisfactory outcomes and potential complications should have been thoroughly discussed prior to surgery, and the hospital (office) records should reflect this. These adverse happenings should be immediately discussed with the family and with the patient. Never give the impression that you are in a hurry or that you are not really concerned with the patient, particularly when problems develop. Be honest, sympathetic and committed in every way to improving the situation for the patient.

This is the 'golden rule': *know your patient*. Nothing can keep you more out of 'harm's way' of litigation than this single personal, professional practice.

WHAT SHOULD THE NEUROSURGEON DO IF HE OR SHE HAS BEEN NOTIFIED THAT MALPRACTICE LITIGATION IS BEING BROUGHT AGAINST THEM?

In some ways the requirement of a professional response is relatively simple (Table 3). First and foremost, do not panic and simply try to relax. You must obtain the services of a good lawyer and you will want a legal expert who is experienced in medical malpractice, especially in neurosurgical litigation. Certainly if you are a member of a good, practicing neurosurgical group, then your associates will know who these people are. If you are not in such an association, then you can certainly enquire within the framework of the hospital or the American Medical Association, or even the neurosurgical societies for assistance. In the final analysis you must have somebody who is highly experienced in medical malpractice as it affects the neurosurgeon.

Second, review all of your office and hospital records (these should include not only the patient history and examination, but also the operation note itself, all of the hospital records, order sheets, nurses' notes and so forth). Everything should be carefully examined, but at no times should you or anyone else be inundated nor should they make any changes to these records, under any circumstances. It might be advisable to place carefully made copies of all of these data into a loose-leaf notebook, appropriately labeled and with the pages numbered.

Third, suggest to your lawyer several expert witnesses who are known to be very competent, with outstanding reputations in neurosurgery. These

Table 3   Program for the neurosurgeon involved in malpractice litigation

(1) Immediately obtain the services of a highly capable and experienced lawyer who
preferably limits his/her practice to malpractice litigation brought against
neurosurgeons

(2) Suggest to the lawyer several neurosurgeons who are known experts in testifying in
malpractice litigation cases, preferably with experience in the particular area of
litigation

(3) Have your lawyer review all the materials relevant to the case with you and request
an in-depth examination of these case records by the neurosurgical experts. An
opinion as to defensability should be provided by the experts, and if a decision is
made to proceed a strategic plan should be provided

(4) Obtain a legible copy of all hospital records (including nurses' notes, laboratory
data, operative procedures, professional consultations and all your entries – in
essence everything). Combine this information with your office records
in a loose-leaf notebook. Separate into appropriate marked sections.
Number all pages chronologically

(5) Literature search, emphasizing the details of the case for which you are being
sued. Become an expert yourself on the disease, indications for your treatment
and outcomes as published in articles in the pertinent medical literature*

(6) Meet frequently with your lawyer so that you become thoroughly familiar with court
procedure. If time permits, visit the court yourself during ongoing trials dealing with
malpractice litigation.

(7) Take courses in public speaking. Have your own lawyer question you as if they were
opposing counsel for the patient, so that you will become (to the degree that you can)
comfortable with this form of interrogation

(8) Do not discuss your legal predicament with family, friends or other physicians.
Try to forget about the case (albeit difficult) and go on with your professional life

*Editor's note: As a lawyer, I would suggest contacting your attorney *before* undertaking any
literature search. If you research the literature prior to your discovery deposition, plaintiff's
counsel may request the citations you have read. If that literature is at variance with your diagnosis or treatment, it will be used to attack your care at trial. Many lawyers advise their physician clients to delay review of the medical literature until *after* their discovery deposition is taken.
If you believe that a particular issue must be researched prior to your discovery deposition, ask
your lawyer to do the research and communicate his findings to you. Such communication is
protected by attorney/client privilege and is not subject to inquiry at a discovery deposition.

individuals should review the case in detail and be prepared to testify for
you during the court proceedings.

Fourth, begin an extensive literature search yourself, and review the articles that deal with the particular pathophysiology and the operative procedures involved in the case of the patient for whom the malpractice
litigation has been brought against you. This should give you an excellent
background so that you can speak with some authority regarding this

wound needs to be stained with sterile fluorescein solution, and the passage of the green dye to the anterior chamber evaluated under slit lamp magnification. Metallic foreign bodies are easily seen on scout X-ray film or on computed tomography (CT) scans. Foreign bodies of glass can be detected by CT scan or direct observation when suitably located, but generally do not show up on X-ray films unless their size is a minimum of 2–3 mm and the lens material involved is photosensitive by virtue of containing silver halides. These compounds of chloride, fluoride and bromide are like the light-sensitive silver on X-ray films. Such fragments must be removed more quickly than conventional ground glass which is largely inert. A slit lamp with clean oculars and good magnification becomes inherent in the detailed examination of a potential foreign body injury.

Delayed treatment of intraocular infections, especially histoplasmosis, which are close to or encroaching upon the area of macular or central vision   Choroiditis, retinitis and retinal detachments may also threaten the macula. Once these highly epicritic cone cells are disturbed mechanically or by inflammatory activity, there will be some permanent loss in the ultimate restoration of vision.

Failure to recognize concurrent causes of early visual loss in the older patient with incipient cataracts, early corneal dystrophy or retinal impairments where partial cataracts alone may be interpreted to reduce vision   It is essential to analyze the potential acuity of such eyes with a dilated pupil and by reading with a 'potential acuity meter', as well as a full examination of the fundus through the enlarged and dilated pupil.

Inadequate triage of the patient with sudden, painless, non-traumatic loss of vision   Not only the physician, but also his telephone receptionist, must be aware of the urgency in the presentation of such symptoms. Particularly acute optic neuritis, retinal arteriolar obstruction or venous occlusion must be recognized as requiring prompt evaluation and therapy by the ophthalmologist. Delayed care may mean irreversible visual loss.

Awareness of the three major visual loss epidemics of recent time in the United States   Richard Lindstrom, MD, of Minneapolis has carefully analyzed these in sequence:

(1) The epidemic of corneal decompensation following early anterior chamber and iris plane lens implants: the obvious superiority of the posterior chamber lens has gone a long way to reduce this complication which provided the major source of corneal transplantation a decade ago.

(2) Hyperopic shift or reduction in myopic correction over a period of months following radial keratotomy for developmental or congenital myopia previously well corrected with spectacles: unlike the epidemic of corneal decompensation which is largely over, this epidemic is now under way; its numbers may also be increased by broadened excimer use.

(3) The developing apparent plane of corneal light scattering following excimer laser sculpturing of the anterior cornea: this epidemic is just emerging in the USA, and positioned to flower with recent Food and Drug Administration (FDA) clearance of broader indications for photo-refractive keratectomy in moderate myopia (1.5–7.0 diopters with < 1.5 diopters of astigmatism).

The basic needs are personal courtesy, thoughtful discussion with patients and explanation of risks in all activities. The concept of a patient (one who suffers) being a client or customer breaks down the unique mutual confidence that is part of all medical care. Similarly, an office, home or bedside visit is not an encounter or adversarial duel. No patient ever calls to schedule an 'encounter', but most seek a professional visit, appropriate examination and thoughtful analysis of their signs and symptoms.

REFERENCE

1. Bettman JW Sr, Demorest BH. *Practice without Malpractice in Ophthalmology.* San Francisco, CA: Ophthalmic Mutual Insurance Co., 1995:207

16

Urology

Shafquat Meraj, MD, Robert K. Luntz, MD,
and Harris M. Nagler, MD

INTRODUCTION

Urological surgery is a broad field which encompasses a vast array of procedures and responsibilities. This breadth is accompanied by a multitude of opportunities for liability that can be incurred by the urologist when there is a perceived or real deviation from a community's 'standard of care'. The purpose of this chapter is to highlight specific areas in the practice of urology that are associated with identifiable exposure to liability.

Suits may be brought against a urologist for a multitude of reasons, including lack of informed consent, failure to diagnose a malignancy and complications of surgical procedures. Current data demonstrating the distribution of lawsuits brought against urologists from one series in a metropolitan area are listed in Table 1.

These percentages are a function of frequency with which various procedures are performed, as well as the frequency of suits filed for each procedure. For example, cystoscopy is associated with a low morbidity and a low frequency of litigation. However, since it is performed so frequently, the percentage of total suits brought against urologists involving cystoscopy is relatively high (6.1%). The remainder of this Chapter focuses on specific areas of urological practice that are potential sources of liability (Table 2), and ways to protect oneself from litigation (Table 3).

TRANSURETHRAL PROSTATE SURGERY

The introduction of alpha-blockers has radically changed the management of patients with benign prostatic hypertrophy (BPH). However, a certain percentage of patients will fail medical therapy and require surgical treatment. Transurethral resection of the prostate has remained the most commonly performed surgical procedure in these patients. While this

Table 1   Major categories associated with urological claims in order of frequency

Procedure	Percentage of total claims
Prostatectomy	28.1
Other urological surgery	11.7
Urological treatment without surgery	11.2
Removal of renal/ureteral calculi	7.1
Gynecological surgery with injury to genitourinary tract	6.1
Cystoscopy	6.1
Prostatitis	5.1
Nephrectomy	5.1
Resection of renal/bladder tumor	4.1
Laser procedures	3.6
Circumcision	3.6
Penile prosthesis	3.6
Hernia repair	2.6
Infertility	1.5

Table 2   More common litigation problems in urology

Urinary incontinence after transurethral resection of the prostate
Transurethral resection (TUR) syndrome
Failure to diagnose testicular torsion
Vasectomy-related complications
Percutaneous procedures on kidneys
Failure to diagnose: malignancy
Penile prosthesis: placement/infection
Endoscopic procedures

Table 3   Avoiding litigation

Thorough preoperative evaluation (medical and urologic)
Informed consent (documented)
Communication with patient/family
Appropriate expectations (surgical or medical)
Appropriate differential diagnosis (failure to diagnose)
Expeditiously and effectively addressing complications
Detailed and accurate documentation (daily progress reports, operative dictations, etc.)

procedure can be performed with relatively low morbidity, certain aspects of this procedure can expose a urologist to liability.

Urinary incontinence

Damage to the urinary sphincter during transurethral resection of the prostate is a common urological complication and is frequently a source of litigation against the urologist. Incontinence most commonly results from violation of certain surgical boundaries and, therefore, may represent deviation from the standard of care. However, the etiology of incontinence after transurethral surgery may also be due to underlying neuro-urological problems that were not diagnosed prior to the procedure. Therefore, obtaining a thorough history and performing a thorough physical examination is imperative before assuming that a patient's lower urinary symptoms are due solely to bladder outlet obstruction. Urodynamic evaluation may be useful to help determine if a patient's presenting symptoms are secondary to bladder outlet obstruction as opposed to bladder dysfunction. These tests are not routinely needed but are useful in patients with complex medical histories or atypical symptoms.

Once it is determined that a patient's symptomatology is caused by bladder outlet obstruction necessitating surgical intervention, resection of the prostatic tissue must be limited to the tissue proximal to the verumontanum. With present equipment and the widespread use of videocystoscopy, photography of the external urinary sphincter at the end of the procedure may be utilized to document that the anatomical boundaries were respected during the surgical procedure. Careful preoperative evaluation and adherence to surgical principles can minimize the patient's risk and the urologist's exposure.

Transurethral resection syndrome

Transurethral resection (TUR) syndrome is another area of potential litigious activity. This entity is caused by hemodilution from absorption of irrigation fluid during transurethral resection of the prostate. The symptoms of hyponatremia can start as mental confusion and muscle cramps, and progress to convulsions, coma and death. For a patient who is sedated or under general anesthesia, the subtle findings of mental confusion and muscle cramps can be masked, resulting in a delay in detection until the problem has become more profound with the potential for dire consequences. The syndrome may be avoidable by limiting resection time to less than 1.5 hours, since the volume of irrigant absorbed is proportional to the length of the procedure. It is also important to use glycine as the irrigant. TUR syndrome must be suspected in a patient who experiences hemodynamic changes, including hypertension and bradycardia. These may be the only signs of hyponatremia in the anesthetized patient. In more severely affected patients, seizures may occur. The anesthesiologist must be relied upon to note these changes. Communication between the anesthesiologist and surgeon is imperative. Awareness of the symptoms of hyponatremia and aggressive therapy once the diagnosis is suspected is critical to optimally manage the patient with this syndrome.

PROSTATE CANCER

Prostate cancer is the most commonly diagnosed malignancy in males in the United States and the second most common cause of cancer death. A wide variety of options are now available for the treatment of localized prostate cancer. These include radical prostatectomy, radiotherapy and cryosurgery. While it is still controversial as to which one of these treatment options provides the best balance between cure and quality of life, the fact remains that these procedures have significant morbidity associated with them that can expose a urologist to potential law suits.

Radical prostatectomy

Radical prostatectomy remains the 'gold standard' for the treatment of localized prostate cancer. However, this procedure is associated with significant intra- and postoperative morbidity. It is not uncommon to incur large blood loss in the perioperative period, which often requires blood transfusions (10% of patients)[1]. Therefore, the need for blood transfusions should be discussed with the patient along with the option of preoperatively autologous blood donation. Injury to the rectum is one of the most feared complications during a radical prostatectomy. While it is possible to perform a primary repair of an injury to the rectum, some patients may require a temporary colostomy. Appropriate bowel preparation (mechanical and antibiotic) preoperatively often allows the general surgeon to perform a primary repair of the rectal injury, thereby avoiding a colostomy. Hence, it is important that the urologist provides the patient with instructions for a proper bowel preparation and explains the potential risk of rectal injury as part of the informed consent. In the event of a rectal injury, intraoperative consultations should be obtained as needed and the injury repaired appropriately.

Long-term complications associated with radical prostatectomy include incontinence, stricture formation at the bladder neck and impotence. These complications can be managed medically or may require surgical treatment depending on the severity of the symptoms. Again, the possibility of these complications should be discussed with the patient as part of the informed consent.

As with any cancer surgery, there is always the risk of not achieving tumor-free margins. This rate has been shown to be approximately 25–35% for radical prostatectomy in most recent series. Positive surgical margins can be quite distressing to a patient who expects to achieve a full cure after undergoing a radical prostatectomy. The surgeon must explain to the patient that despite an extensive preoperative evaluation, it is not always possible to predict the local extent of the disease. In these cases, additional treatment in the form of radiotherapy or hormonal therapy may be required.

Brachytherapy

Insertion of radioactive seeds within the prostatic tissue or brachytherapy has gained significant popularity over the last decade. Improvements in imaging technology have allowed mapping of the prostate and precise radioactive seed placement. This procedure is routinely performed on an ambulatory basis and does not require prolonged catheterization unlike radical prostatectomy. As with any treatment of prostate cancer, appropriate patient selection is important. Recent studies looking at 10 year data for disease recurrence rates have demonstrated that brachytherapy is efficacious for appropriately selected patients. As a result, more patients are choosing to undergo brachytherapy than ever before.

As benign as brachytherapy appears to be in the short term, its long-term complications are not insignificant. Morbidity following brachytherapy can include urinary incontinence, urethral stricture, impotence and recto-prostatic fistula formation.

Cryosurgery

Cryosurgery of the prostate gland for prostate cancer is an additional therapeutic option that should be discussed with the patient. Currently, cryosurgery is being performed for both primary and recurrent disease. With the routine use of urethral warming device and rigorous temperature monitoring within the prostate and at the denonvilliers fascia, the extent of the tissue that is frozen can be controlled with precision. Despite these technical advances, significant potential for both short- and long-term morbidity exists with cryosurgery. Urethral sloughing, irritative voiding symptoms and recto-prostatic fistula formation are some of the commonly seen complications. Patients choosing to undergo cryosurgery of the prostate should be made aware of these complications and the potential effect on the patient's quality of life.

Failure to diagnose prostate cancer

As with all malignancies, failure to appropriately screen for or diagnose prostate cancer can expose a urologist to potential litigation. The use of prostate-specific antigen (PSA) testing, digital rectal examination and improvements in biopsy techniques have allowed prostate cancer to be diagnosed in more males at an earlier and, therefore, presumably at a curable stage. While there is still some debate as to whether screening for prostate cancer has led to a decline in prostate cancer-related mortality, the American Urological Association recommends that all males over 50 years of age should be screened for prostate cancer. Screening should be performed on a yearly basis using PSA and digital rectal exam. For African-American males or males with a family history of prostate cancer, the screening should begin even earlier (40 years). The urologist should offer prostate cancer screening to all males who meet these criteria.

SCROTAL SURGERY

Testicular torsion

Conventional wisdom in urology dictates that scrotal pain in the prepubertal male is testicular torsion until 'proven otherwise'. It's the 'proven otherwise' that creates lawsuits. It must be borne in mind that testicular torsion can occur at any age, and must be in the differential diagnosis of any male with acute onset of scrotal discomfort. The most common mistaken diagnosis is epididymitis for which the patient is given a prescription for antibiotics and anti-inflammatories and sent home. A urologist may or may not have been consulted. Several days later, the patient may re-present with an edematous and tender scrotum and the correct diagnosis is established.

History and physical examination may be highly suggestive of torsion. An anterior lie of the epididymis and absence of the cremasteric reflex on the symptomatic side may be signs of testicular torsion. Furthermore, most emergency rooms have access to either Doppler ultrasonography or nuclear scrotal scintigraphy to aid in the diagnosis of acute testicular pain. When these modalities are appropriately utilized by trained personnel, they can be considered definitive in ruling out the diagnosis of testicular torsion.

Occasionally a physician may entertain the possibility of torsion and may mistakenly make the diagnosis of epididymitis. This error in diagnosis, whether it is secondary to atypical patient presentation or incorrect radiologic assessment, does not protect the physician from litigation. However, recent studies looking at the medico-legal aspects of missed testicular torsion have shown that in such cases the rate of indemnity payment is somewhat smaller. Urologists and emergency-room physicians have also been named in lawsuits in which the patient presented with a fairly long duration of symptoms (greater than 8 hours). Despite the low probability of salvaging the testicle in the setting of delayed patient presentation, error in diagnosis of testicular torsion has led to successful lawsuits against the involved physicians.

The worst mistake that a urologist can make is to try to diagnose the problem without examining the patient. In any situation involving scrotal pain, a thorough history and physical examination is warranted and should be followed with appropriate radiologic examination or even scrotal exploration if indicated. The role of the emergency-room physician in terms of obtaining appropriate and timely consultations and ordering diagnostic tests is critical. Past litigation has ruled that it is the emergency-room physician's responsibility to ensure that standards of care have been upheld in spite of the inaction of the urologist on call.

Vasectomy

Recovery for failed vasectomy resulting in unplanned birth has been somewhat limited. Except for cases in which the child was born with birth defects, it is felt that the potential benefit to the parents more than offsets the financial burden. Therefore, most suits brought against urologists after vasectomy are related to surgical complications after the procedure. The most common complication is hematoma formation. Hematomas may occur as a result of vasospasm during the procedure with delayed bleeding after wound closure, or suture material or surgical clips which fall off, etc. In the worst-case scenario, a hematoma may become infected resulting in loss of the testis. The standard of care, however, is careful observation and patience, as the great majority of scrotal hematomas will resolve spontaneously over a period of several months. Variations in the procedure including the 'no scalpel technique' may reduce the incidence of complications.

Although infection after vasectomy is uncommon, epididymitis and orchitis may occur even with antibiotic prophylaxis. It is virtually impossible to prove deviation from standard of care in these cases.

As with any surgical procedure, patients must receive appropriate pre- and postoperative counseling. In the case of vasectomy, patients should be aware of risks, complications and alternatives. They also must be informed that the effectiveness of the procedure must be demonstrated by semen analysis before the cessation of contraception.

KIDNEY SURGERY

Nephrectomy

The advent of laparoscopic surgery has revolutionized the field of urologic surgery. Both radical and partial nephrectomy for renal cell cancer can now be performed laparoscopically. The benefits to the patient in terms of a shorter hospital stay, less pain and faster recovery to baseline are well documented in recent literature. Therefore, any patient who is a candidate for nephrectomy must be given the option of having the procedure performed laparoscopically. Furthermore, informed consent should consider all possible treatment options including open/laparoscopic radical nephrectomy, partial nephrectomy or cryosurgical ablation of the lesion. While the complication rate in the hands of experienced surgeons is very low, patients must be informed of potential injury to bowel, blood vessels and other adjacent structures during any of these procedures. As a result, a second additional procedure (for example, repair of bowel injury) may be necessary and the patient should be willing to undergo such a procedure if needed.

Percutaneous procedures of the kidney

The development of percutaneous procedures performed on the kidney has resulted from advancements in radiographic technology as well as development of new wires, catheters and endoscopes. Percutaneous nephrolithotripsy is a 'minimally invasive' procedure that is generally associated with reduced morbidity, compared with open procedures. As guidewires and needles are blindly introduced via the flank into the kidney, perforation of the kidneys, arteries, veins and even bowel can occur. In the event of such complications, a nephrectomy or other procedure to repair lacerated blood vessels or bowel may be necessary. The patient must be informed of these potential complications despite the minimally invasive nature of this procedure and should be willing to undergo an additional procedure in the event of an intraoperative complication. Obviously it is best to avoid these complications. In the event that such injury should occur, it is important to make the diagnosis early and intervene expeditiously.

Failure to diagnose a renal mass

With the increased use of ultrasonography, there has been a marked increase in the diagnosis of 'incidental' renal masses. Many urologists will perform renal sonography in their office when evaluating a patient with bladder outlet obstruction. During this evaluation, it is imperative to evaluate for renal masses in addition to hydronephrosis. Owing to the poor outcome in patients who are diagnosed with advanced renal cell carcinoma, early diagnosis is paramount.

Furthermore, patients must be made aware that radiographic studies are not definitive modalities for the diagnosis of malignancy and, despite the malignant radiographic appearance of a renal mass, pathological diagnosis may demonstrate the lesion to be benign.

PENILE SURGERY

Penile prosthesis

In spite of the recent advent of effective oral medications for the treatment of erectile dysfunction (ED), there continues to be significant interest and need for penile prosthetic surgery. Proper patient selection prior to prosthesis placement is essential. The patient must be motivated and, in the case of inflatable prosthesis placement, must possess the dexterity to utilize the device effectively. Furthermore, patients must be properly evaluated prior to the surgical procedure. The etiology of the impotence must be determined. Placement of a penile prosthesis in a patient with psychogenic impotence could be a source of liability for the urologist. Patients must have realistic expectations and understanding of the risks, benefits and limitation of prosthetic surgery.

Once the patient has been properly selected, lack of adherence to sterile technique, poor placement with cross-over of the penile cylinders, or improper sizing can result in penile deformity, curvature and or erosion of the prosthesis through the penis or urethra.

The most common cause of action against the urologist after placement of penile prosthetic devices is as a result of postoperative infection. In spite of the best possible aseptic technique, infections occur. The critical issue is timely diagnosis and intervention. Most litigation in these cases focuses on when the prosthesis was removed. Although most urologists are reluctant to remove a prosthesis, it is the attempt to save the prosthesis through conservative management that results in the lawsuit. Waiting too long to remove the prosthesis can have disastrous results, including Fournier's gangrene and septic shock. Therefore, it is critical to intervene expediently and aggressively in these cases.

Priapism

Priapism may result from underlying systemic disease such as sickle cell anemia or malignancy, or pharmacological therapy for impotence. Additionally, it may be idiopathic in nature. The advent of alternative treatments and greater familiarity with this complication has reduced its incidence. Careful titration of the dosage of the intracorporeal agent to be administered is essential. Furthermore, patient selection and patient education regarding the frequency, dosage and injection technique, as well as complications, is essential prior to a patient's initiation of self-injection therapy. When priapism does occur, aggressive therapy with oral alpha adrenergic or intracavernosal irrigation is indicated. These methods may be ineffective, necessitating surgical intervention. Shunt procedures may render the patient impotent and result in future ineffectiveness of intracavernosal therapy. It is imperative, therefore, to inform patients of the risk and potential sequelae of priapism prior to initiation of an intracavernosal injection therapy program. Furthermore, the patient must understand that immediate medical attention must be sought when priapism does occur, to minimize the morbidity of the condition.

ENDOSCOPIC PROCEDURES

Cystoscopy

Cystoscopy is generally regarded as a procedure with low morbidity. Owing to the frequency with which it is performed, however, there are a number of complications that have become associated with it. Urethral tears, creation of false passages into the urethra, urinary tract infections, bleeding, undermining of the bladder neck and bladder perforation are all possible during urological manipulation of the penis or urethra. The most frequent site of urethral perforation is the bulbar urethra, because of the curvaceous course of the urethra at this point. Undermining the bladder neck with perforation of the urethra at the bulb is not uncommon, but is usually of little clinical significance. Perforation of the urethra into the rectum is a rare but serious complication. In this case, a diverting colostomy may be necessary, resulting in legal action in most cases. Of course, the best way to deal with this situation is to avoid the injury. Care must be taken when manipulating the urethra, especially when there has been prior injury to the urethra. With the excellent fiberoptic and the bright illumination provided by modern cystoscopes, cannulation of the urethra can be performed under direct vision minimizing the risk of causing urethral trauma and subsequent litigation.

Failure to remove a ureteral stent

The advent of internal, self-retaining ureteral stents has resulted in improved patient comfort and reduced likelihood of stent migration. However, because of the inconspicuous nature of these devices, one may easily lose track of them until complications arise. The most common complication is a bacterial or fungal urinary tract infection. Encrustation of the stent from prolonged retention, making endoscopic removal of the stent impossible, is another complication for which legal action may be brought against the urologist. One preventive measure is to keep a log of all stents placed, and indicate the date of stent removal. Utilizing the log, patients with stents can be carefully tracked, and those who have not been followed-up can be contacted for stent removal, hence avoiding potential complications.

GYNECOLOGICAL AND GENERAL SURGERY-RELATED ISSUES

Ureteral injury

The ureter is vulnerable to injury during abdominal hysterectomy. Trauma may be the result of devascularization, ligation, cauterization or transection of the structure. Although the diagnosis may be made at the time of surgery, often there is significant delay in diagnosis. Often the first indication of injury is flank pain and fever 24–48 hours after surgery. Radiographic studies will usually confirm the diagnosis. Once the diagnosis is made, surgical intervention is often indicated. Although, in almost all cases, urologists are required to repair the ureter, the urologist should not be considered to be an expert in the litigation of these cases. The urologist's expertise relates to the diagnosis and treatment of the injury and not in performing the initial surgery.

Damage to the testicle during herniorraphy

Owing to the vast numbers of hernia repairs performed, and the intimate relationship between the hernia sac and spermatic cord, injury to the testis or vas deferens may occur. As in the case of ureteral injury during abdominal hysterectomy, urologists should not be relied upon to determine the standard of care in a general surgical procedure.

The most common cause of testicular injury during herniorraphy is due to compression or occlusion of the vasculature of the spermatic cord as a result of the closure of the internal inguinal ring. Direct clamping or cutting can also result in damage to the cord structures. Injury to the testicular artery may manifest itself as a painful, tender and swollen testis. Although some minor testicular discomfort is common after inguinal herniorrhaphy, protracted discomfort may suggest ischemic injury. The long-term result of such an injury may be testicular atrophy with loss of testicular function

Recently, the damaging effects of the mesh used in inguinal herniorraphy on the spermatic cord structures have also been reported. The mesh can erode into the vas deferens or cause a fibrotic reaction around the vas deferens leading to vasal obstruction. Thus, bilateral hernia repair can lead to infertility especially when mesh is utilized during the repair. The vas deferens may also be injured during dissection of the hernia sac from the cord structures or during ligation of the sac. The majority of cases of vasal injury secondary to hernia repair go unnoticed, however, one must be cognizant of this potential problem in young males undergoing inguinal herniorraphy.

COMMENTS

Urology is a swiftly evolving field. Although the application of technology to urology is enabling the field to advance rapidly, these new territories and techniques may result in increased liability for the urologist in the future. The standard of care must be maintained when applying newly developed techniques and instruments to one's daily practice.

During urological procedures, as with all surgical procedures, care must be taken to avoid complications. Aseptic techniques must be employed, meticulous hemostasis must be achieved, sponges must be carefully counted prior to wound closure, and adequate follow-up care must be provided. With regard to medical malpractice, as Benjamin Franklin stated: "An ounce of prevention is worth more than a pound of cure". Avoiding trouble is the ideal, however, once a problem is encountered, it must be recognized and dealt with expeditiously and effectively, and at all times the standard of care must be upheld.

REFERENCES

1. Goad JR, Eastham JA, Fitzgerald KB, *et al*. Radical retropubic prostatectomy: Limited benefit of autologous blood donation. *J Urol* 1995;154:2103
2. Morton WJ. *Medical Malpractice – Handling Urology Cases*, Shepard's Medical Malpractice Series. New York: McGraw-Hill, 1990
3. American Medical Association. *Risk Management Principles and Commentaries for the Medical Office*, 2nd edn. Chicago: AMA Specialty Society, Medical Liability Project, 1995
4. Focus [Quarterly Publication]. New York: FOJP Service Corp.
5. Matteson JR, Stock J, Nagler HM, *et al*. Medico-legal aspects of testicular torsion. *Urology* 2001:(in press)

17

Orthopedic surgery

Patrick J. DeMeo, MD, Gerald W. Pifer, MD,
and Nicholas G. Sotereanos, MD

The practice of medicine and surgery entails risk. Every time there is an encounter of any type between a physician and a patient, there is the potential for risk. How that risk is managed will influence the outcome of the chosen treatment and the satisfaction of the patient and the physician. With that said, it behoves the orthopedic surgeon to obtain the appropriate training and experience so that risks can be minimized. The reality is that most orthopedic surgeons will be the subject of a malpractice claim at some time during their career. Some cases have merit and others do not.

The American Academy of Orthopaedic Surgeons (AAOS) Committee on Professional Liability reviewed overall data for orthopedic surgeons derived from closed claims of 20 insurers, who reported 351 claims over a 6-to 15-year period[1]. These companies insured 98 000 physicians, but the number of insured orthopedic surgeons was unknown. Closed claims are defined as those cases which have been resolved either out of court or by trial. In the cases studied, an orthopedist was the defendant 81.6% of the time. When Board Certification was known, 82.3% of the defendants were certified. Less than 1% of the defendants were considered impaired, and 75% had a prior history of malpractice claims. Analysis of the disposition of claims revealed that the majority was resolved prior to trial: 30.8% were dismissed; 26.2% were withdrawn; 31.3% were settled; and for all other claims, 9.1% resulted in a defendant verdict, 2.6% in a plaintiff verdict.

Both the defense costs and indemnity payments were highest for spine surgery (with or without spinal fusion). Thus, either form of spine surgery appears to be associated with significant risk. Claims resulting from knee arthroscopy and treatment of tibial fractures showed the lowest indemnity payments and defense costs.

A general discussion will follow, and then more specific topics will be presented regarding various anatomical areas of the body where the orthopedic surgeon will encounter risk and how that risk can be managed.

Before embarking upon a treatment option, the patient must be made aware of the pros and cons of the various treatments available. A thorough discussion with the patient, and family if necessary, needs to be accomplished prior to the initiation of any treatment. A procedure should not be forced upon a patient because it is a favorite procedure of the surgeon when other treatment options may be just as good or better. If it is a new procedure, the patient must be made aware of this; and if the physician has little experience with the procedure, the patient needs to be informed. It does not mean that new procedures cannot be performed with only limited experience. However, it is imperative that the surgeon prepares for the procedure with the appropriate training, i.e., spending time with others who are more familiar with the procedure, doing cadaveric surgery in the laboratory and/or obtaining training at special courses. It may also be necessary to obtain additional delineation of privileges through the surgeon's hospital. Health-care institutions should have, through their credentialing and reappointment process, a procedure where delineation of privileges is recorded for each member of the medical staff. The surgeon must be sure that any procedure being performed is included on this list.

Some orthopedic surgeons believe that the only time they are at risk is when they are performing surgery. As stated, however, risks are present with every patient encounter. This includes prescribing medication such as non-steroidal anti-inflammatory medication, which may have gastrointestinal side-effects, including bleeding, and other medications such as narcotics and sedatives which may become habit-forming. The physician and the patient need to be aware of these and other risks.

Anytime there is a patient encounter, whether it is a phone call, a message left on a message machine, or a curb-side consultation, a detailed note should be made in the patient's record. In general, however, curb-side consultations should be discouraged. Since surgeons work in hospitals, it is almost impossible not to have questions asked of us by hospital personnel and others. The *best* policy is to tell the inquiring person to make an appointment in the office where an appropriate history, physical examination and review of treatment options can be accomplished. A detailed, chronological medical record is mandatory to ensure that a clear and concise record is maintained of the physician's treatment. This makes it much easier for follow-up visits and, just as important, for coverage when the physician is absent.

It is imperative that a correct diagnosis be made prior to the commencement of any surgical procedure. Procedures need to be planned before surgery and the surgeon must have a thorough knowledge of the anatomy through which the surgical approach is to be made. During the procedure, the surgeon must be constantly aware of anatomical structures that may be harmed by the surgeon or the assistant. Preoperative templating for total joint arthroplasties is mandatory to eliminate surprises during surgery. The appropriate equipment must be available at surgery to ensure that the best procedure can be accomplished for the patient. It is the surgeon's responsibility to be sure that the operating room staff are familiar with the implants and instruments to be used during the procedure. It is imperative that the surgeon makes sure the equipment to be used for a procedure is in excellent repair, to minimize failure of an instrument during surgery. Instruments that become dull need to be periodically sharpened. It may be necessary to have training sessions for the operating room support staff so that the procedure will move along smoothly and without error that could result from lack of knowledge or awareness.

If there are complications at the time of surgery, the appropriate steps need to be taken to correct these events. The patient and the family need to be made aware of any complication immediately after surgery to prevent them from being surprised when they see an X-ray image months later in the surgeon's or some other physician's office.

Operative reports are best dictated immediately after surgery and must include all of the pertinent details of the surgical procedure. It is important to include the size of implants in the operative report, as this information may be needed for future care. If operative reports are delayed for days or weeks, details of the procedure become fuzzy or may be forgotten altogether. Most hospital bylaws include the provision that operative reports must be dictated within 24 hours of the procedure. This is also a requirement of the Joint Commission of Accreditation of Hospital Organizations. Operative reports should never be changed unless an error was made in the dictation itself and then this needs to be duly noted, initialed and dated.

It is necessary to have appropriate assistance in the operating room to help with the surgical procedure. Hospital medical staff bylaws, and rules and regulations will all outline what is required for the particular surgeon's institution. A surgeon should not perform any procedure if fatigued, ill, under the influence of drugs or alcohol, or in any other condition that may impair judgment or performance of the procedure. The surgeon should be encouraged to discuss complicated cases with colleagues or present complicated cases at a conference to get collective ideas about a particularly difficult case. If this is done, it should be noted in the medical record. The surgeon must not rush through a surgical procedure or compromise it in any way because of a previous commitment for which the surgeon does not want to be late, i.e., a conference, office hours, etc.

After-care is as important as the surgical procedure *per se*. The patient and the family should be made aware of what their responsibilities are regarding postoperative care. Instructions need to be carefully outlined prior to discharge of the patient from the hospital or ambulatory surgery center. The patient and family need to know how to get in touch with the surgeon or office personnel to answer questions they may have about their care. The patient needs to know that you are there for them. Office personnel must be trained to respond appropriately to the patient's questions and to know when the physician needs to be involved by phone or office appointment.

MOST COMMON AREAS OF LITIGATION

Analysis of the claim data reviewed by the AAOS revealed that the most common allegation involved poor surgical performance by the physician. Table 1 provides the most common allegations.

Patients often expect a perfect outcome when they put their medical care in the trust of their physicians. Likewise, physicians also expect the best outcomes. However unfortunate, though, medicine remains an imperfect science. It is a challenge for the practitioner to prevent litigation when undesirable outcomes occur. Anger is a common thread that is seen throughout a high percentage of cases. An angry patient is more likely to seek retribution through the courts, especially if there is less than an ideal outcome.

Most patients' anger arises from their inability to *communicate* with the physician and/or staff. Physicians must give special attention to communication issues, particularly if there is a complication or unexpected result. Effective communication requires a thorough, honest, easy-to-understand description of proposed treatment options. Include the patient in the decision-making process by outlining different therapeutic alternatives. The physician should discuss alternative forms of treatment in the context of their lifestyles and expectations. Encouraging the patient to be an active partner in the selection of their treatment may help alleviate future problems. With regard to pathology affecting the musculoskeletal system,

Table 1   Most common areas of litigation

Poor surgical performance
Failure to diagnose postoperative infection
Failure to diagnose or manage a complication
Technical complications

Table 2   The essential components of an informed consent

The diagnosis and reasons for treatment
The risks of treatment
Treatment alternatives
Expected and potential unexpected outcomes
Treatment alternatives if the desired result is not achieved

there may be an array of therapeutic options. What one group of patients may believe is a successful outcome, another group may consider an abject failure. Thus, it is critical to ascertain the patient's expectations and to frame this within the context of their lifestyle. A sedentary patient may believe that resolution of a painful problem is a therapeutic success; however, a more active individual would consider anything less than restoration of normal function a failure. The treating physician must discern the patient's expectations and future needs when selecting a treatment option. This can only be performed through expeditious and deliberate patient education. Allowing the patient to participate in the selection of their treatment plan will gain their confidence and lead to a more open dialog concerning the risks, benefits and complications of different therapeutic protocols. Encouraging the patient to ask questions or to follow-up at a future date to address additional potential concerns may help allay their fears. Table 2 provides the essential components of an informed consent.

Following the above discussion about informed consent, these facts should be recorded in the patient's medical record. Asking the patient to sign an informed consent document, which is cosigned by the physician or a witness, is an integral part in the avoidance of informed consent actions.

If litigation does occur, the physician's primary defense weapon is the medical record. The medical record must not only carefully document the actual events as they occur, but the physician's assessment and ongoing treatment plan. Juries are often unwilling to assign blame to a physician if a rational treatment plan is part of the medical record. Given that there may be several ways to address a problem, proper documentation in the

Shoulder

As far as shoulder surgery is concerned, again, it is absolutely imperative that the correct diagnosis is made and the appropriate procedure is being planned to correct the problem. The patient has to be informed as to what is going to be done and what the after-care involves. As with all surgery, the patient needs to be made aware of what they can expect from the surgery. This includes postoperative pain, limitation of motion and level of strength. Is the outcome going to be 'near perfect' or 'something less than perfect'? This is extremely important, especially for athletes who may undergo a shoulder procedure and think that they are going to be able to compete at the same level as they did prior to the surgery.

Upper extremity

In upper extremity surgery, the patient needs to be made aware of what to expect postoperatively as far as hand, forearm and elbow function are concerned. They also need to be made aware of their responsibility regarding exercise and other patient-compliant issues. If a wrist fusion is being contemplated, it may be a good idea to place the patient in a cast, which will mimic the wrist arthrodesis and see whether the patient is willing to swap a painful and perhaps unstable wrist for a solid, and hopefully painless, wrist.

Hip

As far as hip surgery is concerned, by and large, people who sustain injuries to their hip that result in fractures may be less satisfied than patients who have had a degenerative process and require reconstructive surgery. The reason for this is that many people who sustain an injury to their hip had absolutely no symptoms at all prior to the injury. Their hip was perfect in their mind and now it hurts; they have had surgery and they still may have symptoms. The degenerative process is gradual and the patient had pain *prior* to the surgical procedure. The surgery may decrease the pain significantly; therefore, the patient can be extremely satisfied, especially if they have near-painless motion. The surgeon needs to be aware of this dichotomy, and it certainly applies to other joints, as well as the hip.

Patients undergoing hip surgery, especially total hip reconstruction, need to be made aware of the possibility of intraoperative fractures, postoperative dislocation, nerve injuries and infection. They also need to be informed that the hip replacement is a mechanical replacement. It can, therefore, wear or loosen and may need to be revised sometime in the future.

The operating surgeon needs to be aware, along with the assistant, of which tissues may be harmed during surgery; appropriate precautions must be taken to protect these tissues. Patients with total hip arthroplasty also should be aware preoperatively that they may have a leg-length discrepancy postoperatively. If there is a trade-off between stability and leg length at surgery, stability is certainly preferred over equal leg lengths. Patients need to be made aware of the pros and cons of cemented versus non-cemented techniques in total hip reconstruction. It is also necessary to follow patients who have had total joint arthroplasties for the remainder of their lives. After the initial postoperative period, they should be seen every one to two years to monitor their symptoms and the status of the implant. A 'tickler file' should be utilized, so that if the patients do not make an appointment on their own they can be contacted for appropriate follow-up. This also benefits data collection for outcome studies.

As far as the knee is concerned, patients are best made aware of what to expect from a functional standpoint and regarding degree of pain in the postoperative period. They also are to be cognizant of their responsibilities regarding the after-care in the postoperative period.

There are many teaching aids available for patients who are contemplating orthopedic procedures. These aids include brochures, pamphlets and videos that can be used to augment the education of the patient and family. No matter how good these materials may seem, however, it is still the responsibility of the surgeon to discuss the procedure and to assess the level of understanding that the patient has prior to commencing surgery.

Patients who have fractures about the knee, especially intra-articular fractures, need to be made aware that they may develop traumatic arthritis and may need further reconstruction in the future. This is certainly also true of the shoulder, wrist, hand, hip and ankle. If they are made aware of this up front, it does not come as a surprise to them a year or more down the line when they may need reconstructive surgery.

Staged procedures for infected total joint arthroplasties need to be thoroughly discussed with the patient and their family. This is a long process involving several hospitalizations, surgical procedures and parenteral antibiotics.

With surgery on weight-bearing joints, patients must understand that it may be necessary to have long periods of time using ambulatory assistive devices such as walkers, crutches, and canes, and, in some instances, they may not be able to dispense with ambulatory assistance for the remainder of their lives.

Knee

As far as knee replacement is concerned, patients have to be knowledgeable that these are mechanical devices that wear and may need to be augmented or replaced in the future. If a patient is going to require an arthrodesis of the knee, they can be fitted with an immobilizer or a cylinder cast for a month to six weeks, to see if they are willing to trade an immovable knee in an attempt to reduce pain with an arthrodesis.

Ankle

As far as the ankle is concerned, patients need to be made aware that fractures about the ankle can cause traumatic arthritis and they may have pain and decreased motion in the future. These patients also have the risk of further reconstructive surgery. Again, like the knee or the wrist, if the patient is going to have an arthrodesis, it may be helpful to immobilize the ankle in a cast to see if they are going to be satisfied with a permanently fused ankle. This may be more difficult to assess than the knee, the wrist or the hip because, with an ankle arthrodesis, there is usually an increase in motion in the hind foot and mid foot to help compensate for the fused tibiotalar joint. At least the cast will give them some idea of what it is going to be like.

Foot

Since the foot is the first part of the body to make contact during standing, ambulating and running, it is imperative that the patient be made aware of the pros and cons of any surgical procedure being contemplated for the foot. Surgical correction of the hallux valgus and bunions may have a certain incidence of recurrence. Hammer toe deformities may be corrected by permanent fusion of the proximal interphalangeal joint, but patients need to be made aware that this is permanent. Surgery for Morton's neuroma will render the web space permanently numb, and the patient needs to know this. In most patients, this is a small price to pay for relief of symptoms, but the patient should not be surprised by the numbness. Patients also need to be made aware of the footwear that they may or may not be able to use after a surgical procedure. This is particularly important with female patients who may believe that they will be able to wear high-heeled shoes and, because of a surgical procedure or other treatment, this may not be possible. Patients such as those with diabetes, who are at high risk for foot problems, need to have periodic care to try to prevent some of the more major problems. Patients with diabetes often have peripheral neuropathy and have a high incidence of diabetic ulcers and Charcot joints; thus, they need to be followed closely. These patients also need to have appropriate toe-nail care with proper trimming to prevent in-growth. Diabetics with foot problems can often be treated with custom-made molded shoes, casts, splints and braces.

PEDIATRIC AGE GROUP

Orthopedic care of the pediatric age group requires specific knowledge. Physicians must keep in mind the growth potential of children. The growth can be a blessing and a curse. The growth may be very beneficial for the remodeling of fractures; however, if there is injury to a growth plate, there can be premature closure which may cause limb length discrepancies or angular deformities. Orthopedic surgeons and the parents of a minor need to be made aware of that, and when they are making decisions about care for the child, they should do everything possible to be sure that the decision is the same decision the child would make if given the same information upon reaching adulthood.

As stated previously, this discussion is not meant to be totally inclusive of all problems that may arise in an orthopedic surgeon's practice. It is meant to stimulate the thinking and awareness of the musculoskeletal surgeon when contemplating surgery or other treatment plans. Remember, it is important for the surgeon and the patient to have the same level of expectation for *any* treatment plan, and it is imperative for the surgeon to help educate the patient about their pathology, anatomy and any proposed treatment. The orthopedic surgeon must maintain his/her training and expertise by staying up to date, communicating with the patient, being available for their needs and constantly keeping in mind the possibility for therapeutic misadventure. In so doing, the management of risk will be successful and, indeed, there will be many *fewer* misadventures.

'PEARLS' TO AVOID LITIGATION:

A. *Pearls to avoid delays in diagnosis*
   (1) Know what conditions have a high frequency of diagnostic error;
   (2) Follow up laboratory studies, tests and consultations;
   (3) Communicate with consulting physicians;
   (4) Follow up with patients frequently;
   (5) Take detailed histories;
   (6) Maintain appropriate documentation;
   (7) Appeal insurance company denials when necessary.

B. *Communication pearls*

    (1) Review patients' histories;

    (2) Make eye contact;

    (3) Do not interrupt;

    (4) Ask for patient feedback;

    (5) Keep medical terms simple;

    (6) Listen to patients and summarize what they say;

    (7) Do not delay communicating after a complication.

C. *Documentation pearls*

    (1) Document history, tests, procedures and instructions;

    (2) Document non-compliance;

    (3) Date all documentation;

    (4) Write legibly;

    (5) Avoid derogatory comments;

    (6) Keep billing separate from treatment records;

    (7) Do not obliterate original entry when making a correction;

    (8) Do not alter record after receiving notice of a claim.

D. *Follow-up pearls*

    (1) Design systems or protocols to track:

        (a) if the patient obtained test/consult;

        (b) what the results were;

        (c) that the patient was notified of the results and plan of action (or inaction) i.e. was instructed.

E. *Informed consent pearls*

    (1) Physician should conduct discussions;

    (2) Inform patients about risks, benefits and alternatives;

    (3) Document key points in the discussion as well as the patient's consent.

F. *Orthopedic diagnostic specific pearls* (Data obtained from Physicians Insurers' Association of America [PIAA] claim statistics)

    (1) Total hip arthroplasty complications:

        (a) neuropathy (sciatic or femoral);

        (b) leg length inequality;

        (c) infection;

        (d) technical failure (component malposition, dislocation);

        (e) vascular injury;

        (f) pulmonary embolus;

(g) trochanteric nonunion;

(h) persistent pain;

(i) lack of informed consent.

(2) Total knee arthroplasty complications:

    (a) infection (failure to recognize);

    (b) technical (component loosening, wear or failure);

    (c) poor surgical performance;

    (d) deep venous thrombosis/pulmonary embolus prophylaxis.

(3) Femur fracture complications:

    (a) Children – most frequent and expensive complications:

        foot drop;

        skin loss;

        compartment syndrome;

        malrotation/shortening;

        persistent deformity.

    (b) Adults:

        inappropriate fixation;

        malrotation;

        undersized rods;

        poor hardware selection.

(4) Femoral neck fracture complications:

    (a) failure to diagnose;

    (b) poor surgical performance;

    (c) nonunion;

    (d) dislocation;

    (e) avascular neurosis;

    (f) falls from surgical table.

(5) Tibial fracture complications:

    (a) malunion/nonunion;

    (b) skin loss;

    (c) infection;

    (d) pulmonary/fat embolus;

    (e) leg length inequality.

(6) Spine surgery (without fusion) complications:

    (a) failure to improve;

    (b) poor surgical performance (dural or vascular/bowel injury);

    (c) wrong level/wrong side surgery;

    (d) nerve injury;

    (e) retained foreign bodies.

(7) Spine fusion complications:

    (a) neurologic impairment;

    (b) chronic pain/limited recovery;

    (c) vascular injury;

    (d) recurrent deformity;

    (e) impotence;

    (f) neurogenic bowel/bladder;

    (g) infection;

    (h) death.

(8) Knee arthroscopy complications:

    (a) infection (delay in recognition);

    (b) flexion contracture;

    (c) vascular/neurologic injury;

    (d) wrong-side surgery.

ORTHOPEDIC MEDICAL MALPRACTICE: AN ATTORNEY'S PERSPECTIVE

A randomized nationwide survey of medical malpractice attorneys was performed to investigate issues regarding orthopedic medical malpractice[2]. The purpose of this study was to identify risk factors for orthopedic malpractice cases. One hundred and seventy-nine (179) surveys were completed (25.7% with responding attorneys reporting an average experience of 14.4 years in the field of medical malpractice). Fifty of those surveyed indicated that they specialized exclusively in medical malpractice law and the respondents were representative of the entire population in terms of geographic location.

The most common healthcare setting that resulted in all orthopedic malpractice cases was a community hospital (50%). The least common setting was a Veteran's Administration hospital (3%). The most common payer class was private insurance (50%) and the least was self-pay (2%). Of the responding attorneys, 18% believed the number of cases was increasing, 27% thought it was decreasing and 55% believed the number was unchanging.

The most common factors associated with an orthopedic medical malpractice lawsuit are, in order of decreasing frequency, provided in Table 4.

Table 4   Survey of the most common areas of medical malpractice

Physician error during surgical procedure
Error in diagnosis
Incorrect treatment choice
Perioperative complications
Poor physician–patient relationship
Informed consent

The most common factors associated with an orthopedic medical malpractice lawsuit for those cases in which a poor physician–patient relationship was a contributing factor were, in descending order:

(1) The physician appeared rushed and uninterested;

(2) The physician failed to return messages;

(3) The patient had unrealistic treatment expectations;

(4) The physician was rude;

(5) Unhelpful or rude office personnel;

(6) Unhelpful or rude hospital personnel.

This study also revealed that the three most common anatomic areas involved in an orthopedic lawsuit were the lumbar spine, the knee, foot and ankle respectively. The information supplied by this survey seems to corroborate the same issues relating to orthopedic malpractice based on data from the AAOS.

TESTIFYING AT A DEPOSITION OR TRIAL

Should a physician be testifying at a deposition or a trial, the following are helpful hints to remember[3]:

(1) Be persuasive but never argumentative or hostile. Display compassion; be confident; do not become arrogant.

(2) Thorough preparation and attention to details prior to the trial improves confidence. Review all pertinent medical and hospital records, including nurses' and physical therapists' notes.

(3) Refer to the patient by name and know important dates pertinent to the case.

(4) Have a thorough familiarity with the chronology of the case so that you do not appear confused when discussing the pertinent facts.

(5) The medical records should be available at the trial or deposition for physician referral.

(6) The physician should insist on focused questions. Poorly worded or convoluted questions should be clarified before answering them.

(7) The physician should be present in the courtroom throughout the trial.

In summary, medicolegal issues can evoke significant stress for physicians. 'An ounce of prevention is worth a pound of cure.' Establishing effective lines of communication, detailed and accurate record keeping, a thorough understanding of post-surgical complications and their management in consultation with the patient in a timely fashion, and constant monitoring of quality of care are effective methods of litigation prevention. A calm, reassuring and compassionate demeanor in dealing with even the most difficult patients or those with suboptimal outcomes will be helpful in limiting potential litigation.

REFERENCES

1. Committee on Professional Liability. *Managing Orthopaedic Malpractice Risk*. Rosemont, IL: AAOS, 1996
2. Klimo GF, Dajm WJ, Brinker MR, *et al*. Orthopaedic medical malpractice: an attorney's perspective. *Am J Orthopaed* 2000;29:93–7
3. Peimer CA, Goblatt S, Medical malpractice: perspective of the physician's team. In Baratz ME, Watson AD, Imbriglia JE, eds. *Orthopaedic Surgery: The Essentials*. New York, NY: Thieme Publishers, 1999;927–31
4. Bode FW, Medical malpractice: the attorney. In Baratz ME, Watson AD, Imbriglia JE, eds. *Orthopaedic Surgery: The Essentials*. New York, NY: Thieme Publishers, 1999; 933–4

18

Plastic surgery

Gerald D. Verdi, DDS, MD

Plastic surgery, like other surgical disciplines, is experiencing an increased claims frequency. In addition, the awards are climbing steadily. Overall, between 1990 and 1995, 85% of all malpractice settlements were more than US$100 000; 43% of the settlements were in excess of US$500 000; and 22% were for more than US$1 million.

What are the factors that precipitate a lawsuit? The most important is lack of communication with the patient and family. Good communication is a key component to decreased claims frequency. Rapport and communication established by the surgeon and his or her office staff with the patient create a trusting relationship and reduce the possibility of an adversarial one, even if the result is less than desired. There are other factors in addition to communication: the staff and the doctor must be courteous and friendly in every situation; there must be immediate access to the physician in emergency situations, and clear guidelines for phone policy, including the scope of authority of the individuals responding to the patient's concerns; important phone calls need to be recorded and logged on the patient's records; there must be privacy in communication both visual and auditory. The office staff must keep the office clean and in good repair, and provide seating equal to the patient population. The waiting room must be monitored at all times. We must remember that the surgeon is responsible for all of the acts of his or her staff. This requires that the staff enhance their training and experience through office meetings and with the plastic surgeon, and continuing-education courses. Most important again is communication between the physician and the patient. The physician needs to inform the patient of the diagnosis, the prognosis, the treatment plan, the alternatives and the expected outcomes. Defining exactly the patient's goals and expectations are extremely important, particularly in plastic surgery.

One of the most important ways to reduce the legal risk is to keep accurate and complete records. Never, ever alter a record or white-out sections

Table 1 Factors precipitating a lawsuit. Reproduced with permission of P.I.E. Mutual

Poor communication
Pressure for payment
Lack of continuity of care
Practice out of scope
Bad outcome
Abandonment

of entries. Rather, a straight line through a sentence with an initial and the date is adequate and better from the legal perspective. Never leave a record in an examination room with the patient, and never allow a patient to transport their records within the facility. It is an axiom that misinformation and/or incorrect data are a common basis for a lawsuit, and that 'if it is not written, it did not happen'.

A summary of the factors precipitating a suit are summarized in Table 1.

Let us now look at plastic surgery, specifically, and determine what is occurring in this specialty. Esthetic surgical procedures exceed reconstructive procedures in frequency overview: note Figure 1. It is also true that esthetic procedures exceed reconstructive procedures in claim severity (Figure 2). Figure 3 reviews frequency by specialty in the last decade, and it is important to see that the frequency by specialty is headed up by plastic surgery frequency, seconded only by neurosurgery, but when one reviews the severity in the same decade, 1990 to 1999, one finds that plastic surgery and neurosurgery have a much reduced severity as compared to other specialties, particularly obstetrics (Figure 4). Finally, claims for breast procedures far exceed the severity averages of all other procedures (Figure 5). These three figures are from the Doctor's Company, and represent both open and closed claims for the studied years.

One of the significant problems in plastic surgery is full financial disclosure. The patient needs to know what to expect financially. This includes the surgeon's fee, the anesthetic fee, the hospital or surgical-center facility charge, medications, office visits and the possibility of reoperation with additional fees.

Studies have shown that there is no demonstrable correlation between quality of care provided by a physician and their prior claims history. In fact, quality of care does not appear to be a major determinant of whether a patient initiates a malpractice claim. In fact, there are many true injuries to patients for which patients do not seek compensation. It is the breakdown in communication between physician and patient and the resulting

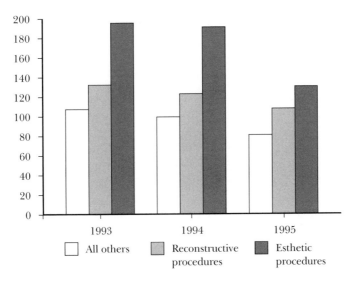

Figure 1   Frequency overview: open and closed claims by report years 1993, 1994, 1995. Reproduced with permission of the Doctor's Company

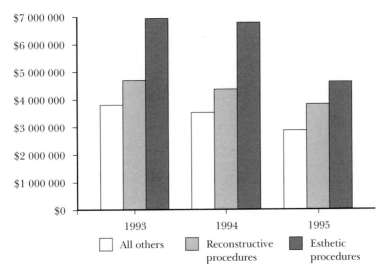

Figure 2   Severity overview: open and closed claims by report years 1993, 1994, 1995. Reproduced with permission of the Doctor's Company

patient dissatisfaction which lead to malpractice; patients report feeling rushed, feeling ignored, receiving inadequate explanations or advice, and spending less time with their physician than they desire. The result is that he or she feels deserted, and that the physician devalues the patient's

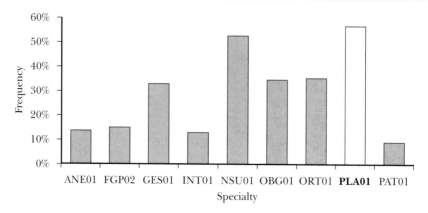

Figure 3 Plastic surgery (PLA01) frequency is higher than all other specialties. Reproduced with permission of the Doctor's Company

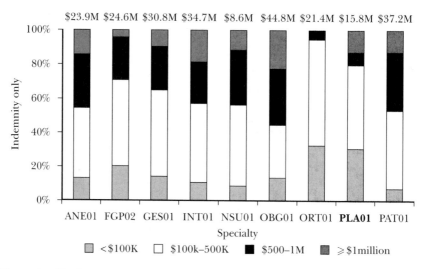

Figure 4 Plastic surgery (PLA01) severity is lower. Reproduced with permission of the Doctor's Company

views, delivers information poorly, and fails to understand the patient's perspectives. It appears that patients want to be active participants in discussing treatment options and understanding the benefits of different surgical approaches. They want their questions answered. Physicians have to transmit to their patients that they are caring and respectful.

In summary, patients are more likely to sue their physicians if they feel that the physician did not care or did not inform them adequately. Physicians need to improve and maintain their communication skills, and

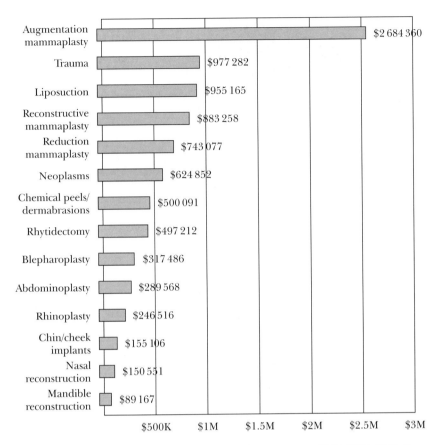

Figure 5 Severity averages: open and closed claims by report years 1993, 1994, 1995. Reproduced with permission of the Doctor's Company

provide enough time in their daily schedules to give each patient the feeling that their problems have been heard and discussed, and that solutions have been provided. All of these are especially true in plastic surgery, where often we are doing surgery that is elective, but is designed to improve self-image. So the physician must spend additional time listening, comprehending and defining the expectations of the patient. It is not uncommon for a plastic surgeon to feel a level of discomfort after the first interview, and that is why it is particularly important for the patient to return for additional consultation, particularly when the surgeon is not sure that he or she can achieve the goals of the patient. Not only are the objectives of the patient important, but it is also critical that the facts of the procedures are transmitted, i.e. that scarring will occur, and that there is a possibility of bleeding, infection, deformity or a lack of symmetry, and all

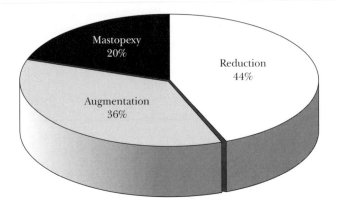

Figure 6   Reduction mammoplasty is the most common cause of claims in breast surgery. Reproduced with permission of the Doctor's Company

other potential hazards and complications of any surgical procedure. It is particularly important that the patient understands that complications may well require additional surgeries and additional expense. It is strongly recommended that all of these facts be transmitted in an informed consent sheet which the patient signs prior to surgery.

Figure 6 shows that the greatest number of claims with breast surgery is now shifting towards reduction mammoplasty, away from augmentation mammoplasty which was once the leader in breast surgery claims made and claims paid.

It is also important to note in plastic surgery, when dealing with the esthetic surgical patients, that many times the nurse and the office staff can receive information about the patient that the physician does not pick up, either because he or she is very busy, or, more likely, because the patient has unintentionally or intentionally tried to mask some of their feelings; but in a one-to-one conversation, the nurses can often sense these feelings and report them back to the physician.

Finally, when the impressions of the staff and/or the doctors are negative, then the surgeon needs to revisit the patient for an additional in-depth consultation.

19

Pathology

Dennis M. O'Connor, MD

Litigation problems have traditionally been less of a concern to pathologists than to their clinician counterparts, such as obstetricians and other surgical specialists. Laboratory administration is well controlled by numerous state and federal regulations, and quality assurance is usually closely monitored. Nevertheless, because 'failure to diagnose cancer' continues to be one of the most common reasons for lawsuits, the pathologist can be investigated as a source of malpractice. Although liability risk can occur in clinical or anatomical pathology, this chapter is limited to anatomical pathology. Potential litigation in anatomical pathology results from errors in cytology screening and interpretation, errors in matching the correct diagnosis with the appropriate patient, errors in histological interpretation and errors in transcription. Unfortunately, many lawsuits occur because of simple miscommunication between clinicians and pathologists.

CERVICAL CYTOLOGY LIABILITY AND THE FALSE-NEGATIVE PAP SMEAR

Exfoliative cervical cytology (the Pap smear) is the prototype screening test. It is inexpensive, is easy to perform on an accessible site, has a good degree of accuracy and can identify a preinvasive condition that, when treated, can prevent cervical cancer. Nevertheless, cervical cytology claims are among the most rapidly increasing areas of liability for pathology laboratories. Although cytology usually involves a very small amount of a clinical laboratory's daily routine, lawsuits in this area have risen to the point that they represent up to a quarter of total pathology claims. The severity of claims now places cytopathology on a par with many of the surgical specialties. The reasons for this include[1]:

(1) The introduction of the Bethesda System and the concept of the Pap smear as a medical consultation;

(2) The Clinical Laboratory Improvement Amendments (CLIA) regulations that require a 'look-back' or review of all Pap smears in patients with diagnosed high-grade dysplasia or carcinoma;

(3) The advent of the 'expert' witness eager to testify regarding laboratory error rates and misdiagnoses;

(4) The impression that the Pap smear must have a zero standard of error, which is an impossible goal.

Because of heightened concern over misdiagnoses and communication problems among laboratories and clinicians, the Bethesda System of classification for reporting cervical/vaginal cytology was developed. The Bethesda System consolidated diverse cytological terms into reproducible categories (Table 1). A major advantage of the Bethesda System was the evolution of descriptive terms ('inflammatory atypia', 'mild dysplasia') into diagnoses that could predict cell behavior ('benign cell changes', 'epithelial cell abnormalities'). In addition, the diagnosis of 'atypical cells of undetermined significance' (a category having no predictive value) emphasizes the subjectivity and irreproducibility of Pap smear screening. It was noted that the cytology report could no longer be regarded as a laboratory test similar to a peripheral blood count, but as a medical consultation. The pathologist should therefore expect adequate clinical information, and should also comment on the quality of the specimen. This also means, however, that the pathologist must take responsibility for the report and its implications regarding predictability of disease.

The Clinical Laboratory Improvement Amendments of 1988 (CLIA–88) now require that laboratories must re-examine all previous Pap smears screened as normal or benign in patients with newly diagnosed high-grade dysplasia or carcinoma. This requirement has presented numerous problems for laboratories. What was originally designed as an educational tool and a quality-assurance probe within a laboratory has provided a wealth of new material for use by malpractice attorneys. Using 'outside experts' who review the material with a prior knowledge that high-grade dysplasia or cancer was eventually found histologically, laboratories are now brought to task for smears that, on second review, are diagnosed as 'limited for evaluation', or contain 'atypical cells of undetermined significance'.

Much has been written concerning the false-negative Pap smear, with numbers quoted between 5 and 50% for any particular laboratory. Nevertheless, the public and the legal profession expect that Pap smears should have a screening error rate of zero. The latter is an unattainable goal for any laboratory. Approximately two-thirds of false-negative smears

Table 1   The Bethesda System[2]

(I) The quality of the smear
(A) Satisfactory for examination
(B) Satisfactory for examination but limited by various factors (obscuring blood, inflammation, drying artifact, lack of transformation zone elements)
(C) Unsatisfactory for examination
(II) The diagnosis
(A) Within normal limits
(B) Benign cell changes
(1) Due to infection (trichomonas, shift in vaginal flora, candidiasis, herpes virus, actinomyces)
(2) Due to reactive or reparative changes (inflammation, IUD placement, radiation, atrophy)
(C) Epithelial cell abnormalities
(1) Squamous cells
(a) Atypical cells of undetermined significance
(b) Low-grade intraepithelial lesions (equivalent to mild dysplasia or human papillomavirus cellular changes)
(c) High-grade intraepithelial lesions (equivalent to moderate or severe dysplasia/carcinoma-*in-situ*)
(d) Carcinoma
(2) Glandular cells
(a) Endometrial cells identified in a postmenopausal woman
(b) Atypical cells of undetermined significance
(c) Adenocarcinoma
(3) Other cells
(a) Sarcomas
(b) Lymphomas
(c) Metastatic neoplasms

IUD, intrauterine device

represent sampling errors (failure to transfer abnormal cells from the cervix to the slide); screening errors probably represent only about 5–10% of false-negative smears. To calculate this number, most laboratories use the false-negative fraction ratio, which utilizes the number of estimated false negatives (calculated from the prevalence of an abnormality, usually a squamous intraepithelial lesion, and the laboratory's total Pap smear volume) as the numerator, and the number of true positives (cases with squamous intraepithelial lesions) and estimated false negatives as the denominator. This number is reproducible from laboratory to laboratory.

Probably the most useful way to decrease the number of lawsuits in cervical cytopathology is education of clinicians and their patients regarding what the Pap smear represents. They must understand that it is a screening test and not a diagnostic test. It is accomplished by human examination and interpretation of the material, which is fraught with human error. Even in the best of hands, this error rate can never be zero. In many cases, laboratories are now including disclaimer statements that emphasize these facts.

Pathologists who interpret smears must examine the slides carefully. All dotted cells should be examined closely, and cells outside the marked areas should also be checked. The pathologist should have a good working relationship with the cytotechnologists under his or her supervision, and the pathologist should be cognizant of their skill levels and any limitations. Any errors in screening made by the cytotechnologist will ultimately be the pathologist's responsibility.

It is possible that, in the future, new adjunct technologies to traditional cytology processing and screening may enhance the accuracy of the Pap smear. At present, the expense of these technologies limits their use. Sadly, in the end, laboratories today are comparing the benefits and the risks of evaluating exfoliative gynecological cytology. Many are now finding that the reimbursement rate (extremely small) and the malpractice liability (extremely high) are too great a burden to bear, and they are considering dropping cervical cytology screening as a service. This is tragic, as it is well known that the best way to prevent cervical cancer is repeated periodic cytological screening.

NON-GYNECOLOGICAL CYTOLOGY

Evaluation of non-gynecological specimens includes examination of aspirated material from suspicious solid lesions, or examination of various body fluids. Of all sites, the most litigated is the breast. It is important for the pathologist to examine carefully the specimen for adequacy and preservation, and not render diagnoses on suboptimal material. Optimally, aspirated material from the breast should not be assessed without knowledge of the clinical findings and review of any relevant radiographs. Direct communication with the clinician is essential to minimize misinterpretation of diagnostic comments.

AUTOPSY PATHOLOGY

In the past, autopsies were extremely useful as a learning tool. Not only did an autopsy provide information regarding the pathogenesis of disease processes, but it also indicated errors in diagnosis and management that,

Table 2   Surgical pathology: most common areas of litigation[3]

Failure to diagnose malignant lymphoma
Failure to diagnose melanoma
Diagnostic problems with prostate
   needle biopsies
Problems with expert consultants

when identified, could be avoided when similar clinical situations occurred in the future. More recently, because of a fear of litigation from a 'medical mistake found at autopsy', the percentage of medical autopsy requests has fallen significantly.

For an autopsy to be performed, a valid consent must be signed by the next-of-kin. In most states and the District of Columbia, a specific order of next-of-kin is described and can be followed if certain members are unavailable. Telephone consents are usually acceptable if witnessed. It is important that the person consenting understands the procedure, and any limitations requested must be noted and observed.

The pathologist should be cognizant of potential medical-examiner cases (deaths outside the hospital or within 24 hours of hospital admission or on the operating table, deaths from violence, trauma or otherwise unexplained) and perform these autopsies only after these patients have been released to the local hospital. If on gross examination an unsuspected error in management is found, the pathologist should stop the autopsy, document the findings and immediately notify the clinician and the medical examiner, if appropriate. Conversely, a medical examiner can be held liable if an autopsy is performed without appropriate justification.

SURGICAL PATHOLOGY

Adverse legal action can occur from errors in specimen identification and description, and errors in diagnosis. A review by a professional liability insurer in California identified the most common areas in surgical pathology. These are addressed in Table 2.

It is important that all specimens submitted from a particular patient match any written materials submitted. Accession numbers on microscope slides should follow an easy-to-understand order and should also match any written report. If not, it is possible for a patient to receive an incorrect diagnosis, which can result in treatment delay or unnecessary invasive procedures. If an error in identification is found, any specimen processing should stop and the clinician should be called to the laboratory to correct the error. If the error is discovered after microscope diagnoses are finalized, all clinicians must be notified immediately and corrected diagnoses issued as amended reports.

Small specimens should be carefully described as to size and number. It is important that all material examined microscopically matches the material submitted. If no material is found on the microscope slides, the specimen blocks must be checked to document the presence or absence of any unsampled fragments.

Errors in diagnosis can occur as part of an intraoperative consultation ('frozen section' diagnosis), or as a final interpretation of permanent sections. It is important to remember that the frozen section should be done only in those cases where an immediate diagnosis will change intraoperative management. Close communication with the surgeon is essential to confirm specimen orientation and appropriate sampling, and to determine exactly what information is anticipated. Realistically, frozen section diagnoses should be kept as simple as possible as specimen sampling is limited owing to time constraints; usually, 'benign', 'malignant' or 'deferred' is appropriate. All frozen section diagnoses should be documented as part of the written report.

Final diagnoses should be arrived at only after careful examination of all microscope sections. Recuts should be made of any suboptimally sectioned and stained slides. Any unexpected diagnosis (carcinoma, pregnancy tissue without villi, sterilization procedures without tissue confirmation) should be relayed telephonically to the clinician and the fact that this was done documented in the report.

The pathologist should not be afraid to seek consultation on difficult cases. Consultants should be chosen with care, and should be limited to one per case. Preferably, this person should be an expert in the area of concern, and the clinician and the pathologist should accept the opinion rendered. It should be remembered that the individual requesting a consultation could be held negligent, under the doctrine of vicarious liability, if the consultant is shown to have made an incorrect diagnosis. If a consultation is requested, the reason should be clearly stated. As the original slides are considered the true legal record, recuts should be sent if at all possible.

Pathologists working in commercial laboratories that receive material from various states or involved in telepathology evaluations should be aware that some states require licensure before processing and microscope diagnoses can be rendered on material originating in that state.

Table 3   The pathologist as witness[4]

Any notes or written comments are discoverable
In court be cognizant of leading phraseology
Rarely is a text or article authoritative unless you agree with everything
Be informative
Avoid an adversarial posture
Be truthful about your qualifications
Be medically correct and up to date
Avoid any questions outside your field of expertise

THE PATHOLOGIST AS WITNESS

The pathologist may be called to testify either as a witness of fact or as an expert. This is particularly true in placental pathology, where the pathologist may be asked to testify regarding placental changes that may reflect long-standing fetal compromise. While a pathologist may decline to participate as an expert witness, he or she may be compelled to testify as a witness of fact. If called to testify, the pathologist must be knowledgeable of all aspects of the case. Keep in mind that any notes or written comments made during review can be provided to opposing attorneys.

In court, the pathologist must be cognizant of leading phraseology used by attorneys, and avoid traps. One should never agree that any text or article is authoritative without review of the pertinent material and agreement with everything in it. The pathologist should try to be informative, and avoid an adversarial posture. If testifying as an expert, one should be truthful about one's qualifications. The testimony should be medically correct and up to date. The pathologist should avoid any questions that are outside his or her field of expertise (Table 3).

SUMMARY

As with any other medical specialty, the practicing pathologist must meet the standard of care at all times. Laboratory guidelines and established quality-control protocols should be carefully followed. Documentation of all procedures and diagnoses is critical. Finally, close interaction with the clinician is essential to maximize trust and minimize miscommunication.

REFERENCES

1. Frable WJ, Austin RM, Greening SE, *et al*. Medicolegal affairs. International Academy of Cytology Task Force summary. Diagnostic cytology towards the 21st century: an international expert conference and tutorial. *Acta Cytol* 1998;42:76–119

2. The National Cancer Institute Workshop. The Bethesda system for reporting cervicovaginal cytologic diagnoses. *Acta Cytol* 1993;37:115–24

3. Roth LM. Medicolegal issues: an anatomic pathologist's perspective. *Am J Clin Pathol* 1996;106(Suppl 1):18–24

4. Troxel DB, Sabella JD. Problem areas in pathology practice: uncovered by a review of malpractice claims. *Am J Surg Pathol* 1994;18:821–31

20

Otolaryngology – head and neck surgery

Jason P. Lockette, MD, and Jeffrey M. Bumpous, MD

Being named in a medical malpractice lawsuit is something that few, if any, physicians will be able to avoid. It can be an emotionally challenging experience and one that we should all be prepared to face. This chapter examines what otolaryngologists are most commonly sued for. It looks at some ways in which to minimize the risk of being sued, and offers some advice for those facing litigation.

WHAT OTOLARYNGOLOGISTS ARE MOST COMMONLY SUED FOR

According to the National Practitioner Data Bank (NPDB)[1], most surgical malpractice payments come as a result of 'improper performance of surgery' (Table 1). The NPDB does not record their data any more specifically than shown in Table 1; however, most malpractice insurance providers do. The Medical Protective Company's national experience with otolaryngology claims from 1991 to 1999 reveals a total of 398 cases[2]. The company is a large medical malpractice insurance provider that covers most of the USA. The highest percentage of their claims resulted from nerve injury (4.77%), nose injury (2.01%) or ear injury (1.51%) (Table 2). These allegations fall into the category of improper performance of surgery. It should also be noted that 3.51% of claims were the result of retained foreign bodies[2] (see Chapter 33).

Facial nerve injury is the most common nerve injury for which otolaryngologists are sued[3]. Most suits come from injury during parotid surgery, with ear/temporal bone surgery being second[3]. Further review shows that most large settlements were the result of facial nerve paralysis, followed by delay in or misdiagnosis of malignancy and perioperative death associated with elective procedures[2].

Table 1 Surgery-related malpractice payments reported to the National Practitioner Data Bank, 1 January 1998–30 September 1999[1]

Malpractice act	n	Median ($US)	Mean ($US)	Maximum ($US)
Surgery: failure to perform	64	100 000	172 632.73	1 000 000
Surgery: improper positioning	56	75 000	153 642.59	1 305 620
Surgery: retained foreign body	451	29 917	63 301.80	700 000
Surgery: wrong body part	228	29 999	80 276.21	1 750 000
Surgery: improper performance of surgery	2799	104 129	211 716.61	9 500 000
Surgery: unnecessary surgery	199	100 000	199 567.74	3 750 000
Surgery: delay in surgery	134	125 000	256 177.42	3 021 645
Surgery: improper management of patient	431	150 000	230 674.00	2 750 000
Surgery: failure to obtain consent	222	78 906	134 874.84	1 000 000
Surgery: not otherwise coded	2383	95 000	178 328.09	6 000 000
Total	6967	100 000	184 793.12	9 500 000

Table 2 Top categories of allegation in otolaryngology from The Medical Protective Company's national experience, 1991–99[2]

Allegation	Cases (%)
Improper surgery or surgical error	22.61
Improper treatment of a condition	15.33
Failure to prevent condition, e.g. perforation, infection, hemorrhage	10.80
Failure to diagnose condition, e.g. tumor, infection, hemorrhage	10.55
Failure to remove, e.g. packing, tumor, drain, sponge	7.04

The Medical Protective Company made no payment in 66.83% of its cases. When the company did pay, the average award was $US120 845. The severity of injury was classified as 'minor temporary' or less in 30% of cases. An indemnity was paid, however, in almost 23% of these cases. There was an interesting trend seen in the percentage of cases resulting in no payment. This percentage increased every year except 1999, most likely due to the increasing number of frivolous cases filed.

WAYS TO MINIMIZE YOUR RISK OF BEING SUED

There are many elements that come together to make a malpractice claim, with negligent medical care being only one. In fact, the argument could be made that negligent medical care is only present in a minority of cases, since two-thirds or more of claims are settled without payment to patients[4,5]. Why, then, do some physicians experience more claims than others? There have been numerous studies that have examined this issue, in an attempt to define physician characteristics that result in more or fewer malpractice claims. Physicians who are most often sued are obstetrician–gynecologists and surgical subspecialists[4]. Also, those who see higher numbers of patients tend to suffer more claims[4]. There are also personal, educational and professional characteristics, identified by Adamson and colleagues[4] which tend to result in more or fewer claims.

Adamson and colleagues[4] compared 427 surgeons associated with both high and low malpractice claim rates. All were members of a California-based, physician-owned, interindemnity liability-protection trust. Being born in the USA was the most significant personal factor resulting in fewer claims. There was also a trend towards fewer claims associated with those who reported church membership. This trend, however, was not statistically significant. Educational factors were also examined. Surgeons associated with more claims were more likely to have attended medical school outside the USA or Canada, less likely to be fellowship trained and less likely to be board-certified in their field. These were the only educational factors that were statistically significant.

Surgeons associated with more claims were reportedly more socially and professionally isolated than their counterparts associated with fewer claims. Solo practitioners as well as those who belonged to fewer professional societies were more likely to be sued. The group associated with fewer claims also tended to have registered nurses rather than non-professional personnel as office staff. Most of the surgeons with clinical faculty appointments had fewer claims associated with them. One could speculate, based on these data, that there are practitioner characteristics that predict suit likelihood. Surgeons who spend more time with their patients may incur a lower incidence of suits[6]. Clauss and Siglock[6] claim that 'spending time with patients is the single most effective line of defense against malpractice suits'. **They also claim that 'the three Cs' are key factors in avoiding and winning suits. These are compassion, care and competence**. In fact, patients are much more likely to overlook deficiencies in the latter than in the former two. It is important to note, also, that office staff often play as important a role as the physician in avoiding claims[4,6].

The most important time spent as surgeon is in explaining and obtaining informed consent[6,7]. Between January 1998 and September 1999, there were at least 222 malpractice payments in the USA that were due to the physician's failure to obtain adequate informed consent[1]. There are many legal theories surrounding informed consent that attorneys use to prove a case[7]. In most states, the following conditions must be met in order to challenge an informed consent:

(1) The physician has the duty to provide information that a reasonable person would find material as part of the professional duty of due care and the physician breaches the duty;

(2) There is an injury that makes the patient worse off (either in financially measurable terms or by violating the patient's right to privacy) than if the procedure had not been performed;

(3) The injury is the materialization of an undisclosed risk or possible outcome;

(4) Had the patient been informed of the potential outcome or risk, even if none occurs, he or she (or a reasonable person) would not have consented[7].

It should be obvious that true informed consent lies in the mind of the patient and not on a piece of paper, underscoring the need to spend ample time discussing the treatment with your patients, to ensure realistic expectations. For example, the literature states that the incidence of facial paralysis as a postoperative complication is somewhere between 1 : 100 and 1 : 1000 cases[3]. A reasonable, well-informed patient should, therefore, not automatically assume negligence should they experience this statistically possible outcome. Does this mean, though, that every possible complication should be discussed in minute detail? The courts leave this issue open to debate.

Another method to avoid malpractice claims is wise patient selection. Just as there are certain physician characteristics that may result in more claims, there are also certain characteristics that indicate a litigious patient. Patients who are chronically malcontent, manipulative or 'doctor-shopping' represent high risk for malpractice suits[6].

No physician, no matter how compassionate, caring and competent, is immune to bad outcomes. The best way to handle these situations is to tell the truth. Accepting responsibility and admitting fault are not synonymous[6]. If the patient feels that you have acted in their best interests, even if you have made an 'honest mistake', they will be much less likely to sue. Being honest and up-front will afford the patient resolve, and will allow them to begin considering additional treatment if needed. Ideally, the patient should see their physician as an ally rather than as an adversary. Unfortunately, though, this is not always the reality.

It is important to remember that only about two-thirds of cases ever result in an indemnity being paid and that only about 5% of cases ever actually go to trial[2,4,5]. It is also important to know that most of what we can do to improve our chances of winning litigation is done prior to actually being sued. The importance of informed consent is discussed above. The medical record should be accurate and *legible*. If a jury sees a medical record that is incomplete and/or illegible, they are likely to assume that this reflects the quality of care. A Texas jury awarded a large settlement to a family after a patient was dispensed the wrong medication, supposedly as a result of an illegible prescription. This was the first settlement of its kind and will probably set a precedent for others to follow.

ADVICE TO THOSE FACING POSSIBLE LITIGATION

Most physicians feel a certain amount of resentment about being sued, as it can be an insult to their competence. Conquering this resentment is an important first step in preparing for and winning a malpractice suit. There are several other things that should also be done by the physician. When an attorney requests records, this can mean an impending suit. Carefully review the records for completeness and legibility. If there are omissions then add a new note, dated the day it is added. Altering previous records, a criminal act in itself, should never be done. The physician should *insist on quality representation* and, more important, should *participate in the defense*. This includes assimilation of pertinent information as well as selection of qualified experts. It is likely that the entire process, from preparation to the trial, will take 5 full years[6].

Clauss and Siglock[6] describe a malpractice trial as a test of persuasion. If the physician can remain composed and objective, and articulate good judgment under pressure in the courtroom, the jury is more likely to believe that they treated the patient with compassion, care and competence. Regardless of the outcome, it is helpful to review the case and to examine how better to avoid such claims in the future. Most cases are either won or lost on several key factors. Careful examination of these factors may allow physicians to prevent future claims.

REFERENCES

1. *National Practitioner Data Bank Research File of September 30, 1999*, as maintained by the Division of Quality Assurance, Bureau of Health Professions, Health Resources and Services Administration, US Department of Health and Human Services, Washington, DC
2. The Medical Protective Company. *Otolaryngology Claims Statistics 1991–99*. The Medical Protective Company, KY, 2000
3. Wiet RJ, Schuring A. The legal aspects of surgical facial nerve injury. *ENT J* 1996;75:737–9
4. Adamson TA, Baldwin DC, Sheehan TJ, Oppenberg AA. Characteristics of surgeons with high and low malpractice claims rates. *West J Med* 1997;166:37–44
5. Rice B. Where doctors get sued the most. *Med Econ* February 1995:98–110
6. Clauss ER, Siglock TJ. The fundamentals of avoiding and winning medical malpractice suits. *Otolaryngol Head Neck Surg* 1994;110:141–5
7. The Ethics Committee of the American Academy of Otolaryngology–Head and Neck Surgery. Informed consent. *Otolaryngol Head Neck Surg* 1996;115:179–85

21

Dermatology

Ira J.K. Cohen, MD

Dermatology as a specialty is not considered high-risk in terms of professional liability when compared with other fields such as obstetrics–gynecology, general surgery and even internal medicine. There are several factors that account for the majority of malpractice cases.

The most common litigation has arisen in diagnostic errors and mismanagement of melanomas (Table 1). This would include failure to carry out a proper history-taking, physical examination, operative procedure and laboratory error resulting in the misdiagnosis of a lesion.

There are several areas in melanoma cases that account for alleged malpractice: the physician did not take a detailed history, for example. One needs to enquire specifically about changes in size, shape, color, bleeding and non-healing when examining moles. One should specifically ask about new lesions. The family history is important since melanomas may run in families. The clinician should ask about unusual or abnormal moles removed in the past from the patient or family members.

One should remember that a negative history is as important as a positive history in recording changes regarding pigmented lesions. Photographic evidence of nevi is a good method of documenting changes in patients with multiple atypical nevi. It is virtually impossible to describe 100 nevi on a patient's body and try to determine 6 months later whether there has been a change in an individual lesion or the development of a new mole. Digital computerized images are useful in this clinical setting. Most dermatologists do not have this available as yet, but can refer their high-risk patients to a pigmented lesion clinic or university dermatology program for photographic imaging. Patients who present for 'mole checks' and melanoma follow-up need a complete cutaneous examination. If a patient refuses, it should be documented in the chart. Patients have come to my office and have been diagnosed with a benign lesion on the face, and I have discovered melanoma or other malignancies on other areas of their

Table 1 Most common malpractice action

Misdiagnosis of melanoma
Misdiagnosis of other malignant neoplasms
Medication errors and adverse reactions to treatment
Procedures performed when not indicated

Table 2 How to avoid litigation

If a condition is not responding to appropriate therapy:
    rethink diagnosis, re-biopsy, laboratory investigation
Consider a second opinion
Careful documentation
Use dermatopathology laboratory if possible
Follow up all biopsies and inform patient of results

body. The management of a melanoma is as important as the diagnosis for good patient care, as well as the avoidance of a lawsuit (Table 2). The first step is a proper biopsy. Just as important as doing a biopsy on a suspicious lesion is sending the specimen to a qualified pathologist. If a physician suspects melanoma and the biopsy report comes back as a benign nevus, one should question the result. A second pathology opinion may be necessary. It is not uncommon for a dermatologist to be named as a codefendant in a lawsuit even though a pathologist has given a false interpretation of a submitted specimen. A less common occurrence is a benign lesion being erroneously diagnosed as malignant. This may result in unnecessary surgery or treatment. Litigation against the clinician as well as the pathologist may occur. This is frightening, but you are only as good as the laboratory you use. With managed care and health maintenance organizations (HMOs) mandating what facility our specimens may be sent to there has been an increase in alleged malpractice.

One should always use a well-qualified dermatopathologist or general pathologist who is competent in dermatology. Some dermatologists no longer participate in specific managed care plans because of 'weakness' at the laboratory. This is an ethical as well as practical decision for a clinician to make.

Once a diagnosis of melanoma or any malignancy is made, the patient must be informed in a timely manner. *Do not* rely solely on patients to check their results. The task of informing patients of biopsy results and your treatment plan lies with the clinician. This can be done by phone or in person at the time of a visit. A mechanism must be in place in one's office or clinic to ensure that patients are given their test results. An easy method is to record all biopsies in a logbook and check off the results when the patient is informed. Patients with a known malignancy who miss follow-up appointments need to be reached by phone or registered letter informing them of their test results and need for further treatment.

Adverse side-effects associated with prescribed medication account for another area of malpractice. This is included under 'informed consent'. Patients must be told verbally or in writing of potential serious reactions associated with any medication. Recently, there has been an increase in litigation involving the use of systemic steroids causing avascular necrosis. Physicians should document in a patient's chart the need for this form of therapy and that the risk/benefit was discussed. It is extremely useful in malpractice cases when the patient has signed a written statement in the chart, acknowledging that the above discussion took place. Many physicians have written-consent forms that they use in their practices. These forms prove useful when defending a suit.

When using immunosuppressive and chemotherapeutic agents such as methotrexate, cyclosporin or cytoxan, careful written documentation of a risk/benefit analysis is necessary. It does not suffice to say in a chart, 'side-effects discussed'. Below is an example of a simple consent form that is useful.

CONSENT FORM

(A) I have been informed that methotrexate is necessary for treatment of my condition. I voluntarily request my physician _____ to treat my condition.

(B) The treatment has been explained to me. I understand that there are risks and potential adverse reactions associated with this therapy.

(C) I understand that there are serious consequences of my condition without this therapy. Alternative forms of therapy have been explained to me.

(D) I understand the potential for decreased white blood count, anemia, decreased platelet count, diarrhea, sores in my mouth and throat, increased susceptibility to infection, increased risk of malignancy, damage to my lungs and damage to my liver. I understand that liver failure is rare, but could result in a need for a liver transplant.

(E) I understand the need for follow-up appointments and laboratory monitoring. I understand that the need may arise for liver biopsies periodically.

I certify that I have read and understand the above consent:

Name: _____

Date: _____

Witness: _____

Table 3   What to do when sued

Notify malpractice insurance carrier if you feel you were negligent or in case of an adverse event before a suit arises
If you are dissatisfied with your attorney, ask the insurance carrier to appoint another
In selecting an expert witness, choose a physician who is knowledgeable, but who also will make a good witness in the courtroom
Speak to other physicians who have been through litigation about the process. This will reduce your anxiety and stress levels. Your insurance carrier or local medical society will have support networks

Table 3 addresses some advice to those facing litigations.

ACKNOWLEDGEMENTS

I wish to thank Jane L. Conley, Director of Riskcare and PMSLIC for providing information and data: Pennsylvania Medical Society Liability Co., Claims Experience, Dermatology 1/1/85–6/30/98

22

Cardiovascular medicine

George J. Taylor, MD

My perspective is that of an active practitioner and teacher, and as an 'insider' in the medical liability industry. During the last decade I have served as an expert witness in almost one hundred cases, both reviewing charts and giving testimony. Early in this experience I saw myself as an advocate for the doctor. More recently I have learned that it is more effective for the expert witness to recognize that his or her role is education, helping the jury and court understand the case so that they can make a fair and sensible decision. During this experience, I have repeatedly stumbled over physician behaviors that 'invite' suit, or that make effective defense difficult.

While all suits are about money, it is hard for a patient to sue their doctor and friend of many years. More cases involve doctors who are new; emergency room physicians, consultants and surgeons are at special risk. Establishing a relationship and good 'physicianly' behavior are critical for the doctor who is new to the patient. The effective physician is one with a friendly and open manner, who indicates a personal interest ('where are your kids and what are they doing?'), who makes an honest effort to explain the clinical decisions so that the patient understands, and who is careful to answer all questions. That also describes the doctor less likely to be sued for a bad outcome. Unlike the practice of law, medicine rarely is adversarial. Conflict increases your risk. I never find arguments with patients or families productive; at least I have never won one. A doctor who is aloof, curt, arrogant, always right and too busy for the personal touch is more likely to learn words like 'tort' (and does not enjoy practicing medicine as most of us do).

Malpractice suits seem to cluster around a number of clinical issues in cardiovascular medicine.

FAILURE TO DIAGNOSE AND ADMIT

Missing the diagnosis of myocardial infarction (MI) is among the most common claims, and it is 'high yield' for the lawyers. In a Massachusetts series, missed MI accounted for 10% of closed claims but 25% of the total income from those claims[1]. The most common documentable error is a failure to get an electrocardiogram (ECG)[2].

Face it, the evaluation of chest pain is difficult. I talk daily with patients who have chest pain, and feel that I take a careful history and that I have good clinical intuition, but I know that my best guess about etiology is wrong a third of the time. Ischemic discomfort varies from patient to patient, and atypical presentation is common. While symptoms of ischemia are not specific, those of some other causes of chest pain tend to be. For example, typical symptoms of gastroesophageal reflux, pleurisy or chest wall pain exclude a cardiac etiology. As an exception to this, I have seen a few people with chronic back pain whose new angina presented as a worsening of the chronic symptom. At the very least, obtain an ECG on the patient with symptoms referable to the chest who is in the age range for coronary artery disease, particularly if there are other risk factors[3]. But do not be fooled by age, as a missed diagnosis of MI is more common with young patients.

About 10% of MIs are silent. The proportion is much higher in diabetic patients, an apparent result of neuropathy and nociceptive dysfunction. A common anginal equivalent is exertional dyspnea, with a pattern quite like exertional angina ('I get breathless walking, have to stop, and it goes away with rest'). Diabetic ketoacidosis often is provoked by other acute illness, and I have seen a number of cases caused by painless MI. Other acute illnesses may also mask MI such as stroke, pneumonia or injury in an elderly patient. Most of the time, getting a screening ECG is good medical practice, not just defensive medicine.

Dissection of the thoracic aorta is a chest pain diagnosis that can be missed half the time[4]. One feature of the history that helps is that pain is maximally intense at its onset; with angina or MI the pain is mild at the beginning and then crescendos. Radiation of pain to the back suggests dissection, but does not occur when the tear is limited to the proximal aorta. A ripping or tearing quality is described by a minority of patients. Proximal dissection may cause aortic regurgitation. Most with dissection have widening of the mediastinum or aortic root on chest X-ray. Interestingly, acute MI does not exclude dissection, as the tear may clip the ostium of the right coronary artery. If you even think of dissection, exclude it with either a computed tomography (CT) scan or a transesophageal echocardiogram.

Acute MI may occur with a normal ECG. The lateral wall of the left ventricle, supplied by the circumflex artery, tends to be 'electrocardio-graphically silent'. Occlusion of this vessel and transmural ischemia may cause only minor ST segment or T wave changes, or no ECG change at all. For this reason, a strong clinical suspicion of MI (quality of pain and risk factors) is reason enough to admit a patient for serial ECGs and enzyme studies.

When you suspect ischemia and the ECG is not diagnostic, repeat it in a half hour. It is common for ST segment changes to be variable during the early course of infarction.

Normal ECGs and cardiac enzymes exclude acute MI. The next issue is whether the patient is having unstable angina. Those with unstable angina and pain within the last 24 hours are at higher risk for infarction, and merit admission to hospital. The diagnosis of angina vs. non-cardiac pain is a judgment call and is based on clinical history.

FAILURE OF DOCUMENTATION

Suits are always about the medical record. The most common problem I find when trying to defend a case is an inadequate description of symptoms. It is a disaster when the history of present illness is just a restatement of the chief complaint, with no detail about the quality, radiation, duration or frequency of pain, or what provokes and relieves it. The simple things we demand from our second year medical students are missing! Invariably the lawyer turns to a nurse's note that describes 'anginal' chest pain when the doctor was treating reflux esophagitis. Maybe the nurse was right and maybe not, but there is nothing the doctor's note can do to rebut. The medical record is 'the witness with the perfect memory'.

I was wondering why terrible history taking and recording are so common in these cases. Then I realized that is why the suit was filed to begin with. Plaintiffs' lawyers can be expected to pursue cases where the medical record hurts the doctor. The best plantiffs' cases are those with an inadequate H&P, infrequent and superficial progress notes, and a failure to address abnormal laboratory findings in the record.

A FAILURE TO FOLLOW PRACTICE GUIDELINES

The last two decades began the era of evidence-based medicine. Randomized clinical trials have certainly changed the way that we practice cardiovascular medicine. As an example, think of the calcium channel blocker story. Early descriptive studies showed that patients with chronic stable angina benefited from this new treatment, as symptoms and angina threshold improved. However, when randomized studies found little survival benefit, the drug class has taken a back seat to aspirin, LDL cholesterol lowering treatment, beta blockade, and, recently, angiotensin-converting enzyme inhibitor therapy.

You might think of evidence-based medicine as a two-edged sword. It is reassuring to know with certainty the treatments and management choices that improve outcome. On the flip side, deficiencies in management are blatantly obvious when we practice medicine by protocol, especially to plaintiffs' attorneys and juries. Table 1 shows a sample of the practice guidelines issued by the American Heart Association (together with other professional organizations). These guidelines are summarized for the primary care practitioner by Spittell et al.[4]. Table 1 is not a comprehensive review; instead, I have picked issues that are easily identifiable and that can be counted on to nail you if your medical record does not address them. Of course, Table 1 also summarizes what we consider good medicine, our present standard of care.

A failure to follow practice guidelines cannot be defended in court. Most expert witnesses recommend settling before such cases come to trial.

A FAILURE TO RECOGNIZE COMPLICATIONS OF THERAPY

A favorite maneuver of plaintiffs' attorneys is to pull out the PDR. I was called recently about a patient on procainamide who developed neutropenia. I was unfamiliar with that side-effect, even as a cardiologist, but there it was in the PDR along with a recommendation for frequent monitoring of the white cell count. I declined to defend the case and recommended settling. Unless your memory is exceptional, a good rule of thumb in medicine is to limit your repertoire to one or two drugs in each class, and to know them and their side-effects thoroughly.

Complications of procedures frequently prompt litigation. I reviewed a case of a patient with a pseudoaneurysm of the femoral artery after angiography that was missed, then ruptured and dissected into the retroperitoneal space. A commonly missed complication of heart surgery is the postpericardiotomy syndrome, an autoimmune condition that can mimic pneumonia two weeks to three months postoperatively. This occurs in 2–5% of patients having heart surgery, so it is easily recognized by

Table 1 A selection of treatments and clinical issues commonly included in practice guidelines. When they are missed or not addressed by the medical record, the plaintiff's attorney's task is much easier

Condition	Therapy or clinical issue
All patients with vascular disease (CAD, stroke or peripheral vascular disease)	Aspirin (or other antiplatelet therapy) Lowering LDL cholesterol to an accepted target level Risk factor modification (this includes a failure to treat systolic hypertension in older patients) Possibly ACEI therapy (an emerging story)
Unstable coronary syndromes (unstable angina and non-Q wave MI)	Admission to hospital for the appropriate patient Anticoagulation in addition to aspirin therapy Beta blocker therapy Early angiography vs. noninvasive testing
Acute MI	Thrombolytic therapy vs. angioplasty without delay Aspirin ACEI therapy (anterior MI or MI with poor LV function) Risk stratification after MI and screening for late complications
Congestive heart failure	Differentiating systolic vs. diastolic dysfunction ACEI therapy Beta blockade Arrhythmia management
Atrial fibrillation	Anticoagulation Adequate rate control and selection for cardioversion
Preoperative evaluation for non-cardiac surgery	Selection of patients for CAD screening

ACEI, angiotensin-converting enzyme inhibitor; CAD, coronary artery disease; LDL, low-density lipoprotein; LV, left ventricular; MI, myocardial infarction

cardiologists and heart surgeons. But the general physician who sends just a couple patients to surgery each year rarely encounters it, and usually calls after the patient has a second hospitalization for 'pneumonia' unresponsive to antibiotics.

As a general principle, any patient who has problems after a procedure should be evaluated promptly by the doctor who performed it. That doctor is best equipped to deal with complications. For example, as an angiographer, I do not want a general surgeon incising and draining a groin hematoma unless I have evaluated it first; it is a complication that I see frequently, more often than the average surgeon. Plus, it is 'my complication'. I feel that my liability exposure is reduced if I am the one to work with the

23

Pharmacy

Gerald D. Wilkie, MS, RPh

The most obvious concern for pharmacists and pharmacy technicians is medication errors. While it has been reported[1] that 'medication errors are common in hospitals', it is apparent that only about 3% actually result in harm or death to the patient. From the opposite perspective, approximately 10–25% of injuries during hospitalization are due to medication errors[2–6]. One therefore must conclude that medication errors are 'preventable'.

Johnson and Bootman have reported[7] an annual cost of drug-related morbidity and mortality in the USA (1995 statistics) at $US77.6 billion. The majority are related to hospital admissions resulting from drug therapy or the absence of appropriate drug therapy. Increased lengths of stay have also been reported, averaging 1.9 days and resulting in hospital costs per patient of $US1939 (LVS Hospital Survey). Lesar and co-workers[8] noted a rate of 3.1 errors per 1000 orders in a year-long study at one specific institution. Fifty-eight per cent of these errors had the potential for adverse consequences. A quote from *Drug Safety* is worthwhile repeating: 'While a human error may have occurred, the true cause of the accident can be viewed as a defect of the design of the system that permitted operator error to result in an accident.'

One example is a problem related to shelf carton storage, such as vials of midazolam injection. A large number '1' (1 mg/ml) or '5' (5 mg/ml) is prominently displayed. This number does not vary with the total volume in the sealed vials. Thus, the vials may contain 1 ml, 2 ml or 10 ml midazolam of 5 mg/ml concentration. All have the large '5'. The depiction of the concentration in this manner has led practitioners inadvertently to confuse the number with the amount of medication in each vial. Several reported errors with respect to dispensing have been related to the shelf carton. The practitioner fails to recognize the actual amount in the vial, i.e. the total volume, less prominently displayed elsewhere on the label. Overdosages of midazolam can result in respiratory arrest. It has been recommended that the pharmacy stocks only 1-ml vials to solve the problem. The product manufacturer, Roche Laboratories, plans to improve the labeling to reduce or eliminate confusion.

STRATEGIES FOR PREVENTION OF PHARMACY-RELATED ERRORS[9]

(1) Use the formulary system; the pharmacy and therapeutics committee is responsible for formulating policies regarding evaluation, selection and therapeutic use of medications in a hospital setting.

(2) Exercise care and consideration with respect to hiring personnel and assigning specific responsibilities.

(3) Ensure an appropriate work environment.

(4) Clearly establish lines of authority and responsibility within the hospital pharmacy with respect to ordering, dispensing and administration activities.

(5) Establish an ongoing systematic program of quality improvement and peer-review with respect to safety and efficacy of medications.

(6) Pharmacists and other responsible personnel should have access to appropriate clinical information regarding the patient, i.e. medication history, allergies, hypersensitivity profiles, diagnosis and pregnancy status, as well as laboratory values.

(7) Pharmacists should maintain a medication profile for all patients, both in-patient as well as in an ambulatory setting to receive care at a hospital.

(8) A pharmacy department is responsible for procurement, distribution and control of all medications used within the organization.

(9) The pharmacy manager or his/her designee with the assistance of the pharmacy and therapeutics committee and the department of nursing should develop a comprehensive policy and procedure *modus operandi* for efficient and safe distribution of medications.

(10) Unless there is an emergency situation, all sterile and non-sterile drug products should be dispensed from the pharmacy department for individual patients.

(11) The pharmacy director and staff must ensure that all medications are of appropriate (high) quality and integrity.

(12) All discontinued or unused medications should be returned to the department of pharmacy immediately or upon patient discharge.

(13) There should be a computerized pharmacy system to allow automatic checking for dosages, duplicate therapies, allergies, drug interactions, etc.

(14) Adequate drug information resources must be available for all healthcare providers involved in the medication-use process.

(15) A standard drug administration time should be established for the hospital by the pharmacy and therapeutics committee.

(16) The committee should develop a list of standard abbreviations approved for use in medication ordering.

(17) Designated individuals should be responsible for data collection and evaluation of medication-error reporting. Periodic review is mandatory.

(18) The pharmacy department in conjunction with nursing, risk management and medical staff should conduct ongoing educational programs regarding medication errors.

RECOMMENDATIONS FOR PHYSICIANS[9]

(1) Determine appropriate drug therapy, stay up to date with respect to peer-review, consultation with pharmacists and consultation with other physicians who are participating in the patient's care.

(2) Evaluate the patient's total status and current medications.

(3) Be familiar with the medication-ordering system.

(4) Drug orders should be complete, including: generic drug name, trademark names (if a specific product is required), route and site of administration, dosage form, dose, strength, quantity, frequency of administration and clearly stated prescriber's name.

(5) Ensure that the intent of medication orders is clear and unambiguous. Write out instructions, i.e. 'daily' rather than 'q.d.' The latter could be interpreted as 'q.i.d.' Avoid terms such as 'take as directed'.

(6) Specify exact dosage strength rather than dosage form units, i.e. use 'milligrams' rather than '1 tablet' or '1 vial'.

(7) Prescribe by standard nomenclature using a drug's generic name. Avoid 'Dr Doe's Syrup'.

(8) A leading zero should precede a decimal expression of < 1, for example: 0.5.

(9) Spell out the word 'units' rather than writing 'u' in dictation.

(10) Written drug or prescription orders must be legible.

(11) Verbal drug orders should be reserved only for situations in which it is impossible or impractical to write the order or enter it into the computer.

(12) If possible, try to administer by oral rather than parenteral route.

(13) Speak with the patient or care-giver to explain cautions or observations that are recommended.

(14) Follow up and periodically re-evaluate the need for continuing the medication.

(15) Orders to 'hold' a medication must be clear.

RECOMMENDATIONS FOR PHARMACISTS[9]

(1) Participate in drug therapy monitoring.

(2) Remain up to date through the literature, consultation with colleagues and other health-care providers.

(3) Be available to prescribers and nurses for information.

(4) Familiarize oneself with the medication-ordering system, and drug distribution policies and procedures of the organization.

(5) Never assume or guess the intent of confusing medication orders.

(6) Maintain orderliness and cleanliness in the work areas.

(7) Before dispensing a medication in non-emergency situations, an original copy of written medication should be utilized. Dispense medications in ready-to-administer dosage forms whenever possible.

(8) Review the use of auxiliary labels and use the labels prudently when it is clear that this may prevent errors, for example 'not for ingestion', 'shake well'.

(9) Be sure that the medications are delivered to the patient-care area in a timely fashion.

(10) Observe how medications are being used in patient-care areas.

(11) Review medications that are returned to the department with the staff, i.e. in case of errors, omitted doses, etc.

(12) In ambulatory patients, counsel patients or care-givers and verify that they understand why a medication was prescribed and dispensed.

(13) Preview and provide advice on the content and design of preprinted medication order forms or sheets.

(14) Maintain records sufficient to enable identification of patients receiving any erroneous product.

RECOMMENDATIONS FOR NURSES[9]

(1) Be familiar with the medication-ordering and -use system.

(2) Review a patient's medications with respect to desired patient outcomes, therapeutic duplications and possible drug interactions.

(3) Verify before medication is administered.

(4) Verify patient identity before administration of prescribed dose.

(5) All doses should be administered at scheduled times.

(6) When the standard drug concentrations or dosage charts are not available, dosage calculations, flowrates and other mathematical calculations should be checked by a second individual (another nurse or pharmacist).

(7) The drug distribution system should not be circumvented by the 'borrowing' of medications by one patient from another.

(8) If there are any questions of what volume or number of dosage units is needed for a single patient-dose, consultation with the pharmacist or prescriber is in order.

(9) All personnel using medication-administration devices should understand their operation.

(10) Speak with patients or care-givers to ascertain if they understand the use of their medications.

(11) When a patient objects to or questions whether a particular drug should be administered, the nurse should listen, answer questions and double-check as appropriate.

REFERENCES

1. US Pharmacopeia. *Summary of 1999 Information Submitted to Med MARx^SM: A National Database for Hospital Medication Error Reporting*. Rockville, MD: US Pharmacopeia, 2000

2. Barker KN, Allan EL. Research on drug-use system errors. *Am J Health System Pharm* 1995;52:400–6

3. Lesar TS, Briceland LL, Delcoure K, *et al*. Medication prescribing errors in a teaching hospital. *JAMA* 1990;263:2329–34

4. Raju TN, Thornton JP, Kecskes S, *et al*. Medication errors in neonatal and pediatric intensive-care units. *Lancet* 1989;374–79

5. Classen DC, Pestonik SL, Evans RS, *et al*. Computerized surveillance of adverse drug events in hospital patients. *JAMA* 1991:266:2847–51

6. Folli HL, Poole RL, Benitz WE, *et al*. Medication error prevention by clinical pharmacists in two children's hospitals. *Pediatrics* 1987;79:718–22

Table 1 Percentage of malpractice claims/suits in a University

Residency programs	
Obstetrics–gynecology	22%
General surgery	22%
Emergency room	15%
Internal medicine	5%
Family practice	5%
Anesthesiology	4%
Psychiatry	5%
Pediatrics	2%
Orthopedics	6%
Dentistry	5%
Others	9%

attempt to explain to a lawyer why you or anyone else is not responsible for injury to a patient. Never give a statement, recorded or otherwise, to a lawyer without proper representation. Remember that plaintiff lawyers are in business to make money by suing people. They are trained to use your words against you to support their claim for monetary damages. They are highly creative in this exercise, and you are not equipped to engage them in the realm of their expertise.

Second, remember that the hospital, whether represented by their risk management department staff or by their lawyer, may have interests that are adverse to yours. Do not discuss your involvement in any case where litigation is anticipated with a hospital representative without direct communication with your department head or insurance carrier. The hospital may not be on your side after a lawsuit is filed. However, please note that some hospitals may provide their own coverage for you while you are working there. In those cases, you should co-operate with the hospital's legal staff. If you are not clear on the distinction, please consult your department head.

RECORD KEEPING

From a legal perspective, the medical record is your best friend or your worst enemy. Remember that anything written by you can be subsequently read by a lawyer looking to place you at a strategic disadvantage. A favorite ploy of plaintiff lawyers at trial, or in deposition, is to state that if something is not contained in the medical record it must not have occurred. Do not allow yourself to be placed in this legal quandary by inadequate documentation in the chart. Always be explicit in your description of informed consent (including an analysis of the risks, benefits and alternatives of a procedure or course of treatment), discharge instructions, patient non-compliance and communications among other members of the health-care team.

Never alter or destroy any part of the record, since this can be detected through scientific ink analysis and will only serve to ruin your future credibility as a witness or party. Write legibly and sign the notes. A printed name and pager number is preferable.

COMMUNICATION

The first and foremost component of communication from a risk management perspective is the preservation of confidentiality. Never discuss a patient's medical condition or treatment with anyone, including family members, without the express consent of the patient. For instance, never assume that the patient's family knows that he or she has tested positive for hepatitis or human immunodeficiency virus (HIV) when discussing the patient's future course of treatment.

You should also remember that, despite unexpected outcomes, patients often decline to sue the physician if they have developed a good relationship with them. If you have good interpersonal skills, use them. If you do not have good interpersonal skills, develop them and then use them. In many instances, it is most important to be a human-being first and a doctor second. Develop compassion and a sense of empathy for your patients. Learn to listen, and learn to be patient. **Implement the golden rule: treat your patients as you would like to be treated**.

The following represent the most common allegations of negligence and injury for residents at one university in descending order of frequency:

 (1) Failure to diagnose;

 (2) Improper surgery;

 (3) Failure to avoid nerve trauma;

 (4) Failure to remove foreign body;

 (5) Improper use of drugs;

 (6) Improper treatment;

 (7) Failure to prevent infection;

 (8) Inadequate informed consent;

 (9) Failure to utilize Cesarean section;

(10) Delay in utilizing Cesarean section.

Miscellaneous cases but important to consider are the following:

(1) Sexual misconduct;

(2) Civil rights violation/incarceration;

(3) Failure to prevent suicide;

(4) Failure to prevent autoimmune deficiency syndrome (AIDS);

(5) Inadequate drug warnings.

The failure-to-diagnose category includes these most frequently:

(1) Cancer: breast/prostate/lung;

(2) Heart attack/infarction;

(3) Meningitis;

(4) Neonatal distress;

(5) Appendicitis.

The experience at our institution appears to be typical of the problems confronting residents while in training programs. Training in both risk avoidance and risk management is an important part of residency training and must be available to residents. It is important to notify both your department head and your insurance carrier promptly when you are involved in a potential case of malpractice or contacted by an attorney regarding such a potential case.

25

Medical students

Leah J. Dickstein, MD

MALPRACTICE CONCERNS FOR MEDICAL STUDENTS

While most malpractice litigation is against physicians, in an academic medical center, medical students must be aware of potential liability issues for themselves as well, and adhere to appropriate professional standards of behavior and medical practice.

It goes without saying that a medical student is expected to perform at the level of a medical student. However, all students must ensure that all their patient-related activities are known to, and approved by, a responsible physician. In addition, medical students should seek guidance from their superiors at *any* time they feel uncertain about a patient's status or patients' responses to questions regarding their medical history.

Frances Hall of the American Association of Medical Colleges (AAMC) noted that 'Medical schools are required as part of the accreditation process to insure that students have a safe and educationally enriched learning experience and this includes the need to provide adequate malpractice coverage for medical students'[1].

However, students should check with their individual institution about that institution's student malpractice coverage. According to Hall, 'Many clinical institutions have moved away from the purchase of a policy for all health care providers and in the direction of self-insurance.'

While various institutions may have insurance in place for their residents, but not for students, those students should nevertheless concern themselves with that issue. Insurance companies may be able to provide individual coverage for the student. Since there seem to be a wide range of insurance policies available from many companies, the student buying such insurance should prudently compare and evaluate coverage and cost before purchasing any policies, as both can fluctuate widely[2].

Because malpractice claims may be on the rise and health-care providers are understandably concerned, for both financial and personal reasons, seminars and workshops are being offered by health-care professionals and others, and by the insurance industry, to educate and provide more details pertaining to this aspect of the medical profession, such as the workshop *Learning Through Personal Assault: Malpractice Stress Response*[3] and the *Law and Practice of Psychiatry Risk Management Seminar*[4].

Ms Hall says, 'It is better to avoid malpractice suits by practicing medicine in the very best professional manner …' and, 'Patients who trust their physician and who believe that they are getting the best care possible are less likely to sue than patients who have not been treated with as much humanistic skill.'

Medical students should, then, familiarize themselves with the aspects of malpractice at the earliest possible time, in order to practice safe medicine.

HOW MALPRACTICE CAN BE AVOIDED

Above all, *courtesy, tact and respect* for all patients and for their privacy and dignity must be part of all medical student behavior. Being respectful, courteous, attentive and showing interest and remaining calm go a long way towards alleviating alienating situations.

Basic to high standards of appropriate professional behavior are the following:

(1) *Confidentiality* concerning all medical knowledge, including personal intimate data about patients: this information should be communicated by students only to identified, appropriate faculty and other medical personnel. When discussing a patient's health, be conscious that someone else may be overhearing the conversation. Do not talk about the patient, or laugh or snicker, when discussing a patient and/or his/her health information.

(2) *Courtesy, respect and tact* for all patients and for their privacy and dignity must be part of all medical student behavior.

(3) *Sexual harassment and boundary violations* must be avoided at all times by medical students in their professional relationships with patients, their visitors and significant others and all hospital and medical center staff and faculty.

(4) *Avoid criticizing*, in front of patients, other health-care professionals.

(5) *Avoid criticizing*, to patients, their treatment protocol.

(6) *Make no medical guarantee* to the patient, of treatment outcome.

Steps towards *proper conduct of procedures* for patient care are:

(1) Residents and attendings should clearly assign tasks.

(2) Medical students must be certain that they understand assigned tasks.

(3) Medical students must be certain to identify the correct patient prior to any professional contact.

(4) Take a careful general medical and psychiatric history, including known allergies, prescribed medications, chronic diseases and history of abuse and violence in the patient and three generations of the patient's biological family. Prominently and properly code charts, in accordance with the institution's requirements, to alert other health-care professionals to any problems.

(5) If you give professional instructions to others related to patient care, make certain they are complied with.

(6) To avoid mistakes and/or confusion, use only standard abbreviations and use them sparingly.

(7) Write legibly.

(8) As a student performing physical examinations, ensure that, when appropriate, you are properly chaperoned.

(9) Practice prevention of infection, particularly with high standards of cleanliness, e.g. hand-washing between interactions with patients.

(10) Be safety conscious: help to prevent injury to patients, particularly in terms of falls. Observe, evaluate and report unsafe conditions in your surroundings. Medical students should ensure that patients are safe at all times and if they are not, they should contact their superiors.

(11) Label all containers properly.

(12) Store lethal drugs in locked areas.

(13) Be aware that equipment should be kept in safe places and in good working order.

(14) Medical students must seek *guidance* from their superiors at any time they feel uncertain about a patient's status or patient's responses to questions regarding their medical history. Notify the resident and/or attending immediately if the student encounters any apparent problems related to the patient and his/her care.

In addition to scientific knowledge and skills, medical students who take good care of their own physical and mental health are more likely to interact most professionally with patients, their significant others and all other health-care professionals.

WHAT TO DO PROFESSIONALLY WHEN YOU ARE SUED

(1) Immediately notify your superiors (attendings and school authorities, i.e. student affairs office) that you have been made aware that you/they will be sued, and use appropriate steps to inform the malpractice insurance company and legal advisors.

(2) Courteously divulge *no* information regarding liability coverage to anyone, i.e. patient, significant others.

(3) Give *all* the facts to *your* insurance representative. Be aware that the insurance carrier representing you may differ from those of others involved in the suit.

(4) Do not discuss the case nor admit to fault or errors to anyone when talking to the patient(s), their significant others, their attorneys, etc.

(5) Answer factually any questions when giving a deposition, but do *not* volunteer any information.

(6) Plan to participate actively in your defense, i.e. keep detailed notes to refresh your memory (it is amazing what you can forget, when under stress, even in a short time).

(7) *Never* alter a medical record.

(8) Recognize and deal with the litigation stress.

(9) Learn from your experience so that you may avoid similar situations in the future.

WHAT TO DO PERSONALLY WHEN YOU ARE SUED

(1) Share the burden with your significant other(s).

(2) Share with your colleagues and other health-care professionals your feelings, but no details of the case.

(3) If needed, consider sharing your feeling with a mental health professional.

(4) Be kind to yourself.

ACKNOWLEDGEMENT

The author gratefully acknowledges major assistance from Margaret Smith.

REFERENCES

1. Hall FR. American Association of Medical Colleges (AAMC), Division of Student Affairs and Education Services, Section for Student Programs
2. Greeno DG. The Medical Protective Company, Fort Wayne, IN
3. Andrew LCB. Presented at Workshop *Learning Through Personal Assault: Malpractice Stress Response*. Ottawa, ON, Canada, 1994
4. Presented at *Law and Practice of Psychiatry Risk Management Seminar*, Raleigh, NC, 9 March 1996

26

Advanced practice nurses, including midwives and anesthetists, and physician assistants

Marianne Hopkins Hutti, DNS, WHNP-C,
and Paulette Freeman Adams, EdD, RN

This chapter reviews the legal liability risks associated with practice as a nurse practitioner, certified nurse midwife, nurse anesthetist or physician assistant. It also identifies ways in which these health-care providers can reduce their legal liability risk. Medical malpractice is the primary focus of this chapter, and specific malpractice statistics are provided when possible.

No specific statistics are available to report the number of suits filed against physician assistants (PAs). Traditionally, PAs have been protected from malpractice by the supervising physician because the law held the physician responsible for delegated tasks. In recent years, however, PAs have been held responsible for the care they provide using the standard of care for physician assistants, independent of the supervising physician[1].

Advanced practice nurses (APNs), including nurse practitioners, certified nurse midwives and nurse anesthetists, do not appear to be at high risk for being sued for malpractice. Pearson conducted a survey of the readers of the *Nurse Practitioner* journal in 1987 to obtain actuarial data on the malpractice experience of nurse practitioners[2]. Of the 3542 nurse practitioners responding, 48 (1.4%) reported that a professional liability claim or other legal action had been filed against them. Pearson reported that, on average, during any given year in the previous 11 years, only 0.1% of nurse practitioners were sued. Of the 48 nurse practitioners who had been sued, 23 knew what had been paid in the malpractice claim, and 18 of these 23 reported that nothing had been paid to the plaintiff. The remainder reported payments of $US 5000–350 000.

The survey was repeated in 1994, with 1610 responses received[3]. Only 25 nurse practitioners from this group (1.6%) reported that a malpractice allegation or legal claim had been filed against them between 1980 and 1994. One of these had been previously reported in the 1987 survey. Most of these claims fell into two groups: failure properly to diagnose, and negligent treatment. Fifty-four per cent of the claims against the 25 nurse practitioners ultimately did not proceed.

The National Practitioner Data Bank (NPDB) is a computer depository of health-care providers' malpractice payments by insurers (see Chapter 33). The NPDB also reports adverse actions by hospitals, licensing boards and professional societies. These data have been collected since September 1990. Cumulative statistics for malpractice payments and adverse action reports are available for physicians, dentists and other health-care providers. Since the NPDB does not generally break the 'other' group down further, Senator Inouye requested more specific data on nurses, and this data was then reported by Birkholz[4]. Her report included data from September 1990 to July 1993. Birkholz found that advanced practice nurses and registered nurses are sued much less frequently than physicians. As a total group, nurses incur fewer than 3% of the total malpractice and adverse actions reported to the NPDB. When registered nurses are separated from advanced practice nurses, the registered nurses are reported significantly more (688) than nurse practitioners (34), certified nurse midwives (39) or nurse anesthetists (238). The nurse practitioner data from the NPDB demonstrates a malpractice or adverse event report rate of 30 times less than for physicians[4].

When Pearson and Birkholz examined the data for 25 nurse practitioners who had been sued, several characteristics of this group became apparent[3]. Nurse practitioners who had been sued generally had less practice experience, with 48% of nurse practitioners in the claim group having 5 years or less of experience. Nurse practitioners who had been sued were overrepresented in women's health and obstetrics, and underrepresented with adults over 65. Malpractice suits against physicians are also overrepresented in the areas of women's health and obstetrics. The greatest numbers of claims were paid to injured clients in the Southwest or Central regions of the USA. The majority (80%) of the claims occurred in ambulatory settings.

Pearson and Birkholz then interviewed 19 of the 25 nurse practitioners who had been sued to identify suggestions for reducing malpractice risk[3]. Their suggestions, as well as those reported by other authors, may be found in Table 1. Malpractice risks for advanced practice nurses and physician assistants reported in the literature may be found in Table 2.

The most common area of liability for physician assistants, abstracted from the literature on physician liability, is professional negligence[1]. At

Table 1   Suggestions for reducing malpractice risk

---

(1) Develop minimalist protocols that are followed without fail. Update protocols regularly[5]

(2) If reimbursement for further hospitalization that the PA or APN believes is needed is denied, protest adverse payment decisions in writing. Provide appropriate follow-up care, including earlier or more frequent appointments, especially for clients discharged before the provider is sure that they are ready[6]

(3) Never take short-cuts when charting in the medical record[1,3]

(4) Consider refusing to be the care provider for a client who is very angry, or whose situation is likely to be problematic[3]

(5) Perform proper medical histories and examinations[1]

(6) Make proper diagnoses and obtain informed consent for procedures or treatments[1]

(7) Fully evaluate clients who frequently complain; do not assume that a frequent complainer is a hypochondriac[3]

(8) Use 'standard of care' treatments only, and practice only within your defined scope of practice[3]

(9) Consult with the supervising physician and refer to that physician or to a specialist as appropriate[1]

(10) Document any job training/education received[3]

(11) Keep abreast of new medical knowledge[1]

(12) Know the state laws regarding abuse, sexually transmitted disease reporting and care of emancipated minors[1,3]

(13) Use good interpersonal skills. Do not abandon the client[1]

(14) Fully document client education regarding side-effects of medications that you have provided[3]

(15) Avoid using the word 'counseled' in charting. It may open you up to the care standards and liability of a mental health counselor[3]

(16) Work only with physicians who are excellent clinicians, and who are honest and will stick to the truth if a malpractice suit is filed[3]

(17) Consider not carrying malpractice insurance; plaintiffs' lawyers always look for the 'deepest pockets' to sue[3]

(18) Personally recheck findings that you question, especially those documented by others[3]

(19) To avoid a defamation suit, never complain to a client about another health-care provider or client[1]

(20) Clearly identify yourself as an advanced practice nurse or physician assistant when meeting a client for the first time. Explain your role and scope of practice related to the client's care. Make certain the client is aware that you are not a physician[1]

(21) Recognize that all clients may accept or reject treatment. Document refusal of treatment or failure of the client to follow through your recommendations[1] and the consequences of such

(22) Treat all clients with dignity[1]

PA, physician assistant; APN, advanced practice nurse

Table 2   Malpractice risks for advanced practice nurses and physician assistants

(1) Failing to diagnose properly[1,6]

(2) Prematurely discharging a client from the hospital because a payer denies further reimbursement[6]

(3) Using ideal practice protocols instead of realistic protocols based on a minimum safe level of practice[5]

(4) Lack of lengthy practice experience[3]

(5) Working in the Southwest or Central region of the USA[3]

(6) Working in ambulatory settings[3]

(7) Scope of practice includes women's health, obstetrics or administering anesthesia[3]

(8) Having poor interpersonal skills[1]

(9) Promising specific results[1]

Table 3   Nurse practitioner and physician assistant medical malpractice checklist. Reproduced with permission (modified) from reference 7

(1) Diagnosis is the critical area where physicians need to limit the role of the physician assistant (PA) and nurse practitioner (NP)

(2) Regard PAs and NPs as an extension of a physician's practice, but not as a substitute for making decisions that the physician should make

(3) For the first 3 months after an employee is hired, he or she should be closely supervised

(4) If an employee is called upon to do anything invasive, with which he or she is not yet adequately familiar, the physician should supervise

(5) If it is a 'nurse's diagnosis', it should be so labeled in the patient's chart

(6) One of the most serious errors is a report of an abnormality that is filed in the patient's record before it is seen by the physician

Allied health professionals continue to assume increasing responsibility with respect to healthcare delivery. They play an essential role in primary care. Specific guidelines regarding regulation of services rendered are delineated by specific state statutes to which you are referred for additional information

present, performance is judged by how a reasonable PA from the same locale would act under similar circumstances. The standard of care for PAs is determined by experience, education, state or national regulations, job descriptions, employment contracts, and statements from professional organizations, the professional literature and expert witnesses. The standard of care for advanced practice nurses is determined similarly. Therefore, it is necessary for PAs and advanced practice nurses to remain up-to-date in their areas of practice to meet the standard of care.

Another area of potential liability for PAs as well as APNs is the doctrine of informed consent. This doctrine is based on the client's right to refuse treatment. Informed consent should be obtained only by the person performing the procedure or treatment. PAs and APNs should not obtain

Table 4 Guidelines for physician assistants (PAs). Reproduced with permission (modified) from reference[7]

The Ohio Law prohibits the PA from the following:
(1) Making a diagnosis of a disease or ailment or the absence thereof, independent of the complying physician
(2) Prescribing any treatment or regimen not previously set forth by the employing physician
(3) Prescribing any medication, signing or stamping a prescription blank on behalf of the employing physician
(4) Having prescription blanks available that have been presigned or prestamped by the employing physician
(5) Signing a physician's name to authenticate any prescription or orders, or in any situation that gives the indication of the physician's approval
(6) Supplanting the employing physician in making visits outside the physician's office
(7) Initiating or changing any orders on the patient's chart in the hospital, nursing-home or clinic, or places other than the physician's office
(8) Maintaining an office, independent of the employing physician
(9) Admitting a patient to, or leasing a patient from, a hospital, independent of the employing physician

informed consent for the supervising or collaborating physician[1]. Therapeutic privilege excuses full consent if disclosure would harm the client, or if the client's emotional response to disclosure would impair his or her decision-making ability. However, PAs and APNs should document consultation with the physician before deciding to withhold full disclosure to the client[1].

The issue of proper consultation with the physician is critical for APNs and PAs. Any time a PA or APN is practicing outside his or her usual practice boundaries, consultation with and/or referral to the physician should occur. This consultation or referral should always be documented in the medical record.

Advanced practice nurses and physician assistants generally practice under protocols with collaborating physicians. These protocols should be reviewed and updated regularly, since they will be used to judge the performance of the PA or APN if a malpractice claim is ever filed. Rather than developing ideal guidelines for care, protocols should be written as a series of realistic steps that will usually apply to a certain problem or set of presenting symptoms. They should identify the minimum requirements for safe competent care. 'Ideal' protocols may not always be followed in every situation, and failure to follow protocols increases malpractice risk[5].

Malpractice risk may also be reduced through the use of complete and accurate charting in the medical record. The record should contain client consent to procedures, and must reflect the dialog between the health-care provider and the client, indicating that the client understood the information presented. All entries should be legible, signed and dated, and should also include patient data, medical analysis, assessment and treatment plans[1].

Further guidelines for nurse practitioners and physician assistants are given in Tables 3 and 4.

In conclusion, advanced practice nurses do not appear to be at high risk for medical malpractice. The literature on physician assistant liability is sparse, and actual statistics are not yet available. Practice areas of increased risk, such as women's health and obstetrics, are consistent for both physicians and advanced practice nurses. Risk of malpractice can be reduced through using good interpersonal skills, following protocols without fail, consulting appropriately, and practicing only within one's identified scope of practice. Readers are referred to Chapter 12 for further details on obstetrics and gynecology and Chapter 10 for anesthesiology.

REFERENCES

1. Tozzini SS. Risk management for physician assistants. *Physician Assist* 1989;13:127–8, 131–4, 143–4
2. Pearson LJ. Comprehensive actuarial data on nurse practitioners … at long last. *Nurse Practitioner* 1987;12(12):6–10
3. Pearson L, Birkholz G. Report on the 1994 readership survey on NP experiences with malpractice issues. *Nurse Practitioner* 1995;20(3):18–30
4. Birkholz G. Malpractice data from the national practitioner data bank. *Nurse Practitioner* 1995;20(3):32–5
5. Moniz DM. The legal danger of written protocols and standards of practice. *Nurse Practitioner* 1992;17(9):58–60
6. Hogue EE. Managing your risk of legal liability. *Pediatr Nurs* 1993;19:366–8
7. Brutton KE, Chapman S. *Malpractice. A Guide to Avoidance and Treatment.* Orlando: Grune & Stratton, 1987

27

Dentistry and oral surgery

Greg C. Nunnally, DMD, and Joseph S. Sanfilippo, MD, MBA

The dental profession has witnessed an increase in malpractice cases. In 2000, a jury in Pennsylvania awarded $1 100 000 for death in association with general inhalational anesthesia during filling of dental caries by a general dentist. The most common problems encountered in all dental specialties are outlined in Table 1. The majority of large awards involve general dentists, for example $900 000 awarded for minor permanent damage and improper treatment in association with tooth extraction in Illinois. TMJ related cases have resulted in awards, including a $600 000 award against a general dentist who performed orthodontia in a patient presenting with malocclusion. Other malpractice claims resulting in an award for the plaintiff include parasthesia from nerve damage with extraction; a dry socket claim was associated with a $570 000 award. A $425 000 award in Kentucky for loss of an eye, related to abscess formation following an extraction and failure to refer the patient for treatment of the infection, which involved the ocular site.

The subject of amalgam fillings has continued to provide controversy in the profession. Dentists do not usually consult patients with regard to what materials to use for fillings since most feel such a dialogue is inappropriate. The concern with respect to amalgam fillings has been addressed by the American Dental Association (ADA) and provides support for use of such fillings. Furthermore, the ADA states, 'The American people can be assured that dental amalgam is safe. There is over 150 years of utilization and its safety should not be disputed'.

At this time neither the ADA nor any American dentist is under specific duty to inform patients of the potential hazards of amalgam fillings or to offer patients an option of available alternative materials. However, the ADA has been attacked for failing to acknowledge the importance of providing the public with information regarding the possible dangers of amalgam and thus the 'opportunity to select other available materials'.

Table 1 Allegations in all dental specialties listed by frequency of occurrence

Failure to diagnose – periodontitis
Failure to remove – foreign body reamer or the like
Failure to prevent condition – infection
Unsuccessful treatment – denture related
Improper treatment – root canal

Unfortunately litigation has resulted from a doctor's failure to disclose material information to the patient. This revolves around informed consent and the duty of the dentist to provide such information. To be successful in litigation, the plaintiff must show evidence that there was a breach of duty and that harm resulted, in addition, causation must be established. Development of mercury toxicity with resultant harm must be clearly conveyed to result in successful litigation. Class action against the ADA has been filed, a federal court will decide this issue in the near future.

The most important aspects of practice include good quality care, excellent communication and involving the patient in the decision making process wherever possible. A proactive stance on the part of the dental professional is the best defense against dental malpractice.

REFERENCES

1. MP Co's Experience with Dental Malpractice in all Dental Specialties
2. Royal M. Amalgam Fillings: Do Dental Patients Have a Right to Informed Consent?
3. Freedman S. Safety of dental amalgam. *JAMA* 1988;260:2295
4. Schafler N. *Dental Malpractice: Legal and Medical Handbook* (vols 1–3). New York: John Wiley & Sons, 1996

28

Podiatry

James Brungo, DPM, and Joseph S. Sanfilippo, MD, MBA

The incidence of medical malpractice suits among podiatrists is low: however, we are far from immune. In January 2001, a Philadelphia jury awarded a patient $1 million in a failure to diagnose case in which gangrene developed in a diabetic male who eventually underwent below the knee (BK) amputation. This is an unfortunate precedent that has entered into the podiatric medical malpractice arena. The case involved a podiatrist and a family foot care center who were sued for negligence and loss of consortium. The plaintiff, who was 63 years of age and an insulin dependent diabetic, fell and sustained a crushed bone of the bridge of his foot. He was evaluated at the emergency room of Northeast Hospital, where the podiatrist ordered immobilization of the fracture in a cast. Follow-up occurred on five occasions within the year. An ulcer developed under the cast and infection spread without the podiatrist focusing on the problem. This was interpreted as neglect by the jury. A second Emergency Department visit occurred at Episcopal Hospital for the compliant of a 'malodorous' lesion that was now noted to have gangrene, edema and cellulitis indicative of ongoing infection. The patient was brought to the operating room for debridment of the gangrenous tissue. At this point the talus was involved along with other segments of the ankle joint. This then resulted in a BK amputation. The jury found for the plaintiff based on the premise that the podiatrist was negligent for failing to appropriately evaluate and diagnose the condition, failure to perform surgery in a timely manner and failure to hospitalize the patient and treat with the appropriate antibiotics. The award was reduced to $800 000 based on the plaintiff's lack of compliance, i.e. not returing to the podiatrist as instructed for change in condition of the lesion. The end product was $600 000 awarded to the plaintiff and $200 000 to the patient's wife for loss of consortium. Furthermore, the foot care center was not found liable because the podiatrist had adequate insurance coverage of his own. For additional details refer to www.law.com (January 24, 2001).

Failure to diagnose is the number one cause of malpractice for podiatrists. This is followed by deviation of standard of care with respect to management of specific diagnoses. The current trend of malpractice, as conveyed by The Podiatry Law Group (http://www.Podiatrylaw.com) is in the area of managed care. The prediction is that more litigation against HMOs and managed care entities in general will result. Obtaining clearance to proceed with patient care as you feel appropriate can be 'interfered with by the managed care company'. Choice of medications, practice guidelines, economic incentives and modes of practice all appear to be under the auspices of the particular company. As aptly stated by The Podiatry Law Group, the managed care entities 'actually practice medicine'.

Few of us have the luxury of avoiding all managed care in our practice. The fine print on the contract reflects 'the devil is in the details'. The practitioner is wise to read the specifics of the hold harmless clause that is in most managed care contracts. Inquire if they can be deleted from the contract and if not, be sure you fully understand the consequences. This may translate into 'if a podiatrist is sued by a managed care patient, the DPM, will be held liable for the entire settlement award'. You will in all probability also be responsible for the legal fees of the managed care attorneys.

We can all agree that there is a dire need for tort reform. A number of reform provisions in the Patient Protection Act continue to be considered. These include a non-economic cap on medical malpractice damages of $250 000. Similar caps on punitive damages have been proposed. Other reforms include limitation on joint and several liability, restrictions on statutes of limitations and admission of evidence of collateral payment sources.

Standard of care remains a critical point in a court of law. Patients now can go to a website and get an opinion from either a DPM or in many cases an individual who carries both the DPM and JD credentials. This may well fuel a patient's desire to sue. The case is dissected with regard to radiologic evaluation, medical alternatives, informed consent, and clinical judgement. Moreover, the increase in television advertisements by personal injury lawyers makes litigation seem an attractive option to dissatisfied patients.

Podiatrists must be cognizant of websites such as Footlaw.com. This is a medical malpractice resource sponsored by trial attorneys who are DPM, JD individuals with a special focus on foot, ankle and leg treatment. They are board certified podiatrists with 14 or more years of practice experience.

The website tells the consumer how they will review your case, obtain experts, prepare the legal proceedings, assist with discovery, conduct depositions, assist in settlements and 'act as second chair at trial'. Details regarding cost to the client are provided. Furthermore, attorneys perhaps less experienced with medical malpractice can be assisted by Footlaw.com.

Details regarding a specific insurance company and the statistics of podiatric awards, communication with Podiatric Medical societies regarding the subject can be obtained from entities such as DPM/PICA. They do not force those insured to settle cases as some insurance companies do. Also Podiatry Online has conducted consumer surveys regarding malpractice coverage.

WEBSITES:

http://www.podiatryonline.com/forward/netforum.html
Discuss a case at this website, also learn about coding, reimbursement and compliance
http://www.podiatryonline.com/doctorportal.html
http://www.smartfoot.com/codebook.html
http://www.myfootdoc.i-p.com

29

Chiropractic

Craig A. Mueller, DC

In the litigious society in which we live and work today, three strategies will reduce the probability that a lawsuit will be filed against you; quit practicing, continue practicing while doting over every patient and procedure either you or a subordinate performs, or do not buy malpractice insurance.

If you are reading this you are probably still practicing, so cancel my first suggestion. If your practice is of any size, training and supervision can only occupy a limited amount of time. You probably train when you hire, supervise on the job, and train periodically as needed. Patients follow some established procedure that allows safe, effective care within an efficient and profitable office. So, forget the anxiety brought on by doting. Assuming you are practicing and overseeing a viable office, you should realize that national statistics support the fact that more doctors of chiropractic (DCs) are sued today simply because they own malpractice insurance.

Of the three strategies I posed, I suggest you throw out the first and the last and settle somewhere in the middle. If you are passionate about your profession, never let the fear of malpractice scare you away. If your practice is small, never try to save a dollar and forego malpractice insurance. Accept the responsibilities you have towards yourself, your patients and your profession, and be wise, be insured.

Accept the idea and the coexisting improbability that, as a doctor of chiropractic, you may be sued by any disgruntled or injured patient. This person needs only to convince an attorney that you acted in a manner inconsistent with other DCs in your area or in violation of a state statute, and/or caused them harm through that negligence or incompetence. This being the case, some very simple and common-sense steps are suggested to avoid such an ordeal. Remember, these suggestions are not intended to create neurosis or paranoia. Although one lawsuit was filed against me, I contend that you have to run your practice to serve patients efficiently and effectively. The chances are strong that your prudent approach and character judgment will assist you in discerning potential problems.

Attentiveness will only protect you to the extent that you know what is expected of you and abide by it. It is likely that you will not know the intimate details of your state law regarding such topics as: informed consent, the professional contract, medical necessity, warranties, quality of care and standards of care. To gain more insights into these issues, I recommend *The Chiropractic Physician's Guide* by R. C. Schafer, D.C., F.I.C.C., distributed through the National Chiropractic Mutual Insurance Company. In this handbook, Dr Schafer points out common pitfalls doctors make which lead to malpractice suits. The 'nice doctor' who forgoes a test or X-ray to save the patient money may later find that same patient confronting him in the courtroom. Other common oversights Schafer lists are: failure to obtain an informed consent, charges of abandonment, failure to conduct a thorough examination, using excessive force, failure to base the treatment on a diagnosis, poor records, unethical behavior and failure to heed clinical contraindications. The list is extensive and, taken in its entirety, may be intimidating.

When striving for the malpractice-proof practice, remember that the 'vital factor' is human relations. Before addressing clinical mishaps, consider the office design and staff selection as your initial safeguard. Towards this end, I suggest the following. Avoid entirely open adjusting rooms. Keep plants or furniture as a visual impediment in a wall-less space. If women change into gowns, incorporate small changing rooms that open into a common hallway. When examining female patients, consider keeping the door open or have an assistant present. Bear in mind that assistants must respect the patient's privacy and maintain professional decorum in a doctor's office. Assistants are an extension of you, so train them regarding appropriate behavior and ask them to sign an agreement outlining such an understanding when they join your staff. Be prompt. Respect others' time and apologize when you have had an unexpected interruption to your schedule. Do not rush. How would you like your doctor to 'catch up' using you?

While my front desk appears to be open when patients walk in the front door, the counter height allows patients to write checks on it and the front-desk assistant to speak on the phone behind it while her voice is blocked. This keeps eavesdropping to a minimum while creating a cordial reception-desk area. I also train staff to discuss finances in an adjacent area, and never risk embarrassing a patient by alerting the reception area to sensitive financial matters! Instruct your staff to keep all conversations at the front desk to a 'matter of fact' tone. Staff must avoid discussing accounts or patients in an open area.

All legal proceedings commence when someone exceeds their tolerance threshold. One case may be dismissed and forgotten; however, the accumulated irritations may cost you a patient, an explanation to your licensing board or a full-blown malpractice suit. If you demonstrate a sincere attitude towards all aspects of patient care and you take steps to show it, minor mishaps or oversights are often forgiven.

If an infraction or a potential weak-spot in your design or staff is apparent, address it promptly and note it in an office memorandum. If the situation demands, have a special office meeting and note in the minutes those who attended. Persistent disregard for a known deviation from standards of care may be used against you.

When I began practicing, my understanding of malpractice consisted of forgetting to perform the worthless, but expected, cerebrovascular test and causing a stroke in some otherwise perfectly healthy young person who would lose 25 years of earning capacity. Worse yet, I would miss a rare bone disease even Russell Erhardt would have missed. Now I understand and appreciate malpractice better. Having a suit filed against me certainly helped. Malpractice claims are generally filed for acts of commission and omission. Remember that you can only be held to a reasonable standard, and it is only a lawsuit. Have you asked yourself what a reasonable standard is for your area?

For the sake of brevity allow me to assume that you have established office procedures for all new and established patients. If not, learn them and implement them now! Some cases will necessitate a 'consent to treat' form, outlining inherent risks in any procedure that challenges the body to divert its current course and return to vibrant expression. Omitting this form is often pointed out in deposition or court by plaintiffs' attorneys to establish you as inept. Posting a sign in your report room, or mentioning inherent risk in the report, may serve as passive consent. It is unlikely that you will ever be accused of malpractice over a form, but providing the patient with one that they complete in their own handwriting establishes you as considerate of professional conduct at a minimum.

During history taking, follow established protocol to determine the patient's need for your services. At least, learn the frequency, intensity, duration, character, onset and prior history of their presenting complaint. Review body systems rather than focus only on the chief complaint. Be able to show how you arrived at your diagnosis, your decision to take or not to take X-rays, and the treatment plan you suggested. Have in writing your collected thoughts on the case. This could be in a SOAP (subjective, objective, assessment, plan) format or some structured notes: just have them!

If you want to take minimal notes at each visit, I suggest spaced progress examinations. Meet with the patient at 30, 60, 90 days to update their file, and re-establish what your treatment objectives are and how successfully they have been accomplished. This is the necessary reality check that ensures the patient's well-being is served.

Pay close attention to swings in patient remarks as treatment moves from day to day or week to week. It is your responsibility to know how a case should progress through the healing process over time. Review recommendations regarding home care and life-style management with the patient, and note such conversations and suggestions in your progress notes. Are you considering a change in treatment or referring to someone else? Put it in your notes!

Recording your every word is not the intent of note taking and documentation. The key to remember is that you must demonstrate attentiveness to your patient. I have reviewed numerous files where there are scant notes, no progress examinations, no change in treatment when there is no change in the presenting complaint after reasonable effort. A recent case involved a DC preparing to retire at the year's end when an 'old' patient returned for care. An 'update' form was completed citing a single chief complaint: neck pain. The form included one- and two-word answers for such questions as: History? none; Injury? none; Diagnosis? subluxation C2; Exam Findings? limited extension and right rotation C-spine. The patient received no X-ray on the initial visit. After the first adjustment, the patient remarked, and the doctor noted, 'severe arm and hand pain following the first adjustment'. Still, the treating DC did not take a radiograph or alter his treatment. Or maybe he did alter his treatment, but his notes showed the same entry 'C2' at every visit. The patient developed lower-extremity dysfunction subsequent to the upper-extremity weakness. His legs gave way on several occasions and his wife accused him of being drunk! The patient said he was reassured by his doctor that his condition was not unusual, and would heal with time and treatment. After 12 visits the patient admitted himself to the emergency department and underwent magnetic resonance imaging (MRI) that revealed his ruptured disc. Surgery ensued and his arm pain and cord tension resolved.

I was asked to give an opinion for the patient, and testify against a colleague and the company that insures me. After reviewing the data, I concluded as you probably have that what really happened and what should

Table 1 Loss types representing more than 5% of total claims 1994–98. Reproduced with permission of the National Chiropractic Mutual Insurance Company

Loss type	Percentage of total claims
Disc	
Cervical	12
Thoracic	0.5
Lumbar	13.4
Total	26
Fracture	
Rib	8.1
Total	12.5
Failure to diagnose	
Cancer	3.4
Total	11.1
Cerebrovascular accident	5.3
Vicarious liability	5.1
Aggravation of condition	9.4

have happened were different. The doctor let down his guard, did not proceed intelligently, dismissed the patient's remarks, and did not re-evaluate, refer or alter his care. I concluded that a reasonably prudent chiropractor should have responded to the adverse response to care, drawing no firm conclusion as to causation, and at minimum performed some test to compare against on future visits.

This case had many small oversights that could have been rectified. One that caught my attention was the repeated adjustment to an area that was worse than before the patient commenced treatment, especially without verifying the need for the type of care provided. This happens often in cerebrovascular accidents (CVAs). Although CVAs are statistically rare in our profession, records show that DCs often 'readjust' patients complaining of syncope. In an effort to help, they may provoke or at least not allow the situation to stabilize and, if injury has occurred, increase the risk of exacerbating an already precarious state.

Cerebrovascular accidents are not the most common injuries attributed to DCs. According to Richard Choate at the National Chiropractic Mutual Insurance Company (NCMIC), the loss types given in Table 1 are those representing more than 5% of the total claims NCMIC received from 1994 to 1998.

It is important to note that malpractice is not determined exclusively by the treatment outcome. People are injured and die every minute in hospitals. This does not indict hospitals or doctors. Malpractice exists when the failed outcome is a result of something you could have and should have known or done to protect the patient against the failed outcome. Malpractice carriers report that the most frequent malpractice claims involve failure to diagnose accurately, aggravation to an underlying condition, disc rupture requiring surgery, broken ribs and injury by ancillary modality.

An all too common reaction to a severely adverse situation in your practice is to delay that dreaded call to your malpractice carrier. Never hesitate to make it. However, until you receive a formal letter requesting information from your patient's attorney, your call typically nets you reassurance from a claims agent and instructions regarding file handling, records and what steps to take next. If you are notified that a suit is being considered, remain calm, stay the course and begin taking direction from the person assigned to your case at the malpractice insurance company. Do not bother perusing the *Yellow Pages* for legal representation, the malpractice carrier will provide one. You will meet the attorney to discuss the situation and chart a course. The attorney will be experienced in this field and guide you from start to finish. If you agree to keep the attorney assigned to you, minimal contact will occur between you and the carrier.

Your attorney will thoroughly review your file and daily office notes. Let me tell you in advance: never change or alter your notes after you are notified that a suit is being considered. Do not speak to anyone, including staff, regarding the issue. They may eventually testify or give a deposition in the case. Bear in mind that any notes you write, or tape-recordings you make to remind yourself of your account, will probably be subpoenaed. Do not initiate contact with the patient and do not accept any calls from them. Keep any correspondence they send to you. Unless your case is settled promptly, you will give a deposition to the plaintiff's attorney. Your attorney will take the plaintiff's deposition and the two sides will decide how far apart they are. Do not worry about this step; your attorney will walk you through a 'rehearsal'. No one is out to badger you; just answer the questions and nothing more.

Regardless of the outcome, the insurance company is required to notify your state board and the National Registry in Washington, DC. Be prepared to present your version to your board, and any managed care carriers you apply to.

The information discussed above is intended to prevent legal action being taken against you, and assist you in understanding the defense process. My strongest suggestion is to know your craft! Know how your craft works, when it is effective, and when it is not! Know what is expected of you as a DC where you practice. Keep your eyes and ears open and do what is right for the patient seeking your care and advice. Since you cannot foresee all the possibilities, be wise, be insured.

30

Words from a plaintiff's attorney

Gary M. Weiss, JD

Having spoken to many groups of physicians, lawyers and others across the country over the years, I have always been impressed by the level of attendance, participation, attention and interest by physician groups. There may, indeed, be no professional group who studied and worked harder to be trained, and continued after training to be retrained and re-educated and recertified. If that is true, and I for one believe that it is, it is no wonder that most physicians are in turn astonished, appalled, chagrined and anguished by the level of litigation against them. The purpose of this chapter is to sort out, from a plaintiff's attorney's view, what 'risk management' can and cannot do to reduce this incredible level of anxiety, as well as the level of litigation.

WHAT IS MALPRACTICE?

Malpractice is generally defined as the negligence or carelessness of a professional in his or her professional capacity. In a technical sense, malpractice is defined as a 'deviation from the accepted standard of care'. The 'accepted standard of care' is generally defined as a reasonable consensus on what is supposed to happen under a given set of medical facts. For example, when a pregnant woman's membranes rupture at home, she is told to go to the hospital. When a patient develops pneumococcal pneumonia, he or she is put on antibiotics. These are consensus opinions as to what is supposed to happen, and the failure to meet that 'consensus' is the 'deviation from the accepted standard' which touches off a malpractice case.

That, however, is not the end of the story. The 'deviation' must be the 'proximate cause' or a 'substantial factor' of some physical injury caused to the patient. In simple English (which lawyers detest), did the 'deviation' make the patient worse? If so, it is a case, and if not, it is not, despite the egregiousness of the alleged 'deviation'.

In order to have a 'malpractice case', the plaintiff must prove 'deviation' and 'causation'. If, for example, the patient calls the doctor and says, 'I've got a splitting headache and I've had it for 11 days', and the response is, 'Take two aspirin and call me in the morning', it would almost certainly be a deviation from the accepted standard or consensus but may not be a case. Let us assume that the result of the doctor's advice is that the patient dies of a stroke during the night. That arguably could be a case because faster action would probably have prevented at least some of the effects. Certainly death would not have ensued. On the other hand, let us assume that the patient dies in the middle of the night of a form of brain cancer. No action would have prevented it and, thus, there is no 'causation'.

THE CAUSES OF MEDICAL MALPRACTICE

As can be seen below, there is a clear-cut distinction between what causes malpractice and what causes malpractice cases. Malpractice is caused by simple human error. The laws of probability apply equally to physicians, lawyers and truck-drivers. Thus, there is basically a largely irreducible number of instances when physicians will be negligent. Luckily, most of those instances will cause no harm or only slight temporary harm. Some, however, will have devastating results. While it may be possible to reduce these errors slightly, particularly those that can cause devastating harm, all the care and concern in the world will probably not much reduce the number of justifiable malpractice cases. The real issue is how to reduce the number of unjustified cases, not the number of justified ones. Below are some suggestions. Thus, I believe that no amount of 'bedside manner' will dissuade the badly injured who have truly been victims of malpractice from proceeding.

THE CAUSES OF MALPRACTICE CASES

The real question is: how can medicine reduce (hopefully to zero) cases that clearly have no merit? To say that you should just be more caring begs the question. All professionals should be caring. In my view, physicians need to have a higher degree of respect for the intelligence and common-sense of their patients. A case in point illustrates this. When the prostate-specific antigen (PSA) test became available, I knew about it, and requested one, because I subscribe to many medical journals. The first year, my PSA level was 2.5, which is acceptable. The second year, I inadvertently skipped the test. Last year, the level was up to 3.7, slightly elevated for my age. My internist suggested that I consider an evaluation by a urologist and perhaps a biopsy. I discussed the situation with two urologists and obtained some medical literature on the subject. Based upon their advice and the literature, I skipped the biopsy and had another PSA test done in 6 months. The last one was back to the 2.5 level, thus eliminating the necessity for the biopsy. The point of the story is that my physicians discussed the options, handed me some literature and let me make the decision. Obviously, many patients are not in a position to review calmly the medical literature, but many are. Standard diagnostic questions come up every day, and there is literature that discusses these issues which could easily be photocopied and properly underlined for the patients. Thus, if something goes wrong which is not necessarily malpractice, at least the patient has been able significantly and meaningfully to participate in his or her treatment, and is much less likely to point the finger at the doctor. On the other hand, the dictatorial-type physician may have clearly dictated an acceptable choice for a treatment plan, but when the result is bad, has a much higher risk of facing an unjustified but time-consuming and aggravating malpractice case. In my practice, when the issue of settlement comes up, I routinely hand appropriate literature to the client to see what verdicts and settlements have been brought in similar cases. It is their case and it is certainly their body, and the more you get them to participate, the less likely they are to blame you unjustifiably when the inevitable bad result occurs.

Below are my suggestions for reducing the number of unwarranted and unjustifiable claims. This list is based upon a quarter of a century of hearing tales of woe from potential clients, all of whom had no justifiable case:

(1) Return your patients' telephone calls promptly. This alone will avoid half of the crank cases that I deal with on a daily basis.

(2) If it is practical, and if you have a long-time patient, when test results come back negative, call the patient yourself. It was a pretty nice feeling when my internist left a message, unsolicited by me, that my PSA test was normal.

(3) Schedule so that the patients do not wait, if at all possible. I realize that this is easier said than done, but an hour sitting in a waiting room makes a sick person very, very angry. A case in point: some years ago I needed to see a doctor and was 'worked in'. Since we were friends and probably since I was a malpractice lawyer, 'worked in' turned out to be that the moment I hit the waiting room, I was immediately ushered in ahead of 30 or 40 people sitting there. Their anger was visible and a clear prescription for disaster when the inevitable 'known and accepted complication' occurs.

(4) When faced with a bad but non-negligent result, it is imperative to deal with it directly, immediately and face to face. I would strongly recommend that you explain to the patient not only what occurred but why the 'bad result' is not evidence of malpractice. I would strongly suggest that you use the term 'malpractice' in your discussion with the patient. Nothing arouses the suspicion of a person whose medical treatment made him or her worse than the runaround or an insincere letter of some kind. A case in point in our office: a man underwent bypass surgery and died on the table. A bad result but one that does occur. There was no direct explanation by the surgeon as to what happened. A letter which brought the widow to my office stated as follows:

> 'Dear Mrs _____: Please let me take this opportunity to express my deepest and utmost sympathy upon the passing away of your husband, last _____ Thursday following *successful* triple bypass surgery.'

(5) If you have a pleasant personality, use it. If you do not, be aware that you do not and hire a nurse with one. Even if you are not a stand-up comic-type, politeness and courtesy is a necessity. How many of you routinely apologize to the patient for having to make them wait?

HOW I SELECT MY CASES

In order to reduce your risk of unjustified lawsuits, it might be helpful to know how I pick my clients with an eye towards reducing my risk of unjustified lawsuits. My criteria are quite similar to the criteria of all malpractice lawyers around the country. The criteria are as follows:

(1) Is the potential defendant somebody I know and respect as a person who has been helpful and courteous to me in the past? If so, I may have a conflict of interest.

(2) Is the claimed injury to the plaintiff permanent, disabling and/or likely to bring a jury award of in excess of $US250 000? If not, I will almost certainly reject the case as being economically not feasible, given the enormous cost of bringing malpractice actions where experts and other court costs run into tens of thousands of dollars.

(3) Is the plaintiff a clean-cut, pleasant, honest person trying hard to get well? No case is better than the appearance of the plaintiff, and if that appearance is not good, we often refuse those cases.

(4) Is the client reasonable? Unreasonable people make unreasonable demands, such as asking us to make sure immediately that the defendant doctor's license is revoked. Those clients want more than the law

Table 1   The plaintiff's attorney: items of concern for the medical professional. Reproduced with permission (adapted) from reference 1

(1) Innocent and seemingly innocuous requests for charts by the plaintiff's attorney can be dangerous
(2) Review your legal obligations
(3) If you suspect a claim, number pages of the record, impound the original, and immediately contact your malpractice carrier and defense attorney
(4) A simple cover letter should accompany the records you send to the plaintiff's attorney: no comment should be made
(5) Beware of phone calls from a plaintiff's attorney, making a request for medical records. (Get it in writing)
(6) Discovery tools are not available to an attorney before a lawsuit is filed
(7) Unless your personal attorney is 'bird-dogging' the carrier, the case could be settled without your permission
(8) On receiving a summons, immediately notify your medical malpractice carrier
(9) Beware of plaintiff's attorneys' attempts to pin you down 'on authoritative textbooks': no textbooks *per se* are authoritative
(10) When in doubt, ask to see the record when testifying
(11) Do not speculate, do not guess
(12) Leave the impression of being courteous, yet in control
(13) Do not lose your temper
(14) Your attorney should set a time limit of no more than 4 hours at a stretch during deposition
(15) It is important that you set the pace of questioning during the deposition
(16) Three areas are under attack: your credibility, the validity of your evidence and the logic of your conclusions
(17) As the trial date approaches, co-ordinate your schedule with one or more of your colleagues for appropriate coverage

can give them and we cannot satisfy them. Likewise, those folks want perfect health and are prescription for disaster for the physician. Identify them and attempt to avoid them if possible.

(5) Does the peer-reviewed medical literature on the subject support the plaintiff's contention that malpractice occurred? If not, our expert would have no basis for his or her opinion and we generally reject those cases. (This is a very good reason to give the literature to your patient after an accepted complication has occurred.)

These simple rules have helped my firm to achieve a fairly high success rate and no malpractice cases filed against us by an irate client. By accepting the fact that you are human and may make a negligent error which causes harm, and concentrating your efforts on reducing unwarranted claims by the simple suggestions provided above, a physician ought to be able to go through his or her career without adding to the general pressure of being a professional by fearing every patient as a potential claim, rather than welcoming every patient for the very reasons that you went to medical school.

Table 1 lists items of concern for the physician from the plaintiff's attorney's point of view.

REFERENCE

1. Brutton YKE, Chapman S. *Malpractice. A Guide to Avoidance and Treatment*. Orlando: Grune & Stratton, 1987

31

Deposition–pre-trial–trial

Tracy S. Prewitt, JD, and John T. Ballantine, JD

THE DEPOSITION

What is a deposition?

A deposition is a question and answer session conducted by an attorney of a witness which is given under oath and transcribed by a court reporter. It may be recorded on video. The goal of the deposition is to obtain information from the witness about what he or she knows regarding the facts of the case, or what he or she might testify about at trial.

Your role

In medical malpractice cases, the parties, other treating physicians and expert witnesses are common deponents. As a party (defendant), you are entitled to attend any or all depositions (the plaintiff also has the right to be present). Talk to your attorney to determine whether your attendance would be helpful.

How are depositions used?

Generally, depositions are taken so that attorneys can 'discover' the pertinent facts of a case or the opinions of expert witnesses. The attorney uses the information gained in a deposition to prepare the case for trial. Because deponents are under oath while testifying, an attorney can use the deposition testimony to contradict or impeach the witness at trial if the witness' trial testimony differs from what was said in the deposition. A deposition also may be read at trial in lieu of having the deponent appear as a witness if the parties agree or if, at the time of trial, the deponent is dead, outside the state or unavailable because of age, sickness, imprisonment or any other valid reason. Attorneys often present expert witness testimony via videotaped deposition because the expert witness is unable to be present for the trial.

What happens during a deposition?

The attorney 'noticing' or requesting the deposition will be the first person allowed to ask questions of the witness. All other parties' attorneys will have an opportunity to question the witness too. For example, your attorney may want to take the deposition of the plaintiff to discover the basis for the plaintiff's claims against you. Once your attorney completes his or her questioning of the witness, the attorneys for any other defendants in the case will be able to ask the witness additional questions. The plaintiff's own attorney may ask the plaintiff a few questions if it is necessary to qualify or explain any of the witness' previous answers.

While the witness is being deposed, a court reporter will probably be recording and transcribing everything the attorneys and the witness say. In some instances, the deposition may be videotaped and no court reporter will be present. The court reporter will transcribe the attorney's question, the witness' answer and any other conversation between the attorneys during the depositions. Attorneys are allowed to object if the attorney taking the deposition asks an improper question. The court reporter transcribes all objections to preserve them for the court's review at a later time.

Once the deposition is over it will take several days for the court reporter to produce a written transcript of the deposition. The witness has the right to read the written transcript and make any necessary changes before the transcript is considered final. On occasion, the witness may find typographical errors in the transcript and these can be corrected without any further testimony. If the witness wants to make a substantive change to his or her testimony, however, the parties have a right to redepose the witness about that change.

Who may be present at a deposition?

In addition to the witness, the attorneys and the court reporter, the presence of other individuals at a deposition depends on the local laws and customs of the jurisdiction where the deposition occurs. Parties are entitled to attend depositions; generally the public and the press are not. Occasionally one or more of the attorneys will ask his or her paralegal to be present to take notes or help with exhibits. A common tactic used in the deposition is to have the other party present for the deposition in the hope that the witness will be hesitant to criticize the attending party.

Your role

If you are the witness, do not be afraid to be completely honest (Table 1), even if this means saying that the patient was non-compliant. Remember,

Table 1 Tips at deposition

(1) Always tell the truth!
(2) Listen carefully to the question. Do not assume that you know what the questioner is asking. If you do not understand the question, ask the attorney to rephrase it until you do understand it
(3) Answer only the question that is asked
(4) Answer the question as succinctly as possible: 'Yes' or 'No' if possible
(5) Avoid using obscenities, derogatory comments, ethnic slurs or jokes of any kind. The atmosphere at a deposition is often more relaxed than the atmosphere at a trial, but this is no reason to let down your guard. Remember, nothing is 'off the record'
(6) Do not rush to give an answer. Take your time. This will allow you to give a more reasoned response and allow your attorney time to object to the question, if necessary
(7) Keep your composure

Table 2 Preparation for discussion with the insurance company and attorney

(1) Be knowledgeable regarding details of the case
(2) Be sure you have gone through *all* the records
(3) Preparation of a narrative summary is often helpful to 'remember the details'
(4) Try to be both accurate and objective in this narrative as well as in your communication
(5) Remember, all communications with your attorney are privileged and therefore pose no risk (attorney–client privilege)
(6) Formulate questions that you have for the attorney handling your case
(7) It is imperative that you *do not discuss the case with anyone*!
(8) Conversations with the claims investigator from the insurance company may not be protected by the attorney–client privilege, so treat these differently from discussions with your attorney
(9) Establish your own separate litigation file in an effort to preserve confidentiality of the information. Ideally, this file is kept at a location other than your office

your patient has alleged that you were negligent in your treatment. This is not the time to 'sugarcoat' the facts to stay on good terms with your former patient.

How to prepare for your deposition

First, it is important to be very familiar with your own medical records. The plaintiff's attorney undoubtedly will have a copy of your records and ask you about their contents during your deposition (Table 2). You should also review any hospital records, laboratory reports or information documenting the patient's condition before and after your treatment. Your attorney will obtain medical records from other physicians who treated the patient and you should review these as well. It is important to have an idea of your patient's overall medical history before testifying about your treatment in particular.

Next, you should discuss with your attorney the best way to handle difficult issues in your case, or issues that the two of you believe will be covered by the plaintiff's attorney. For instance, the plaintiff may complain that you did not inform her of the risks of a certain procedure. You recall that you did inform her of the risks but that conversation is not recorded in your office chart. Talk to your attorney before your deposition about how to explain that omission.

PRE-TRIAL MOTIONS

As the trial date approaches, you or your opponent's attorney may well make a number of 'pre-trial motions' or 'motions *in limine*'. These might concern a variety of topics including evidentiary issues, allowable experts and the specific legal standards applicable to your case. The judge will consider these motions and hear the attorneys' legal arguments before the trial begins. In most cases, the judge will rule on the motions at the conclusion of the attorneys' oral arguments. The judge might also prepare a written opinion concerning his or her ruling.

These rulings are important because they clarify what the court will and will not allow the parties to present at trial. Except in rare circumstances, the parties cannot appeal these rulings before the trial. If the losing party at trial believes that an adverse pre-trial ruling was improper, he or she may file an appeal with the appropriate appellate court after the jury renders a verdict.

Your role

Your attorney will update you about the results of any pre-trial motions. There is no need for you to attend the hearings on these motions unless your attorney specifically asks you to be present.

THE TRIAL

Now that you have accepted the fact that the case 'will not go away', you must be prepared for the actual trial. Medical malpractice cases are almost always heard by a panel of 12 jurors. The judge is present to rule on any legal questions that arise during the trial and to instruct the jurors on proper trial procedure and the law applicable to your case. The jurors consider the evidence, weigh the credibility of each witness and decide the ultimate factual issues in the case. For instance, it will be up to the jury, not the judge, to determine under the evidence and their collective evaluation of it whether your medical treatment of the plaintiff/patient met the applicable standard of care.

Jury selection

Because so much of your case will be decided by the jury, it is important to select jurors who can listen impartially to the evidence and issues. During 'voir dire' (questioning of prospective jurors), the parties will have an opportunity to discover the backgrounds and potential biases of the jurors. 'Voir dire' is the French term for 'to speak the truth'. This is where your input counts!

On the first day of trial, a panel of 35–40 (or more) potential jurors will be called to the courtroom. Each party will receive an information sheet containing each potential juror's name, age and place of employment. The information sheet also will list whether the potential juror has previously served on a jury. The judge will ask the panel of potential jurors some preliminary questions to make sure no one is familiar with, or related in any way to, the parties or their attorneys.

In most courtrooms, the judges allow the attorneys to question the potential jurors about any possible biases they may have. For instance, your attorney may ask whether any of the potential jurors or their close family members or friends have been treated for the same condition for which you treated the plaintiff. If the subject of the suit is a surgically related problem, you should try to excuse any juror who has had, or whose spouse has had, an adverse experience with respect to medical or surgical care generally, or your type of procedure in particular.

If either side believes a particular juror could not listen impartially to the evidence, that party can ask the court to strike the potential juror 'for cause'. If the judge agrees that the juror cannot be impartial, the judge will excuse that juror from serving on your case. Each party will also have the opportunity to exercise a certain number of 'pre-emptory' challenges. In other words, each party may eliminate a set number of jurors for any reason other than their race. Once the process is completed, the remaining jurors, either six or 12, depending on the state, plus one or two alternatives will be sworn in.

Table 3 Chart to assist in jury selection

Juror 1	Juror 2	Juror 3	Juror 4	Juror 5
Juror 6	Juror 7	Juror 8	Juror 9	Juror 10
Juror 11	Juror 12	Juror 13	Juror 14	Juror 15
Juror 16	Juror 17	Juror 18	Juror 19	Juror 20
Juror 21	Juror 22	Juror 23	Juror 24	Juror 25
Juror 26	Juror 27	Juror 28	Juror 29	Juror 30
Juror 31	Juror 32	Juror 33	Juror 34	Juror 35
Juror 36	Juror 37	Juror 38	Juror 39	Juror 40

Your role

During jury selection, your role is to assist your attorney in selecting jurors who can impartially consider the facts in your case. Look for body language; listen to each juror's answers and the *way* in which he or she answers (or looks when he or she does *not* answer). Identify jurors who you would or would not like to decide your case. Some people find it helpful to make notes on each of the potential jurors. Table 3 gives an example of a chart you can use for this purpose.

Opening arguments

Once the jury is selected, each party's attorney has an opportunity to make an opening statement. The plaintiff's attorney will begin. He or she will give the jury a 'thumbnail sketch' or overview of the claims that the plaintiff is making in the case. Be prepared to hear the plaintiff's attorney criticize the way you cared for the plaintiff/patient. Your attorney will also have a chance to address the jury and tell the jurors the facts from your perspective.

Your role

Sit with a concerned, but 'never surprised', face. You may hear the plaintiff's lawyer make statements with which you vehemently disagree. It is in your best interest to remain composed, even though this may be difficult.

The plaintiff presents his (her) case

Once all parties have given an opening statement, the plaintiff will present his or her case to the jury. The plaintiff's attorney will call one or more persons as witnesses. The questions an attorney asks his or her own witnesses are called 'direct examination'. When the plaintiff's attorney finishes questioning the witness, your attorney will have a chance to 'cross-examine' the witness. The plaintiff's attorney may then ask more questions or 'redirect' in an effort to try to clarify or rebut points that have been addressed by the defense attorney. If necessary, your attorney can 're'-cross-examine the witness but only on points covered in redirect. This process of direct and cross-examination continues until all plaintiff's witnesses have been examined. The plaintiff will then 'rest' his or her case.

At this point, in the absence of the jury but in your presence and that of the plaintiff, your attorney might move for a directed verdict. This means your attorney wants the judge to rule that the plaintiff, as a matter of law, has failed to prove his or her case against you. If the judge agrees, no more facts will be presented to the jury and the case will be over. Although many defense attorneys make motions for directed verdict, do not raise your hopes or expectations. Judges, generally, are reluctant to grant such a motion. They prefer to let the jurors decide the case based on all the evidence. Even if the judge rules against your attorney's motion for a directed verdict, it is possible that further streamlining of the allegations will occur. For example, if the judge believes that the plaintiff has failed to prove specific allegations, he or she may not allow the jury to consider those issues.

On average, trial proceedings unfold for periods of about 1 hour at a time. The judge calls rest-room breaks and allows a lunch break which lasts between 1 and 2 hours. Often the judge will use this 'break' time to hear other motions, totally independent of your case.

The defense presents your case

Assuming that your motion for a directed verdict is overruled, your attorney will call witnesses to present your case. These witnesses might include you, other health-care professionals and expert witnesses. This time your attorney examines the witness first followed by cross-examination by the plaintiff's attorney. Your attorney can follow up with questions on redirect if necessary. Once you have presented all your witnesses, the defense will rest. Once again there may be a motion for a directed verdict or further refinement of the allegations.

Instructions for the jury

Before the trial begins, the judge usually requires each party's attorney to prepare draft jury instructions. These are short statements of the law governing your case, and are designed to help the jurors decide the factual issues raised during the trial. The judge will review each party's draft jury instructions and decide which version, or parts of each, to give to the jury.

At the conclusion of all the evidence, and in the jury's absence, the attorneys will review the version of jury instructions prepared by the judge. Each side has the opportunity to argue for or against the correctness of any of these jury instructions. Routine instructions include those that tell the jurors they may render a verdict for the defense or for the plaintiff. If the jury returns a verdict for the plaintiff, it also must determine the amount of any monetary award due to the plaintiff and the percentages of fault

Table 4 Courtroom–trial checklist

(1) Dress conservatively: avoid 'flashy' jewelry
(2) Arrive at least 30 minutes before the court convenes
(3) During the jury selection process, sit straight and look solemn and concerned
(4) Discuss your reaction to potential jurors with your attorney
(5) Look at the jury at all time when you are testifying: eye contact is important
(6) The jury's attention span is greatest during opening and closing statements
(7) Face the jury squarely during closing arguments but try to show little emotion
(8) Insisting on answering questions without referring to medical records is a big mistake
(9) Never volunteer information: only answer the questions
(10) Convey the impression that you are 100% convinced you acted appropriately
(11) Be aware of your body language (avoid sighing, clearing your throat, rubbing your hands, nervousness)
(12) When you leave the witness stand, do not convey what you are feeling (grin, wave, etc.)
(13) Try to save your questions for your attorney until a break in a witness' examination so your attorney is not distracted

among the various defendants. In appropriate cases, the jury also may find that some of the fault must be borne by the plaintiff.

Closing arguments

Once the judge finalizes and reads the instructions to the jury, closing arguments begin. These are presented in reverse order from the opening statements. In other words, your attorney will make his or her closing argument to the jury first. The plaintiff's attorney will go last. Be prepared for the plaintiff's attorney to criticize vigorously your care of the plaintiff/patient. The plaintiff's attorney will also suggest monetary award amounts to the jurors.

The jurors will then go to a separate room and deliberate in seclusion until they render a verdict. In most states, the jury's verdict does not need to be unanimous (although in federal court it must be). Only nine or more (in a case with 12 jurors) must agree.

Your role

The best advice is to be prepared and patient. A trial may last anywhere between minutes and days. Often your attorney has no control over the speed of the trial, particularly when the judge has other, non-related, matters to deal with during your court recesses. If you want your attorney to ask a witness a specific question, note the question on a piece of paper. Your attorney will almost always check whether you have any questions before releasing the witness.

The verdict

Once the jurors agree on a verdict, the judge, jury, plaintiff(s), defendant(s) and attorneys reassemble. The jury foreperson will present the signed verdict to the judge who then will read the jury's decision to all present.

Your role

While the jury is deliberating, you may wait at your attorney's office or at a site away from the courtroom. This certainly is permissible as long as you tell the court or clerk where you can be reached. It will be impossible for your attorney to tell you how long it will take the jurors to reach a verdict.

Table 4 lists points of advice regarding the courtroom situation.

A trial is an intimidating experience which can be less threatening with appropriate education regarding the process. The good news is that, to date, the vast majority of verdicts are for the defendants.

Good luck! Be calm, cool and collected – easier said than done – but important!

32

Successfully suing
the plaintiff's attorney

Joseph S. Sanfilippo, MD, MBA

Retaliation associated with the frustration of a frivolous malpractice claim
remains an area of debate from a defendant's point of view. 'Counter suing'
when dealing with an unscrupulous attorney and/or the 'greedy' patient
may bear consideration. The Minnesota Medical Association Commission
on Profession Liability[1] conveyed that for every 100 malpractice claims
filed against physicians, 60 are closed without payment, 30 are settled with
payment before trial, and of the remaining 10, eight are won by the defendant physician.

Health care professionals would be in agreement that from a moral perspective, and as a matter of public policy, there is no 'no legitimate reason'
for physicians or anyone else to be required to suffer the damages forsee-
ably inflicted by groundless lawsuits. Justice demands a means of recovery
for the harm generated by the purveyors of meritless litigation[2].

From the perspective that 50–75% of all claims are dropped without any
compensation being awarded, one can imply that a large percentage of cases
filed are without merit[3]. In order to proceed with a counter suit against a
plaintiff and the plaintiff's attorney, the following must be understood. In
most States, a number of requirements must be met. These include:

1. The malpractice suit must have been terminated 'in your favor'. This can
   be either through a defendant verdict at trial, dismissal or a summary
   judgment.

2. The case against you must be demonstrated to have been either groundless or filed maliciously.

However, the fact that in many States it is required that before a plaintiff files a suit, an expert opinion from one other physician is obtained and
there must be agreement that there is evidence of 'malpractice' sets the

stage for an uphill battle. To recover in a suit, the plaintiff (patient) must demonstrate the following:

1. The physician owed a duty to the patient.
2. The physician breeched this duty.
3. The patient suffered a demonstrable injury.
4. There was a causal connection between the breech of the duty and the injury.

Criteria – prerequisite to winning a suit against a plaintiff and their attorney

One would have to prove that the defendant (physician) suffered damages (i.e. loss of income or attorney's fees, etc.); sustained humiliation; had a loss of reputation; loss of other intangibles; and there was a loss of patients, all of which would have to be linked to the malpractice suit.

CATEGORIES FOR PROCEEDING WITH CASE AGAINST THE PLAINTIFF AND PLAINTIFF'S ATTORNEY

The following categories have been utilized for successfully achieving a counter suit precipitated by an initial medical malpractice case:

1. Malicious prosecution.
2. Abuse of process.
3. *Prima facie* tort.
4. Defamation.
5. Intentional infliction of emotional distress.
6. Constructive contempt – invasion of privacy.
7. Professional negligence – violation of professional code of responsibility or ethics by the attorney.
8. Barratry (the offense of frequently exciting or stirring up suits and quarrels between others).

Malicious prosecution

This is the most common basis for a countersuit. The essential elements include:

1. Prior institution of civil proceedings by the defendant in the malicious prosecution action.
2. Termination of the previous proceedings on the merits in favor of the counter suit plaintiff.

3. Lack of probable cause for instituting the proceedings.

4. Malice on the part of the defendant in bringing the proceedings.

5. Damage to the plaintiff.

Malice, which is a necessary element of a malicious prosecution, implies an intentional or willful act designed to bring about a wrongful result. The challenge is proving malice. One could argue that filing a frivolous lawsuit, or failing to adequately investigate appropriate details prior to filing the case, or failing to obtain an ethical expert's input would serve as appropriate grounds for 'malice'. In many instances the problem is while a physician may win their case at a lower court, often the decision is reversed on appeal.

In the case of Berlin *vs.* Nathan, a trial that took place in the State of Illinois based upon a radiologist (Dr Berlin) who was sued for malpractice for 'misinterpreting' the X-ray of the patient's 'little finger', the physician believed that the finger was dislocated and subsequently was noted to have a fracture (chip fracture). The malpractice suit was voluntarily dismissed with prejudice. The physician proceeded to file a counter suit in violation of the Barratry Statute (the offense of frequently exciting or serving up suits and quarrels between others). The case was won but on appeal the decision was reversed. The Illinois Appellate Court stated that Dr Berlin had not met two of the required prerequisites for the malicious prosecution suit, viz the malpractice suit had been brought maliciously and without probable cause and the court had sustained special damages as a result. The court stood behind the 'special damage' requirement in order to limit the number of malicious prosecution suits and, thus, continue to allow patients appropriate access to the courts.

Abuse of process

The essence of abuse of process is the 'misuse of regularly-issued process for any purpose other than that for which it was designed'. The key elements for abuse of process include:

1. That the original plaintiff made an illegal or improper use of the process.

2. That the plaintiff had an ulterior motive in so using the process.

3. That damage resulted to the defendant (physician) because of the misuse of process.

One example of abuse of process is Bickel *vs.* Mackie in which the physician who was sued argued that the patient and her attorney proceeded with a non-meritorious suit. The patient plaintiff and her attorney attempted to use the legal system to accomplish 'an improper purpose' – to extort a settlement based on lack of merit. The court found for the original plaintiff attorney feeling that the major objective of the initial lawsuit was for the purpose of settlement which *per se* was a legitimate goal of proper process. However, at the Appellate Court level the decision was for the physician and $35 000 in compensatory damages was awarded and $50 000 in punitive damages.

Although abuse of process is defined as the misuse or perversion of a regularly issued legal process after it has been issued, to achieve some collateral purpose not justified by the nature of the process, it infrequently stands up with a counter suit. One advantage with abuse of process is that there is no need to prove lack of probable cause or previous favorable termination. Unfortunately, the initiation of a meritless medical malpractice case *per se* is insufficient to allow one to counter sue based on abuse of process because 'process' does not include a civil complaint or summons to appear in court[4].

Prima facie tort

A *prima facie* tort is defined as 'the infliction of an intention to harm without excuse or justification by an act, or series of acts, which otherwise would be lawful and results in special damage'. The focus is on the negotiation between the parties rather than 'the issuance of formal use of the process *per se*'. For *prima facie* tort the key elements include: (1) an intent on the part of the original plaintiff to injure the defendant; (2) a lack of justification; and (3) special damages. The difficulty here is that the physician plaintiff must prove an actual intent to injure occurred.

Defamation

The physician plaintiff must find that there is damage to one's professional reputation – 'good name'. This requires an untruthful publication of defamatory material detrimental to the physician's reputation in the community, thus the physician is exposed to ridicule or contempt in the eyes of citizens of the community.

The tort of defamation is an 'intentional tort' because malpractice trials are of public concern and there is potential for it to 'lessen the physician's image' in the community or deter patients from seeking the medical care of the physician *per se*.

In Hanley *vs*. Lund a patient plaintiff's attorney as well as the newspaper were found liable for defamation. This was both libel and slander.

Dr Hanley was sued for wrongful death and the plaintiff's attorney made defamatory statements about the physician which were published in the newspaper. The judgment was for the physician and the court awarded $13 500 in compensatory damages and $5000 in punitive damages, based upon the proof that the statements attributed to the lawyer were published in the newspaper and were indeed defamatory with respect to the physician.

Intentional infliction of emotional distress

This tort is an intentional or reckless act amounting to extreme and outrageous conduct which causes severe emotional distress to another by one not privileged to do this[5]. Here the physician plaintiff must prove that he or she was damaged by conduct 'so outrageous so as to shock one's conscious'. This of course is difficult to prove even when a frivolous malpractice suit is pursued by the patient and their plaintiff's attorney.

Constructive contempt – invasion of privacy

In the case of Wolfe *vs.* Arrogo, the physician sued the patient plaintiff's attorney for 'constructive contempt' on the grounds that the malpractice suit filed against him was without merit. The physician sought $750 000 for damages related to embarrassment and probable cause of action for constructive contempt from actions of invasion of privacy[6]. The basis of constructive contempt is extremely difficult to prove and unlikely to be meritorious in a counter suit.

Professional negligence – violation of professional code of responsibility for ethics

The problem is that liability for malpractice from the attorney's perspective is extremely difficult to establish because of the necessity of 'privity'. The 'sacrosanct' client–attorney privilege discussion with their client often serves as protection. For professional negligence the suits must be based on two claims: (1) the physician–plaintiff alleges that the patient's attorney was negligent in bringing an unfounded lawsuit against the physician; and (2) the physician usually charges the attorney with a breech of the American Bar Association Code of Professional Responsibilities for Lawyers DRG-10 (A) (2). Specifically this code states 'a lawyer shall not handle a legal matter without preparation adequate in the circumstance(s)'. DRG 7–102 (A) (1) states 'In his representation of a client, a lawyer shall not file a suit, assert a position, conduct a defense, delay trial or take other action on behalf of his client when he knows or when it is obvious that such action would serve merely to harass or maliciously injure another'.

In general, claims against the malpractice plaintiff's attorney for professional negligence are usually similarly dismissed because the patient has a 'fundamental constitutional right to present their case in court and thus have the claim adjudicated'.

In Freese *vs.* Lemmon, a physician was sued for negligence in failing to meet the standard of care and determine if the patient was susceptible to seizures and, thus, warn him not to drive. It was alleged that as a result of this negligence the patient suffered a seizure while driving which resulted in injury to the plaintiff. The problem is that the physician should know when his or her patient is not fit to drive and has a duty to the patient, as well as the public, to warn the patient accordingly. The counter suit by the physician needless to say did not result in a decision in the physician's favor.

Action based on attorney unethical conduct

If a physician feels that an attorney has filed an unjust malpractice suit and should the plaintiff's attorney be held liable for violation of the legal profession's rule of professional conduct, this could lead to a counter suit based on unethical conduct. Once again it is difficult for the physician plaintiff to utilize this concept as appropriate grounds for successful litigation in a counter suit. The concept is that a physician feels that there is a duty on the part of the plaintiff's attorney not to file the suit when such action would serve merely to harass or maliciously injure another and the duty of fairness to the opposing party and Counsel must be taken into consideration[7].

Actions for intentional infliction of emotional distress

This cause of action has been attempted in counter suits. Without exception, this has been an unsuccessful principle. In Sullivan *vs.* Birmingham and Williams *vs.* Coombs it was stated that the communication between the attorney and his or her client was privileged and the privilege as a matter of law nullified action for intentional infliction of emotional distress[7].

FILING A SUIT

If the decision has been made to proceed with a suit against the plaintiff and the plaintiff's attorney, the complaint must be lodged with the State's

Attorney Disciplinary Commission. The required form is frequently available from the State Bar. In many States the complaint filed against the attorney is associated with 'immunity' for the physician. Hence, there is no risk of liability to the physician for filing such a case.

WINNING THE CASE

Judges are not supportive of frivolous claims when indeed the patient's claim is 'groundless'. The physician who does not pursue a counter suit theoretically is recognized as an individual who is less likely to stand tall and thus would allow a frivolous suit to proceed in the future. Hence, this is clearly an important issue to consider. One should give a counter suit due consideration but fully comprehend the undertaking.

The chance of winning a counter suit and what the award can be must also be taken into consideration. If you are able to show the plaintiff's attorney acted with malice or blatant disregard for the truth then you stand a chance to win. Unfortunately, the case may take a significant amount of time, i.e. more than one year, depositions must be obtained, and the settlement may well be minimal.

Cases

Huene vs. Carnes – The original lower court decision was for the defendant in the countersuit. The appellate court reversed a summary judgment for the defendant and the case was ultimately settled.

Mahaffey vs. McMahon – In this counter suit the Kentucky Supreme Court reversed a directed verdict for the defendant and remanded the case for re-trial. The case was never retried and no monetary award was given to the physician plaintiff.

Nelson vs. Miller – In this Kansas case the Supreme Court reversed a summary judgment for the defendant and remanded the case for trial. As time progressed, the case was settled. In this situation, the physician's complaint alleging malicious prosecution was dismissed. The specifics of the case were that a malpractice suit had been initiated against Dr Nelson and a number of other physicians alleging that the patient and her son – 'an undetected fetus' at the time of the incident – had been injured while being surgically treated with a dilatation and curettage without first ruling out pregnancy. The trial court dismissed Dr Nelson from the suit without prejudice and subsequently granted a summary judgment in favor of the remaining defendant-physicians. The ruling was upheld on appeal.

Subsequent to this event, Dr Nelson initiated a counter suit for malicious prosecution in the State of Kansas. The key point here is that the Kansas Court stated that the voluntary dismissal of a prior action without prejudice may constitute a termination on the merits for the purpose of the malicious prosecution action and remanded for resolution of this issue. The court rejected the requirement that the plaintiff alleged or approved special damages. On remand, the trial court concluded that the dismissal of Dr Nelson in the initial lawsuit was not a favorable determination on the merits, and granted summary judgment in favor of the defendants in the malicious prosecution action.

Etheredge vs. Emmons – The court reversed the physician's victory on appeal and remanded the case for trial.

Wong vs. Tabor – The Indiana Court of Appeals established a new standard for attorneys contemplating whether or not probable cause exists when a client approaches with a potential medical malpractice case. The Indiana legal system has established a litigation review board which has significantly decreased the number of cases that proceed to trial. In addition, a more restrictive statute of limitations and time requirement has been established. In McCullough *vs.* Allen, the court felt that for the physician to establish a malicious prosecution case, the physician would have to show either that the attorney did not subjectively believe that the patient's claim merited litigation; or that no competent and reasonable attorney familiar with the Law of the Forum would consider that the claim was worthy of litigation, on the basis of facts known by the attorney who instituted the suit.

Weaver vs. Supreme Court of Orange County – The question of malice was addressed and the California Court stated it is a necessary element of malicious prosecution that could be inferred from the lack of probable cause: 'the quantum of culpable conduct which must be proved to prevail as a plaintiff in a malicious prosecution case is significantly greater than that required to prevail in a case alleging only'.

Rodgers vs. Robson – This was not a counter suit, however a physician proceeded with an action against attorneys retained by the physician's insurer when the attorneys settled a malpractice claim without the physician's consent. The case went to the Illinois Supreme Court which held that the physician was 'entitled to a full disclosure of the intent to settle the litigation without his consent and contrary to his express instructions'.

Berlin vs. Nathan – The Illinois Appellate Court concluded that 'willful and wanton conduct' is not necessarily malice but that a suit brought with an improper motive may be malicious. A successful malicious prosecution case occurred with *Peerman vs. Sidicaine* in which the Tennessee Court of Appeals affirmed compensatory and punitive damages in a counter suit action brought on the theories of malicious prosecution and abuse of process. The court felt that the initial lawsuit against the physician was without the consent of the client and groundless. The action against the attorney in the counter suit stood in the eyes of the court.

REFERENCES

1. Minnesota Medical Association Commission on Professional Liability. *Am Med News* 1985
2. Sokol D. Countersuits deter frivolous malpractice actions. *Dental Econom* 1994;
3. Parker JDT. The failure of the Medical Malpractice Countersuit Movement – a reply to David J. Sokol, DDS, JD, FAGD. *Am J Law Med* 1986;12:323
4. Hirsh H. Physician countersuits: a chronology of losses and wins, Part I. *Med Law* 1987;6:13
5. Hirsh H. Physician countersuits: a chronology of losses and wins, Part II. *Med Law* 1987;6:23
6. Hirsh H. Physician countersuits: a chronology of losses and wins, Part III. *Med Law* 1987;6:35
7. Witlin L. Countersuits by medical malpractice defendants against attorneys. *J Leg Med* 1988;9:421
8. Gerber P. Malpractice countersuits won by physicians. *Physician Management* July 1983
9. Sokol D. The current status of medical malpractice countersuits. *Am J Law Med* 1985;10:439–57

CASES

Berlin *vs.* Nathan – Ill Cir Ct, Cook County, Dkt No 75-M2-542 (1 June 1976)
64 Ill App 3d 940, 381 NE 2d 1367
381 NE 2nd 1367 Ill app Ill 1975. Cert denied 444. US 828, 2 Ill 682 (1979)
Bickel *vs.* Mackie – 447 F. Supp. 1376, 1381 (N.D. Iowa), *aff'd*, 590 F.2d 341 (8th Cir. 1978)
Freese *vs.* Lemmon – 210 N.W. 2d 576 (Iowa1973)
Hanley *vs.* Lund – 218 Cal. App 2d 633, 32 Cal Rptr 733 (1983)
Sullivan *vs.* Birmingham – 11 Mass. App. 359, 416 N.E. 2d 528 (1981)
Williams *vs.* Coombs – 179 Cal. App. 3d 626, 224 Cal. Rptr. 865 (1986)
Huene *vs.* Carnes – 175 Cal Rptr. 374 (1981), *h'g denied* (Sept. 16, 1981)
Mahaffey *vs.* McMahon – 630 WS 2d 68 (Ky Sup Ct 1982)
Nelson *vs.* Miller – 233 Kan. 122, 660 P.2d 1361 (1983)
Etheredge *vs.* Emmons – No. AO14929 (Cal. App. 1985)
Wong *vs.* Tabor – 422 NE 2d (1979) (Ind App 1981)

McCullough *vs.* Allen – 449 NE 2d 1168 (Ind App 1983)

Weaver *vs.* Supreme Court of Orange County – 95 Cal App 3d 166, 156 Cal Rptr 745 (Cal App 1979)

Rodgers *vs.* Robson – 81 Ill. 2d 201, 407 N.E. 2d 47 (1980)

Peerman *vs.* Sidicaine – 605 S.W. 2d 242 (Tenn. Ct. App. 1980)

Wolfe *vs.* Arrogo – 543 S.W. 2d 11(Tex Giv App 1976)

33

Living will

Joseph S. Sanfilippo, MD, MBA

An advanced directive is a document written by a competent adult convey-ing instructions for future health-care in the event that the individual becomes incompetent or unable to communicate, or loses decision-making capabilities. Two types of advanced directive are recognized in most states: the living will and health-care power of attorney.

A living will is a written statement that tells the physician and family what type of health-care the patient will accept or refuse if he or she is unable to express his or her wishes. The laws about living wills vary from state to state, but, in general, living wills tell physicians what patients want to be done to prolong their life. This might include the types of life-sustaining therapy to be undertaken, such as respirator, cardiopulmonary resuscitation, feeding tubes and administration of intravenous medica-tions. The living will goes into effect only if the patient has a terminal condition and cannot make decisions.

For a number of reasons, including the limitations of the living will, indi-viduals also prepare another document: a health-care power of attorney. In this, the person chooses a health-care agent to make medical decisions when he or she is unable to do so. In the health-care power of attorney doc-ument, a person may state his or her wishes about medical care, but the agent is not necessarily required to follow them because the power to make decisions may be transferred to the agent. Patients can specify exactly which powers they are giving their agent. These may include the power to choose physicians, the right to decide on hospitalization, and the right to accept or refuse treatment.

Approximately 5–15% of the population have completed a living will. The most common reason for not having a living will is young age. Health status of the individual is also a factor. Functionally independent persons are less likely to have a living will; the frequency of completion of such a document increases with one's dependency on others. Patients who die of cancer or pulmonary disease are more likely to have documented a living will (16% and 11%, respectively).

The federal Patient Self-Discrimination Act of 1990 requires hospitals and nursing-homes to tell patients of their rights to make advanced directives. They must put in the patient's medical record whether he or she has an advanced directive.

In addition, states have their own laws about health-care powers of attorney. State laws will determine what advanced directives may contain, and how and when they must be followed.

Increased use of written advanced directives prevents many ethical dilemmas about life-sustaining interventions for patients who are no longer competent to make decisions. Acting on a living will may, however, present a dilemma for the physician. Ethical concerns may also arise for the patient's family and health-care professionals in general. Quality-of-life considerations in treatment decisions as well as physicians' obligations regarding the implementation of living wills can raise a number of questions with respect to the right of patients to self-determination. Nevertheless, adults have the right to make their own health-care decisions. That right includes defining one's wishes regarding life-prolonging treatment and artificial nutrition and hydration.

Advanced directives should be kept in a safe and accessible place in case of emergency, and a list of people who have copies should be kept with the document. Copies should be given to one's physician, agent, spouse or trusted family member, attorney and health-care providers upon admission into a hospital or nursing-home facility, but there is no requirement that advanced directives must be filed with an attorney. These documents may be changed or may be revoked orally or in writing at any time. It is important to replace all outdated documents.

There is no restriction regarding the validity of a living will if the patient is the sole supporter of dependent minors, or changes his or her marital status. Most states limit the rights of pregnant patients to refuse certain treatments in order to protect the developing fetus. These limits may not be explained on the state's recommended forms. Physicians should check with legal counsel to understand specific state statutes.

DURABLE POWER OF ATTORNEY

A durable power of attorney is similar to a health-care surrogate designation in that it provides another individual with the power to make health-care decisions when the patient is unable to do so. The difference between the living will and the durable power of attorney is that the latter involves decisions beyond health-care. The designated individual, known as an 'attorney-in-fact', may be asked to make personal and financial decisions as well. In the living-will directive, a person can designate an individual adult to make health-care decisions if he or she is unable to do so. This individual is designated one's 'surrogate'. In general, living wills authorize the surrogate to proceed with withdrawing or withholding artificial nutrition and hydration only under the following circumstances:

(1) Death is imminent;
(2) The patient is permanently unconscious and the decision is consistent with an advanced directive of the patient;
(3) Artificial nutrition and hydration cannot be absorbed by the body, or the burden of providing artificial nutrition and hydration outweigh the benefit.

Living wills must be in writing and must be witnessed by two adults unrelated by blood or marriage to the person making the declaration.

REFERENCES

1. American College of Obstetricians and Gynecologists. *End-of-Life Decision Making: Understanding the Goals of Care.* ACOG Committee Opinion 156. Washington, DC: ACOG, 1995
2. Faden RR, Beauchamp T. *History and Theory of Informed Consent.* New York: Oxford University Press, 1986
3. Hanson LC, Rodgman E. The use of living wills at the end of life. *Arch Intern Med* 1996;156:1018
4. Park DC, Eaton TA, Larson EJ, Palmer HT. Implementation and impact of the Patient Self-Determination Act. *South Med J* 1994;87:971
5. Walker RN, Schonwetter RS, Kramer BR, Robinson BE. Living wills and resuscitation preferences in an elderly population. *Arch Intern Med* 1995;155:171

34

National Practitioner Data Bank

Ronald L. Scott, JD

INTRODUCTION

The Health Care Quality Improvement Act (HCQIA) of 1986[1] established the National Practitioner Data Bank (NPDB) as a central information clearing-house to collect and release information related to the professional conduct and competence of physicians, nurses, dentists and other health-care practitioners. The NPDB contains information about health-care practitioners' malpractice payments, adverse licensure actions, restrictions on professional membership and negative privileging actions by hospitals. The intent of the HCQIA is to support professional peer-review by encouraging hospitals, state licensing boards, professional societies and other health-care entities to identify and discipline health-care practitioners who engage in unprofessional conduct. The HCQIA offers limited immunity from damages in civil suits under federal or state law for peer-review bodies and individual participants assisting such bodies if two conditions are met. First, the peer-review action must be taken in the reasonable belief that the action was in the furtherance of quality health-care. Also, the practitioner must be afforded due process protections, including adequate notice and hearing procedures fair to the practitioner under the circumstances. As a national database, the NPDB helps to prevent incompetent practitioners from moving between states without discovery of the practitioners' incompetent performance.

HEALTH-CARE PRACTITIONERS

The NPDB specifically applies to physicians, including doctors of medicine or osteopathy legally authorized by a state to practice medicine or surgery, and dentists legally authorized to practice dentistry by a state. Additionally, the NPDB applies to other practitioners who are licensed or otherwise authorized (i.e. certified or registered) by a state to provide health-care. The NPDB *Guidebook* gives examples of health-care practitioners other

Table 1 National Practitioner Data Bank (NPDB) examples of other health-care practitioners

Acupuncturists
Audiologists
Chiropractors
Dental hygienists
Denturists
Dietitians
Emergency medical technicians
Homeopaths
Medical assistants
Medical technologists
Mental health counselors
Nuclear medicine technologists
Nurse aides
Nurse anesthetists
Nurse midwives
Nurse practitioners
Nurse, registered
Nutritionists
Occupational therapists
Occupational therapy assistants
Ocularists
Opticians
Optometrists
Orthotics/prosthetics fitters
Pharmacists
Pharmacists, nuclear
Physical therapy assistants
Physician assistants
Physical therapists
Professional counselors
Psychiatric technicians
Radiation therapy technologists
Radiological technologists
Rehabilitation therapists
Respiratory therapists
Respiratory therapy technicians
Social workers, clinical
Speech/language pathologists

than physicians or dentists (Table 1), with the caveat that inclusion or exclusion from the list should not be interpreted as either a mandate or a waiver of NPDB reporting requirements, since licensing and certification requirements vary among the states.

QUERYING AND REPORTING
REQUIREMENTS/ELIGIBLE ENTITIES

To date information about individual practitioners contained in the NPDB is not available to the public. Only eligible entities are entitled to participate in the NPDB. Entities eligible to *query* the NPDB include state licensing boards, hospitals, other health-care entities that provide health-care services *provided that* they also follow a formal peer-review process, and professional societies that follow a formal peer-review process. Practitioners are also permitted to 'self-query' the NPDB for their own records only. Entities eligible to *report* to the NPDB include entities that make medical malpractice payments for the benefit of a health-care practitioner, state licensing boards, health-care entities that take adverse privileging actions as a result of professional peer-review, and professional societies that take adverse membership actions based on peer-review. A plaintiff's attorney who has filed a medical malpractice claim against a hospital may query the NPDB where evidence is submitted that the hospital failed to make a required query of the NPDB about the practitioners named in the claim. Defense attorneys are not allowed access to the NPDB since a defendant practitioner is permitted to self-query the data bank. Payors of medical malpractice claims must report such payments to the NPDB and state licensing boards within 30 days of payment. Hospitals, professional societies and other health-care entities must submit reports to the NPDB and state licensing boards within 15 days of an adverse action. More detailed information on querying and reporting requirements is provided in Table 2.

DISPUTES

An individual health-care practitioner may submit a self-query to the NPDB. The practitioner may be advised that no information exists in the data bank. Alternatively, he or she will be provided with a list of all querists to whom information has been reported if the practitioner has been the subject of an Adverse Action Report (licensure, clinical privileges or professional membership) or a Medical Malpractice Payment Report. In each case where the NPDB receives a report on a practitioner, a notification of such a report will be provided to the practitioner. If a practitioner disputes the accuracy of a report, the practitioner has two options. First, the practitioner must contact the reporting entity to request that the entity files a correction. If the entity refuses to file a correction, or the practitioner still believes that the report is factually inaccurate, he or she may add a

Table 2   National Practitioner Data Bank (NPDB) reporting/querying requirements

Entity	Reporting to the NPDB	Querying the NPDB
State medical and dental boards	must report adverse licensure actions related to professional competence or conduct	may query at any time
Hospitals/other health-care entities	must report professional review actions that adversely affect clinical privileges of physician or dentist for more than 30 days, or physician's or dentist's voluntary surrender of clinical privileges while under investigation, and revisions to such actions; may report on other health-care practitioners	hospitals must query when screening for medical staff appointment or granting/expanding clinical privileges (and every 2 years thereafter); may query at any time when necessary; health-care entities other than hospitals may query for medical staff appointment/granting privileges, and in support of peer-review activity
Professional societies	must report peer-review actions that adversely affect professional memberships for physicians and dentists; may report on other health-care practitioners	may query when screening applicant for membership or affiliation, and in support of peer-review activity
Medical malpractice payors	must report payments on behalf of physicians, dentists and other health-care practitioners in settlement of claim or judgment	not permitted to query the NPDB
Health-care practitioners	no self-reporting	may self-query the NPDB at any time
Plaintiff's attorney	no reporting	a plaintiff's attorney who has filed a medical malpractice claim against a hospital may query the NPDB where evidence is submitted that the hospital failed to make a required query of the NPDB regarding the practitioners named in the claim

Table 3 Examples of disputes

Type	Description	Secretary's decision
Alleged denial of due process	practitioner alleged denial of due process because peer-reviewers ignored testimony of medical experts or other witnesses	outside the scope of review
Licensure completion: trigger date	pharmacy student in training allegedly committed malpractice, with payment made on student's behalf after student received license; report disputed on basis that practitioner must be licensed at time of incident for report to be made to NPDB	report voided from NPDB since appropriate trigger date for determining if practitioner is licensed is date of incident rather than payment
Residency status	medical student disputed malpractice payment report on basis that he/she was in training at the time of the incident	outside scope of review: payment reportable if practitioner (regardless of residency status) is named in claim and payment is made on his/her behalf
Settlement: practitioner disagrees	practitioner disputed malpractice payment report because he/she did not concur with settlement	outside scope of review since practitioner's agreement to settlement is irrelevant to reportability of payment
Settlement: practitioner dismissed from lawsuit	practitioner disputed malpractice payment report on basis that he/she was dismissed from the lawsuit by summary judgment before settlement	report voided since no claim existed against the practitioner and no payment was made on his/her behalf

NPDB, National Practitioner Data Bank

statement (of up to 2000 characters) to the report or initiate a dispute with the NPDB, or both add a statement and initiate a dispute. If a reporting entity refuses to change a disputed report, the Secretary of Health and Human Services will, upon request, review disputed reports for accuracy of factual information and to ensure that the information was required to be reported. However, such a review will not consider the merits of a medical malpractice claim in the case of a payment, or the appropriateness of a health-care entity's peer-review action or a state licensing board's action. Detailed time requirements for the dispute process are set forth in the NPDB *Guidebook*. Most reports may be filed via the Internet at the NPDB's web site. Table 3 gives examples of disputes.

HEALTH-CARE INTEGRITY AND PROTECTION DATA BANK

The Health Insurance Portability and Accountability Act of 1996[3] established the national Health-care Integrity and Protection Data Bank (HIPDB). The HIPDB was created to combat fraud and abuse in health insurance and health-care delivery. The HIPDB contains information regarding civil judgments, criminal convictions, or actions by federal or state licensing agencies against a health-care provider, supplier or practitioner related to the delivery of a health-care item or service. The HIPDB also contains information relating to the exclusion of a health-care provider, supplier or practitioner from participation in federal or state health-care programs. All licensing boards and some reporting entities are required to report to both the HIPDB and the NPDB. However, reports on medical malpractice payments, clinical privileges actions and professional society membership actions will only be in the NPDB. Civil judgments and criminal convictions will only be contained in the HIPDB. The HIPDB will collect and maintain some licensure actions; for example, adverse licensure actions from 21 August 1996 must be reported to HIPDB. Access to information in the HIPDB will not be available to the public, but will be available to federal and state government agencies, health plans and via self-query, similar to the NPDB. A joint web site has been established for the NPDB–HIPDB[4].

OTHER PRACTITIONER DATA BANKS

In addition to the NPDB, hospitals and other entities use a number of other practitioner data banks when credentialing physicians and other health-care practitioners. The Federation of State Medical Boards maintains a Board Action Data Bank containing disciplinary actions including license revocations, probations, suspensions, consent orders and Medicare sanctions. Other data banks include the Physician Masterfile of the American Medical Association, the Drug Enforcement Administration Controlled Substances Act Registration Database, and the Chiropractic Information Network/Board Action Databank (CINBAD).

REFERENCES

1. *Health Care Quality Improvement Act of 1986*, Title IV, PL 99–660 See also: *NPDB regulations*, 25 C.F.R. Part 60(2000). See also: Baldwin LM, Hart G, Oshel RE, *et al.* Hospital peer review and the National Practitioner Data Bank. *JAMA* 1999;282:349

2. National Practitioner Data Bank. *Guidebook-hipdb.org*. http://www.npdb (1996, 1999)
3. *Health Insurance Portability and Accountability Act of 1996*, PL 104–191
4. National Practitioner Data Bank – Health-care Integrity and Protection Data Bank. http://www.npdb-hipdb.org (visited 8 February 2001)

35

A patient Bill of Rights

Peter A. Schwartz, MD

The concept of a patient Bill of Rights was born in the early 1970s as an expression of patient demand for autonomy or choice in an era governed by beneficence: the obligation of the physician to act for the well-being of the patient. As the millennium approached, the Bill of Rights had a renaissance. Both the patient reveling in their new found autonomy and the physician coming to terms with the balance between beneficence and autonomy spoke out against care 'managed' by a 'third party'. It was untenable that the provider organization (the third party), contracted to provide care by the employer, would usurp control of the patient–physician dynamic.

The patient Bill of Rights is a list of rights that a patient may expect in his/her interactions with the health care system. Conversely it is a list of obligations that the health care system has towards patients. The list, as iterated in this chapter, will include both obligations the physician has in his/her office and those obligations the physician has towards the patient in the hospital setting. The euphemistic 'bill' is a collection of legal and ethical obligations.

For the purpose of ease of presentation, the Bill of Rights has been grouped as general principles and specific or evolved principles. It is believed that the former are or should be constant whereas the latter have evolved significantly over the past few decades and their further evolution might be assumed.

GENERAL PRINCIPLES

1. A patient has the right to his/her civil and religious liberties. This would include the right of a person 16–18 years of age or older (depending on state law) to request release from care.

2. A patient has a right to effective bi-directional communication, i.e. the physician ensures that the patient understands the information that an

average patient would want to know. This includes the physician's obligation to attempt to enhance communication limited by educational level, cultural and language of origin differences, and hearing disability.

3. A patient has the right to courteous treatment at all times, regardless of concurrence with the caregivers' choice of care.

4. A patient has the right to appropriate medical care which is individually based.

5. A patient has the right to know the identity of his/her caregivers at all times. Physicians should introduce themselves, have visible signs of their identity, etc. The health care provider also has an obligation to disclose his/her position in the health care team (physician, other provider, resident, student etc.)

SPECIFIC RIGHTS

Patient communication/patient right to informed consent (choice)

A patient has the right of informed choice both as a legal requirement and as appropriate medical care. The concept of informed consent has evolved significantly in both the medical and legal disciplines over the past decade or two and will undoubtedly continue to evolve. The practicing gynecologist must understand the differences between the ethical and legal perspectives. Ethical standards describe optimal behaviors and the law outlines the minimal level of compliance demanded of the physician. This chapter focuses on the ethical aspects of informed consent. Ethically, informed consent is a *process* not a signed document. A signed informed consent is simply documentation that the process has occurred. The process helps create and enhances fundamentals of the physician–patient relationship. The increasing obligation of informed consent during the latter half of the 20th century derived from the increased emphasis placed on patient autonomy during that period of time.

The process of informed consent serves the values of trust, patient self-determination without coercion, and mutuality of respect that are fundamental to the physician–patient relationship. The process of informed consent should include:

1. Evaluation and documentation of the patient's capacity for understanding and decision making.

2. Communication/explanation of the:
   a) diagnosis
   b) anticipated prognosis or clinical course without therapy

c) recommended therapy (with anticipated risks and benefits)

d) alternative therapies (with anticipated risks and benefits)

e) the physician's ability or experience in effecting the recommended therapy, and

f) any incentives or inducements that might influence the physician's choice of therapy.

3. Documentation of the patient's free choice.

Informed consent might preferably be named informed choice as the patient should feel free to refuse treatment, consent to it, or choose among alternatives. The physician should be as diligent in noting and recording informed refusal as informed consent.

Patients' right to privacy and confidentiality

The physician has the responsibility to protect the patient's privacy whenever possible. Communication should be done in an area that has been chosen to enhance privacy, whenever possible. This includes both physical privacy at the time of examinations and verbal privacy when history or information is being exchanged between the patient and the physician. The patient has the right to expect that all information will be maintained in a confidential and secure manner. This confidentiality includes:

1. Transmission of information only with the patient's permission and then only that information that is necessary for appropriate care of the patient and to serve the patient's best interests.

2. Using methods of communication that are secure in their confidentiality. This would include fax machines, computer screens, phone conversations, and the security of the medical record. All information concerning a patient should be kept in storage that is secure from people that do not have the privilege of receiving it. Moreover, employees who do have access to patient information must be counseled against accessing information for personal purposes or purposes beyond the scope required by their employment. Proscribed penalties for employee abuse of patient privacy should be known by all employees and the employers' reaction should be anticipated and immediate.

Patients' right to voice grievances

Patients have the right to voice their grievances with the physician or the health care facility without fear of retribution. Some would argue the obligation of the system to provide patient advocates or the right of family or a representative to be present at all consultations. (It is interesting to put those concepts into the perspective of physician permission or refusal to allow husbands in the delivery room just a few decades ago.)

Patients' right to accessible health care

A patient has a right to accessible health care. If a physician has a patient–physician relationship, the patient has a right to expect that physician or his designate will be available to the patient at the time of need. The patient can also expect that the physician will make every effort to deliver his/her services at an agreed upon time. Since physicians rarely tell patients the cost of services in advance and patients rarely request that information the physician has the obligation to price his/her services fairly.

Patients' right to honesty

A patient has the right to expect her caregivers to be honest. This would include frank discussions on issues such as potential complications of surgery, use of resident physicians, alternatives that either the patient's health plan or the physician's expertise does not allow him/her to provide (also see informed consent). A patient has the right to expect a clear explanation of the benefits of their health plan. Moreover, a patient has the right to expect that their health plan will cover a full range of basic benefits with exclusions frankly presented.

Patients' right to access information

A patient has the right to access information in their medical record or to designate someone else to access the information.

Patients' right to assistance in communication

Patients have the right to assistance in communication wherever necessary – the services of interpreters and assistance for the hearing impaired is a responsibility of the provider.

Patients' right to accurate accounting of charges

Patients have the right to an explicit and accurate accounting of charges.

Patients' right to access of health care

Patients have a right to recourse if 'third parties' unfairly, or without notice, limit expected and appropriate access to health care providers and modalities of care. (The limits of the recourse is a current topic of both debate and legislative activity at the time of writing.)

Patients' rights as subjects in medical research

If participating in medical research, the patient has the right to be:

1. Informed of the nature and purpose of the research.
2. Explained the procedures of the research.
3. Explained any potential benefits and any side-effects and/or discomforts that are known or reasonably to be expected.
4. Informed of all alternatives of care.
5. Given the opportunity to ask questions.
6. Instructed that their consent may be withdrawn at any time.
7. Given a copy of the signed and dated consent form.
8. Given the opportunity to consent or not consent without duress, deceit, coercion, or undue influence.

SUMMARY

Patient's bills of rights have become rather ubiquitous, suggesting the consumer's rights and demands to be treated appropriately by both provider and third party insurers, or managers of care. This chapter has emphasized the role of the provider rather than the third party or manager of care. It has also attempted to compartmentalize rights into those that appear to have historical and prospective durability, and those that are likely to continue to evolve as the health care system continues to evolve.

BIBLIOGRAPHY

1. *Your Rights and Responsibilities*. Reading, PA: The Reading Hospital and Medical Center, 2001
2. *Patients' Bill of Rights*. St Paul, MN: Regions Hospital, 2001
3. Annas GJ. A national bill of patients' rights. *New Engl J Med* 1998;338:695–9
4. American Medical Association. *Code of Medical Ethics*. Chicago: AMA, 1997
5. Sorian R, Feder J. Why we need a patients' bill of rights. *J Health Polit Policy Law* 1999;24:1137–44

36

Basic legal principles

Clayton L. Robinson, JD, and David B. Gazak, JD, PhD

IMPUTED FAULT

One of the most interesting, and perhaps frustrating, legal doctrines affecting the practice of medicine is 'imputed fault', for through it, a physician whose personal conduct is within all professional standards of medical care can be liable for the wrongful conduct of a third party 'tortfeasor'.

Theory

In contrast to the doctrine of 'negligence', in which a special relationship between a defendant and plaintiff imposes on the defendant a duty to use 'reasonable care', in imputed fault, a special relationship between an 'innocent defendant' and a 'third party tortfeasor' renders the defendant liable to the plaintiff for injuries caused by the wrongful conduct of the third party as a matter of law. Imputed fault is not liability for innocent conduct. Rather, it is a shift of the liability for wrongful conduct from the one who actually engaged in it to the person who, owing to a special relationship, was in a position to have prevented the conduct. The defendant is thus said to be 'vicariously liable' for the actions of those persons over whom he/she maintains such a position of control. This 'master–servant' relationship, which is the legal basis for imputed fault, gives rise to the synonymous phrase *respondeat superior*, or 'let the master answer'.

The master–servant basis for imputing fault is commonly found in an employer–employee relationship. However, in the absence of this social construction, any circumstance in which a position of authority is accompanied by the right to control a subordinate acting within a prescribed set of duties is a sufficient basis for imputed fault. This generic arrangement is legally described in the doctrine of 'agency', in which a principal (master) may control the conduct of his/her agent (servant) within a prescribed scope of agency. In making the master answer for the servant, two broad legal criteria must be met: the servant must be acting within the scope of pre-scribed duties, and the master, either directly or indirectly, either was, or in the exercise of reasonable care should have been, in control of the servant.

The proclaimed social policies warranting imputed fault are largely four-fold. First, it is alleged to be simply 'the cost of doing business'. Second, since the master profits from the good conduct of the servant, he/she should stand responsible for the cost of improper conduct. Third, it is argued that the master stands behind the actions of the servant in the name of an implied warrantee. Finally, in theory, imputing liability to the master places on him/her, who is in the position of control, the incentive to create a prescribed scope of duties which minimizes the risky behavior of the servant.

The ultimate philosophy of imputed fault is that the burden of tortious conduct should not be placed upon the innocent, injured party, but rather should be shifted to the person who is in the best position to prevent the conduct from occurring. Furthermore, since it is not intended to be an imposition of absolute liability, the master is subsequently entitled to indem-nification from the servant, who arguably breached an implied condition of the employment or agency: to perform his/her duties with reasonable care.

Practice

Employer–employee relationships in the medical profession largely involve a hospital's employment of nurses, technicians and assistants. By an appli-cation of imputed fault, a hospital is vicariously liable for the injuries caused by the negligent conduct of these employees in the course of treat-ing patients. As well, a physician is vicariously liable for the conduct of those persons directly employed in his/her practice.

Agency doctrine accounts for the bulk of physician liability exposure based on vicarious liability. This exposure can be subdivided into four cate-gories of agency doctrine: borrowed servant doctrine, dual agency, osten-sible agency and partnerships.

Borrowed servant doctrine

The general principle of the 'borrowed servant doctrine' is that, where a servant of one master is 'loaned' to a second master for the performance of specific services such that the borrowing master assumes a position of control over the servant, the wrongful conduct of the servant is imputed to the borrowing master if the injuring conduct is exhibited in the exercise of those services.

As one of the first applications of agency doctrine to the medical profession, borrowed servant doctrine was used in surgical settings where the surgeon, in charge of an operation, was liable for the conduct of his/her assistants who, although employees of the hospital, were the temporary 'borrowed' agents of the surgeon for the duration of the procedure. The classic scenario of a sponge, clamp or scalpel blade retained in a patient after a surgical procedure, thus, under the borrowed servant doctrine, became the sole liability of the surgeon since he/she could have, or in the exercise of reasonable care, should have, averted the occurrence.

Dual agency doctrine

'Dual agency doctrine' is a more modern version of the borrowed servant doctrine. Its application to medical litigation arguably grew out of the need for a more logical and fair application of the law to an increasingly sophisticated and specialized medical profession. While still recognizing the ability for the servant of one master to be loaned to another, dual agency holds that the position of control by the borrowing master does not necessarily exonerate the lending master from a simultaneous duty of control. A person may, therefore, be the servant of two masters simultaneously as to a single service if that service is within the scope of agency and the furtherance of the duties owed to each principal. Therefore, the tortious conduct of the agent is imputed to both masters such that each is a percentage at fault, presumably dictated by his/her relative ability to control the agent's conduct.

The retained-sponge case of modern day has, in most jurisdictions, moved away from the borrowed servant doctrine, under which the surgeon is solely liable for an erroneous sponge count, to the dual agency doctrine, under which the hospital, as the primary employer of the assistant, bears some responsibility for hiring and training the assistant as well as providing him/her as an agent for the surgeon.

The outcome of cases in which two principals stand liable for the wrongful conduct of a dual agent depends largely on the facts and the key element of *control*. Where a physician is not in a position of control over an agent, is not present during the tortious conduct of the agent, is not negligent in borrowing the agent, and has no knowledge of the wrongful conduct, or in the exercise of reasonable care could not have known of the conduct, that physician is arguably not a principal and, therefore, cannot be liable for injuries caused by such conduct. Consider the following two scenarios.

278   RISK MANAGEMENT HANDBOOK

Case 1: Physician, an obstetrician, provided prenatal care for Patient whose prenatal history placed her in a high-risk category. Patient presents to the hospital in labor where she is seen by Obstetrical Nurse. Subsequently, Physician sees Patient and notes evidence of fetal distress on the fetal heart monitor. Physician orders oxytocin for labor augmentation and leaves. Over the next 2 hours, blatant signs of worsening distress are seen on the fetal heart monitor. Nurse fails to contact Physician. The next day, an emergency Cesarean section is performed; however, owing to the delay, the child is seriously injured and later dies.

Obstetrical Nurse in this scenario is both an employee of the hospital and a borrowed servant of Physician. Given Nurse's furtherance of the duties of both the hospital and Physician in caring for Patient, dual agency applies. The key issue of imputing Nurse's liability to both the hospital and the obstetrician depends on their relative positions of control. The hospital hired, trained and provided Nurse as a capable professional to assist Physician in patient care. This indirect position of control over the tortious conduct renders the hospital liable for resulting injuries. Physician, although not present during the actual moment when the fetus' condition became critical, at a minimum remained in a supervisory position, given personal knowledge of Patient's high-risk pregnancy and her immediate condition, and the subsequent order for oxytocin. In most jurisdictions, regardless of whether Physician was negligent in his/her own conduct, the fault of Nurse, as a dual agent, would be imputed to Physician as well as to the hospital.

Case 2: Physician, an obstetrician, provided all obstetrical care for Patient who is pregnant with her fourth child. No complications were experienced with Patient's past pregnancies or with her current pregnancy. Patient presents to hospital at 03.00 at 34 weeks with mild contractions, where she is seen by Obstetrical Nurse. Nurse performs a sufficient examination and assesses the fetal heart rate with an external monitor. The monitor shows evidence of severe fetal distress, and an emergency Cesarean section is indicated. Nurse calls Physician at home and informs Physician that all fetal signs were normal. Physician instructs Nurse to discharge Patient. Patient returns the next day with intrauterine fetal demise.

For the same reason as in Case 1 above, the hospital is vicariously liable for the injuries caused by Nurse's tortious conduct. But should dual agency apply? While the outcome may vary with jurisdiction, Physician was not present, was not in a position of control, nor should he/she reasonably have been expected to control Nurse under the circumstances. Arguably, Physician should not share the hospital's liability.

Ostensible agency doctrine

'Ostensible agency doctrine', or 'imputed agency', imposes liability upon an *apparent* principal for the injuries caused by the tortious conduct of a non-agent. In ostensible agency, the master–servant relationship which forms the basis for vicarious liability does not exist between the defendant and the tortfeasor; however, the relationship is presumed as a matter of law. Two broad legal elements are required for a defendant to be liable for an ostensible agent. First, the defendant must have intentionally or negligently represented the tortfeasor to be his/her agent, and second, the injured party must have reasonably believed the tortfeasor was the agent of the defendant.

Ostensible agency is rooted in equity. Where an unsuspecting party detrimentally relies on what he/she reasonably believes is a master–servant relationship owing to an intentional or negligent representation by the defendant, the defendant is liable for injuries caused by the tortfeasor.

Via ostensible agency, therefore, a hospital may be liable for the negligence of a physician. The doctrine is generally applied in those cases where the physician, although an independent contractor, is supplied through the hospital rather than selected by the patient, such that the patient reasonably believes the physician is an agent of the hospital. This reasonable belief on the part of the patient is the basis for imputing the liability to the hospital, since it would be unreasonable to expect the patient to ask of each treating physician in a hospital whether he/she is an employee or an independent contractor. Ostensible agency has traditionally been applied to impute the liability of anesthesiologists to hospitals; however, it has also rendered hospitals liable for radiologists, pathologists, emergency-room physicians and physicians of other specialties.

Partnership doctrine

'Partnership doctrine' is a branch of the law of agency; therefore, many cases have held that, where physicians have entered into a partnership to practice medicine, all partners in the practice are liable for the damages caused by the wrongful conduct of one partner in the firm, provided that he/she was acting within the scope of the partnership.

Other physician relationships not based on agency, however, escape imputed liability. For example, where one physician is called in to cover for another physician who is unavailable to care for a patient, or where a physician recommends that a patient sees a second physician, the primary physician is not liable for the subsequent malpractice of the 'called-in' or 'recommended' physician as long as there was no agency or partnership relationship between the physicians and no negligence in the substitution itself.

Similarly, the substituting physician in such cases is not liable for the prior malpractice of the primary physician unless there is an agency or partnership relationship. Likewise, a substituting physician is liable for those acts and negligence of the primary physician he/she observes, or in the exercise of reasonable care, should have observed.

CONCLUSION

Unfortunately, there is little a physician can do to avoid the application of these legal doctrines. Modern medical malpractice litigation appears to have surpassed the goal of restitution for the injured party and moved on to claiming against as many insurance policies as the law will allow. Strategically, the best defensive posture in circumstances of imputed liability is either to argue against the position of control over the tortfeasor, or to take the offensive and seek indemnification.

REFERENCES

1. *Restatement (second) of Agency*, $226, 1958; $227, 1957; $267, 1958
2. *Liability of One Physician or Surgeon for Malpractice of Another*, 85 ALR2d, 1900
3. Phillips J, Terry N, Maraist F, McClellan F. *Tort Law*. Charlottesville, VA: The Michie Company Law Publishers, 1991

37

Medicolegal problems in Britain

John Dewhurst, FRCOG, FRCS

The manner in which medicolegal problems are handled in Britain is different in several respects from the way things are accomplished in the USA. For example, a case alleging medical negligence in Britain will be heard in court only by a learned judge; no jury will be involved, and the judge alone will decide the monetary award.

Despite these and other differences, physicians in the USA and in Britain are concerned with the same thing: how to defend themselves successfully against a charge of medical negligence. In this chapter, ways in which we should approach the problem in Britain are explored.

We cannot prevent ourselves from being sued! All of us have cases from time to time that go wrong through no fault of our own; however, the unfortunate patient may feel that we physicians are to blame and may bring action against us. If we have treated the patient correctly, it should be possible to offer a successful defense, but this is not always the case. I have provided medical expert opinion for many colleagues who, I believe, have managed their cases properly but who were unable to prove their competency in court; thus, judgment has gone against them. How can such a thing happen?

The most common cause of failure to defend correct management is inadequate case records (Table 1). It has been my belief for many years that if a physician examines a patient properly, reaches the correct diagnosis, selects the correct treatment which is then explained to the patient, with mention of the risks involved, then carries out that treatment correctly, *and records all this in the case records*, that doctor has put himself or herself in the best possible position to offer a successful defense in court. He or she has provided the evidence on which the case will be judged; if the records clearly indicate correct management, the action should be decided in favor of the defendant.

Table 1 To prove competency in court

Prepare adequate case reports: if not mentioned, not done
Provide proper evidence of proper management

Table 2 To win or lose the case

If you have managed the case correctly, and
Recorded what you have done accurately
you should win your case, but
If you have not done either of these things you probably
will lose the case

Suppose, however, that everything has been done correctly but not recorded accurately. What then? A court is likely to decide that if there is not mention in the progress notes of, say, a bimanual pelvic examination being performed, none was performed; and if the patient has not been examined thoroughly she is likely to win her case. Let us suppose, as another example, that a doctor carries out a vaginal examination on a patient in labor with a high cephalic presentation, whose membranes have just ruptured. He or she determines all the appropriate assessments such as presentation, position, dilatation of the cervix, etc. and in addition feels beside the presenting part to make sure there is no cord which might prolapse. Let us also suppose that what he or she writes in the case records is:

VE. Head presenting, 2 cm above the spines. Cx 3 cm dilated; clear amniotic fluid and makes no mention of feeling for the cord. When the cord does prolapse 30 minutes later it will be extremely difficult, during any subsequent court action, for that doctor to convince a judge that a specific examination was really carried out to exclude an imminent cord prolapse. Once again, although the right thing was done, the facts were imperfectly recorded. In Britain today, poor recording of events in the case records is the most common reason for inability to defend successfully what was, in reality, correct treatment (Table 2).

It must be admitted, however, that correct management sometimes can be a matter of opinion, not a matter of fact! It may well be that an expert on the plaintiff's side states categorically that your judgment was wrong. You must then rely on your own expert to refute the allegations against you, if at all possible with documented evidence from the literature that what you did was correct.

All this, of course, presupposes that management has been correct (Table 3). If it has not, one cannot expect the case to be defended, and the

Table 3 Successful defense
If the patient is treated incorrectly
successful defense is not possible
If the patient is treated correctly
successful defense should be possible,
but may fail because of imperfect recording of case records

patient thus deserves to be compensated. Often it has been my sad duty to inform the legal advisers of a colleague that his/her management fell below the acceptable standard and so cannot be defended. We have duties to our colleagues, but also to patients.

How should you behave on the witness stand if you are unlucky enough to find yourself there? As this experience can be quite traumatic, a few pointers might help. You should have no problems when questioned by your own counsel; he/she knows your position fully by this time and will direct the questions accordingly (direct examination). Your problem may come from the plaintiff's lawyer who may ask you many awkward questions. It is not easy to advise someone how to deal with this type of determined adversary except to say that you should confine yourself to answering the questions only. You are not arguing the case. Your lawyer is doing that for you. If you have given an honest answer in cross-examination which shows you in a poor light because of the manner in which it was asked, you can count on your own advocate to rephrase it more favorably when he/she has the opportunity to question you again in re-direct examination, and, in so doing, redress any damage your answer might have done.

Keep your answers as brief as you can. Remember that if you elaborate gratuitously on an aspect of the case, this will only give the opposing counsel the chance to explore another angle which, had you not brought it up, he/she might not have mentioned.

Answer what you are asked and leave it at that!

And if you are asked the same question several times, do not hesitate to stress that your answer is the same as it was on the previous occasion(s). Judges do not like repetitive questioning any more than you do.

Never allow yourself to take up a position that you do not really hold; the truth is sure to be found out by a wily counsel and you will end up being forced to correct what you said earlier – a sure way to give a bad impression. Never try to be clever, or to score off your questioner. It is far better to treat him/her with scrupulous politeness even though he/she is giving you a hard time. If there is some aspect of the case that you have forgotten (and in Britain this is not unusual since the time interval between the event and the trial can be years), do not be afraid to say so.

Remember that honesty is generally evident to listeners in court: so is dishonesty! And if you do find yourself on the witness stand, may I express the hope that this information will be useful to you.

38

The Occupational Safety and Health Administration and bloodborne pathogens

Lynn K. Rikhoff, JD

There are millions of health-care workers who are at risk of occupational exposure to bloodborne pathogens, including the human immunodeficiency virus (HIV) and the hepatitis B virus (HBV) and other potentially infectious materials. The Occupational Safety and Health Administration (OSHA) has put forth regulations that address occupational exposure to bloodborne pathogens and prescribe safeguards to protect health-care workers from these hazards. These regulations apply to every employer with one or more employees who can reasonably expect occupational exposure to blood or other potentially infectious materials[1]. However, states may administer their own occupational and safety health programs which must be at least as effective as the federal requirements. This chapter focuses on the federal requirements, but all health-care employers should check their own state's requirements to determine whether there are additional requirements.

OCCUPATIONAL EXPOSURE AND BLOODBORNE PATHOGENS

Before getting to the numerous requirements of this OSHA regulation, it is important to become familiar with OSHA's definitions regarding occupational exposure and bloodborne pathogens. OSHA has defined occupational exposure as:

'Reasonably anticipated skin, eye, mucous membrane or parenteral contact with blood or other potentially infectious materials that may result from the performance of an employee's duties.'

According to the regulation, bloodborne pathogens are defined as follows:

'Pathogenic microorganisms that are present in human blood and cause disease in humans. These pathogens include, but are not limited to, hepatitis B virus (HBV) and human immunodeficiency virus (HIV).'

This standard also protects against potentially infectious materials including human body fluid, any unfixed tissue or organ from a human, and HIV or HBV cultures, tissue, solutions or otherwise.

EXPOSURE CONTROL PLANS

Each employer with employees subject to occupational exposure must establish a written exposure control plan to eliminate or minimize employee exposure. Each employer's plan must evaluate routine tasks and procedures in the workplace that involve exposure to blood or other potentially infectious materials, identify employees performing such tasks and utilize a variety of methods to reduce the risks.

The exposure control plan consists of the following components:

(1) An exposure determination in which the employer must analyze and list those employee job classifications having occupational exposure, and list all tasks and procedures in which occupational exposure occurs. This determination must be made without regard to the use of personal protective equipment.

(2) The schedule and method of implementation of the methods of compliance, vaccination, post-exposure evaluation and follow-up, communication of hazards to employees and the required record-keeping of this regulation.

Each employer must ensure that a copy of the exposure control plan is accessible to its employees and the plan must be reviewed and updated at least annually. The plan must also be updated whenever necessary to reflect any new or modified tasks and procedures which affect occupational exposure in the office, and to reflect new and revised employee positions with occupational exposure.

METHODS OF COMPLIANCE

OSHA has established the following methods of compliance with this regulation.

General This signifies the use of universal precautions under all circumstances. 'Universal precautions' is a method of control in which all human blood and certain body fluids are treated as if known to be infectious.

Engineering and work practice controls   These are the primary methods utilized by employers to control the transmission of bloodborne pathogens. Employers are required to put various controls and protocols in place to isolate or remove the bloodborne pathogen hazard from the workplace. Where occupational exposure remains after the institution of these controls, an employer must provide protective equipment to its employees. Included in the engineering and work practice controls are the following:

(1) Employers shall provide handwashing facilities, which are readily accessible to its employees.

(2) Use of contaminated needles or other contaminated sharps that are bent, recapped or removed is prohibited unless the employer can demonstrate that no alternative is feasible or that such action is required by specific medical or dental procedure. Additionally, all contaminated reusable sharps shall be placed in appropriate containers until properly processed.

(3) Eating, drinking, smoking, applying cosmetics or lip balm, and handling of contact lenses are prohibited in work areas where there is a reasonable likelihood of occupational exposure. This includes prohibiting food and drink from being kept in refrigerators, freezers, shelves and cabinets or otherwise where blood or potentially infectious materials are present.

(4) Additionally, OSHA requires that specimens of blood or other potentially infectious materials must be placed in a container which prevents leakage during collection, handling, processing, storage, transport or shipping.

Personal protective equipment   When occupational exposure is present, the employer shall provide, at no cost to the employee, appropriate personal protective equipment such as gloves, gowns, laboratory coats, face shields or masks and eye protection, mouthpieces, resuscitation bags, etc. The personal protective equipment should prevent blood or other potentially infectious materials from passing through or reaching the employee's clothing or exposed areas. The employer is required to ensure that the employees use the appropriate personal protective equipment.

Housekeeping   Employers must ensure that the work-site is maintained in a clean and sanitary condition. Furthermore, the employer must determine and implement an appropriate written schedule for cleaning and a method of decontamination. Contaminated work surfaces shall be decontaminated with appropriate disinfectant immediately after completion of the procedure, or as soon as possible upon contamination, and at the end of the work-shift. Contaminated sharps must be discarded immediately or as soon as feasible in containers that are closable, puncture-resistant, leak-proof and appropriately labeled or color-coded.

TRAINING

Employers are required to provide free training annually to all employees. This training includes access to a copy of OSHA regulations with an under-standable explanation of its contents. Training must also occur at the time of an initial assignment or task when an employee may be subject to occu-pational exposure. An annual training for all employees shall be provided within one year of the previous training. The employer's training program must contain the following components:

(1) An accessible copy of the regulatory text of the OSHA standard and an explanation of its contents;

(2) A general explanation of the epidemiology and symptoms of blood-borne diseases;

(3) An explanation of the modes of transmission of bloodborne pathogens;

(4) An explanation of the employer's exposure control plan and the means by which the employee can obtain a copy of the written plan;

(5) An explanation of the appropriate methods for recognizing task and other activities that may involve exposure to blood and other poten-tially infectious materials;

(6) An explanation of the use and limitations of methods that will prevent or reduce exposure, including appropriate engineering controls, work practices and personal protective equipment;

(7) Information on the types, proper use, location, removal, handling, decontamination and disposal of personal protective equipment;

(8) An explanation of the basis for selection of personal protective equipment;

(9) Information on the hepatitis B vaccine, including information on its effi-cacy, safety, method of administration and benefits of being vaccinated, and that the vaccine and vaccination will be offered free of charge;

(10) Information on the appropriate actions to take and persons to contact in an emergency involving blood or other potentially infectious materials;

(11) An explanation of the procedure to follow if an exposure incident occurs, including the method of reporting the incident and the medical follow-up that will be made available;

(12) Information on the post-exposure evaluation and follow-up that the employer is required to provide for the employee following an exposure incident;

(13) An explanation of the signs and labels and/or color-coding required for sharps and containers;

(14) An opportunity for interactive questions and answers with the person conducting the training session.

HEPATITIS B VACCINE

An employer is required to make available at no cost to the employee the hepatitis B vaccine and vaccination series to all employees who have occupational exposure, and post-exposure evaluations to all employees who have had an exposure incident. An employee who declines to accept the hepatitis B vaccination offered by the employer must sign the following statement:

> I understand that due to my occupational exposure to blood or other potentially infectious materials I may be at risk of acquiring hepatitis B virus (HBV) infection. I have been given the opportunity to be vaccinated with hepatitis B vaccine at no charge to myself. However, I decline hepatitis B vaccination at this time. I understand by declining this vaccine, I continue to be at risk of acquiring hepatitis B, a serious disease. If in the future I continue to have occupational exposure to blood or other potentially infectious materials and I want to be vaccinated with hepatitis B vaccine, I can receive the vaccine series at no charge to me.

_____

Signed

_____

Date

RECORD-KEEPING

Employers are required to maintain medical records for each employee in accordance with 29 CFR (Code of Federal Regulations) 1910.1020. Each record must include the following:

(1) The name and social security number of the employee;

(2) A copy of the employee's hepatitis B vaccination status including the dates of all the hepatitis B vaccinations and any medical records relative to the employee's ability to receive the vaccination;

(3) A copy of all results of examinations, medical testing and follow-up procedures;

(4) The employer's copy of the health-care professional's written opinion regarding the hepatitis B vaccination or post-evaluation and follow-up.

Furthermore, an employer must ensure that the employee's medical record is kept confidential and maintained for the duration of the employment plus 30 years.

An employer shall also keep training records containing the following information:

(1) The dates of the training sessions;

(2) The contents or summary of the training sessions;

(3) The names and qualifications of persons conducting the training;

(4) The names and job titles of all persons attending the training sessions.

Each employer shall maintain the training records for 3 years from the date in which the training occurred.

FREE OSHA CONSULTATION

OSHA provides free consultation assistance on request to employers who want help in establishing and maintaining a safe workplace. Consultation assistance includes a comprehensive appraisal of all work practices and environmental hazards of the workplace and all aspects of the employer's current plan. This program is distinct and separate from OSHA's inspection program. This service is confidential and employers will not be penalized nor will citations be issued for any safety or health problems identified by the consultant.

RESOURCES

A wealth of information, including publications and forms, are located on OSHA's web page at http://www.osha.gov.

Related publications

Occupational Exposure to Bloodborne Pathogens – Precautions for Emergency Responders. OSHA 3130

Access to Medical and Exposure Records. OSHA 3110
All about OSHA. OSHA 2056
Bloodborne Pathogens and Acute Care Facilities. OSHA 3128
Bloodborne Pathogens and Long-Term Care. OSHA 3131
Controlling Occupational Exposure to Bloodborne Pathogens in Dentistry. OSHA 3129
Occupational Exposure to Bloodborne Pathogens. OSHA 3127
Log and Summary of Occupational Injuries and Illnesses. OSHA 200
Record-keeping Guidelines for Occupational Injuries and Illnesses.

OSHA consultation project directory

State	Telephone
Alabama	(205) 348-7136
Alaska	(907) 269-4957
Arizona	(602) 542-5795
Arkansas	(501) 682-4522
California	(415) 982-8515
Colorado	(970) 491-6151
Connecticut	(860) 566-4550
Delaware	(302) 761-8219
District of Columbia	(202) 576-6339
Florida	(904) 488-3044
Georgia	(404) 894-2646
Guam	011(671) 475-0136
Hawaii	(808) 586-9100
Idaho	(208) 385-3283
Illinois	(312) 814-2337
Indiana	(317) 232-2688
Iowa	(515) 281-5352
Kansas	(913) 296-7476
Kentucky	(502) 564-6895
Louisiana	(504) 342-9601
Maine	(207) 624-6460
Maryland	(410) 333-4210
Massachusetts	(617) 727-3982
Michigan	(517) 332-8250 (H)
	(517) 322-1809 (S)
Minnesota	(612) 297-2393
Mississippi	(601) 987-3981
Missouri	(573) 751-3403

Montana	(406) 444-6418
Nebraska	(402) 471-4717
Nevada	(702) 486-5016
New Hampshire	(603) 271-2024
New Jersey	(609) 292-2424
New Mexico	(505) 827-4230
New York	(518) 457-2481
North Carolina	(919) 662-4644
North Dakota	(701) 328-5188
Ohio	(614) 644-2246
Oklahoma	(405) 528-1500
Oregon	(503) 378-3272
Pennsylvania	(412) 357-2561
Puerto Rico	(809) 754-2188
Rhode Island	(401) 277-2438
South Carolina	(803) 734-9614
South Dakota	(605) 688-4101
Tennessee	(615) 741-7036
Texas	(512) 440-3834
Utah	(801) 530-6868
Vermont	(802) 828-2765
Virginia	(804) 786-6359
Virgin Islands	(809) 772-1315
Washington	(360) 902-5638
West Virginia	(304) 558-7890
Wisconsin	(608) 266-8579 (H)
	(414) 521-5063 (S)
Wyoming	(307) 777-7700

(H) Health
(S) Safety

REFERENCE

1. 29 CFR 1910.1030 (Code of Federal Regulations)

39

Glossary of terms

David B. Gazak, JD, PhD

abandonment   Failure to fulfill a contract. Malpractice charge made when a practitioner stops giving care during the course of a patient's illness.

abuse   Excessive or improper use or treatment of something or someone (see *child abuse*).

ad damnum   'To the damage'. The clause in a complaint that states the plaintiff's claim for money damages.

adverse witness   A witness prejudiced for or against the party questioning the witness (see *hostile witness*).

agent   Someone authorized to act for someone else.

allegation   Assertion or claim in pleadings that states what the plaintiff expects to prove.

answer   Reply written by the defense attorney to the plaintiff's complaint, defining the grounds for the defense, admitting or denying allegations, and listing arguments for preventing recovery of damages (see *pleadings*).

appellate courts   State and federal courts that handle appeals and review lower court cases and decisions.

arbitration   Process whereby a dispute can be settled by a mediator accepted by both parties involved. If the parties have not agreed to follow the decision of the arbitration procedure, the decision is not binding. In some instances, arbitration is used to determine whether the case should go to court.

assault   Willful attempt or threat to injure another person. Assault may occur without any physical contact or bodily harm (see *battery*).

assumption of risk   '*Non fit injuria*'. Subject cannot claim damages for an injury caused by a danger which he or she knew about, yet voluntarily chose to be exposed to and take the risk that the danger entailed.

attorney's lien   Document describing the right of an attorney to obtain payment for services. A copy of an attorney's lien may be given to a defendant as a means of announcing a lawsuit.

authoritative   Person or written-work commonly held to be correct. To state that someone or something is authoritative is to agree implicitly with every detail the person has ever written or every detail in a specified written-work. To concur instead only on the accuracy of particular statements of the author or work is to avoid making authorizations beyond your awareness or intent.

bankrupt   Unable to pay one's debts. The Federal Bankruptcy Act of 1978 allows for reorganizing a debtor's financial condition rather than taking the debtor's assets.

battery   *Criminal battery* is the unlawful beating of or use of force on another person without consent. *Technical battery* occurs when a health-care practitioner administers treatment that goes beyond what has been consented to by the patient. *Assault* and *battery* are punishable under civil and criminal proceedings (see *assault*).

best evidence   Rule that original documents, X-rays and other best evidence be entered in court. Copies should only be used if the originals are not available.

bill of particulars   Statement defining the details of a claim (see *pleadings*).

borrowed servant   A person temporarily working under the direction of a master who is responsible for the actions of that 'borrowed servant' in certain circumstances of close supervision. If a nurse who is an employee of a hospital performs an act under the direct supervision of a physician, the doctor, rather than the hospital, might be held responsible for that nurse who acted as a borrowed servant.

breach of contract   Failure to act as required by a contract. A contract may be implied and initiated when a doctor undertakes the responsibility to treat a patient.

breach of duty   Failure to provide the usual standard of care to a patient.

brief   Written statement, prepared by an attorney for a court, that summarizes a case and tells how specific laws are relevant to the case.

but for   Test whether the plaintiff would have suffered harm 'but for' – or in the absence of – the actions of the defendant.

captain of the ship   Holds the surgeon in an operation responsible for the negligence of nurses and others working under the direct supervision of that surgeon. Some courts have decided not to uphold this doctrine, and thereby made nurses – and the hospitals that employ them – liable for their negligent acts (see *borrowed servant*).

causation   Implication that the damage suffered by the plaintiff was a direct result of the action – or inaction – of the defendant.

child abuse   Mistreating, molesting or causing serious physical or emotional injury to a minor (see *abuse*).

circumstantial evidence   Testimony not based on personal observations of the witness.

civil lawsuit   Legal action designed to protect personal rights, or to correct and compensate for damages done to individuals (see *crime* and *tort*).

claimant   Plaintiff. One who sues.

claims-made policy   Insurance covering lawsuits filed and alleged acts of negligence that occur during the life of the policy. Because many suits are filed years after the alleged acts of negligence occurred, claims-made policies by themselves may provide insufficient malpractice coverage.

closing arguments   Summaries given to the jury by each attorney at the end of a trial.

codefendants   Parties being sued in the same lawsuit.

collateral source   Defendant's payment will not be reduced because the plaintiff has been paid by another source. For example, if a plaintiff who has won a claim of $100 000 in damages has already received $80 000 in insurance benefits, the defendant physician would still be required to pay the plaintiff $100 000 (see reference 12 for exceptions to the rule).

common law   Legal standards derived from custom and court decisions (see *statutory law*).

comparative negligence   When injuries are judged to be due in part to several different parties, including the plaintiff, the negligence – and liability – of each party can be determined on a percentage (comparative) basis (see *contributory negligence*).

complaint   Often the first legal paper filed to announce a malpractice claim and give a brief account of the facts of the case (see *pleadings*).

confidential   Information given by a patient to a health-care practitioner is normally to be kept secret. However, a practitioner may be held liable for not sharing certain 'confidential' information, as in the case of a dangerous or threatening patient who injures someone else. When a malpractice suit is active, considerations of confidentiality are relaxed while in court, but not at other times.

conflict of interest   Situation in which a person in a position of duty and trust is given an opportunity to betray that devotion and trust. For example, an attorney cannot represent two sides of a disagreement simultaneously.

consent   See *informed consent*.

contingency fee   Payment a plaintiff agrees to give an attorney will be a specified percentage of (contingent on) the damages paid to the plaintiff.

contract   Agreement about what will or will not be done. Most contracts in business are made in writing. In medicine, a practitioner has an implied contract with a patient once treatment is undertaken, and will be held to that contract to give competent continuing care, even if the patient fails to follow treatment or pay bills.

contractor   One who performs work under a contract (see *independent contractor*).

contributory negligence   Negligence on the part of the plaintiff that, when combined with the negligence of the defendant, caused injury (see *comparative negligence*).

counterclaim   Claim made by the defendant against the plaintiff. For example, a physician being sued for malpractice might make a counter-claim for the bills for treatment that had not been paid by the plaintiff.

countersuit   Lawsuit brought by the defendant against the plaintiff or plaintiff's attorney. A suit charging the plaintiff with malice would be difficult to prove. Easier to win would be a claim of a poor standard of practice or harassment of the practitioner by the plaintiff's attorney, which would be a malpractice suit against the attorney.

crime   An act judged to be against a state or the country (see *civil lawsuit* and *tort*).

cross-examination   The questioning of a witness by the opposing attorney. The material covered in cross-examination is limited to that introduced previously during direct examination.

damages   The amount of money a plaintiff is awarded for injuries suffered.

deadlocked jury   A jury that cannot reach a decision (see *hung jury*).

defamation   Injury to a person's reputation by acts of libel (writing) or slander (speech).

defendant   The person being sued and asked to pay damages to the plaintiff.

demurrer   Declaration by the defendant stating that even if the accusations made were true, there would be no basis for a suit against the defendant. For example, the claims do not state that the defendant's negligence was a proximate cause of the patient's injury.

deposition   A meeting in which various parties, including the defendant, are asked a series of questions. The deposition will be recorded and used to define the facts of the case, the limits of memory and knowledge of the defendant, and the extent and meaning of entries in the medical record. The record of the deposition can be used as evidence in court.

diligence   Due diligence is the degree of care that could be expected from a prudent practitioner under similar circumstances. This is the standard to which a practitioner is normally held when facing a malpractice charge.

direct examination   The questioning in court of a witness by the attorney who called that witness. This is normally the first questioning in court experienced by a defendant.

directed verdict   The trial judge may enter a decision, a directed verdict, when a party has failed to present a case with sufficient evidence for jury evaluation.

disability   Loss or lack of the ability to work, to enjoy legal rights or to receive governmental payments.

disclosure   Divulgence or explaining of information and evidence.

discovery   The finding of information, e.g. by private investigation, depositions, interrogatories and examination of evidence.

discovery rule   The statute of limitations starts to run when the patient knows about, or when a diligent patient would have been able to recognize, the negligent act of the practitioner.

duty   Obligation or commitment. A health-care practitioner has a duty to continue competent treatment of a patient once treatment has started.

employee   A person hired by an employer to perform duties.

employer   The employer (e.g. family physician or hospital administrator) has the responsibility to control the details of how the duties of employees are performed (see *respondeat superior* and *independent contractor*).

entrap   To bring unexpectedly into danger or to entangle. To entrap in a conversation is to confuse or cause the other person to make contradictory statements.

evidence   Matters of fact or proof on which belief or decision is based.

exemplary damages   Awards beyond what would compensate the plaintiff for injuries suffered, likely to be added when fraud or other deliberate or criminal actions have occurred. Such awards, often not covered by malpractice insurance, are meant to deter future misconduct.

expert witness   Someone recognized by the court as qualified by reason of training or experience to give expert testimony on the case and subject being tried.

fellow servant   Fellow employee.

fellow servant rule   Provision invoked by employers to decrease their liability when an employee injures another by claiming that the injuring employee was responsible for the damage to the other employee. Workers' compensation insurance has eliminated the need for this argument in many cases.

fraud   Deliberate falsification or concealment of facts.

going bare   Practicing medicine without having professional liability (malpractice) insurance.

Good Samaritan law   Statute that protects from malpractice claims the health-care practitioner who renders free and voluntary emergency care outside of medical facilities.

guilt   Violation of a criminal law. A defendant may not be 'guilty' of malpractice, a civil wrong; yet one may be guilty of criminal charges filed along with a malpractice claim.

hearsay   Second-hand testimony provided by rumors or unconfirmed reports (see *inadmissible evidence*).

hostile witness   A witness prejudiced against the questioning party (see *adverse witness*).

hung jury   A jury that cannot reach a verdict (see *deadlocked jury*).

hypothetical question   A question posed to a witness in relation to a situation that is supposedly similar to the case in hand, in order to allow the expert to express an opinion which will help the jury make an informed judgment about the present case.

immaterial   'Matter' that is unimportant, unnecessary and meaningless to the case in hand.

immunity   Freedom from penalty or obligation.

impeach   Denounce, castigate or discredit.

impleader   Document that names a third party as a defendant (same as *third-party complaint*).

implied contract   See *contract*.

inadmissible evidence   Testimony or matter that cannot be legally brought before the court (see *hearsay*).

indemnity   Exemption or protection from liability, penalty or loss.

independent contractor   One who performs under a contract with no controls on how the work will be done; only the result of the work is specified by the contract. A hospital might be held less liable for the act of an independently contracted physician who operated in the hospital than for the practice of a physician employed by the hospital.

in evidence   The facts of a case which have been established as true are considered in evidence.

informed consent   A patient may accept or reject treatment based upon an evaluation of information about the treatment and its possible effects that would be given by a reasonably prudent practitioner. What information is an adequate prerequisite for treatment may depend upon the emotional state of the patient or the urgency of the situation.

injury   Physical or psychological harm. Damages are the amount of compensation the plaintiff is awarded for suffering the injury.

interrogatories   A written list of questions given to witnesses or defendants to obtain information that would be difficult to recall from memory at a deposition.

judgment   The decision of the court.

jurisdiction   The legal and geographical territory in which a court has power to interpret and apply the law (e.g. appeals cases in California).

lawsuit   A case of action placed before a court for decision.

leading questions   Framed to control, direct or cause the witness to answer in a manner that would serve the needs and support the case of the questioning attorney.

liability   Obligation, responsibility or duty to pay.

liable   Legally responsible or under obligation.

libel   Defamation of a party by printed means (see also *slander*).

life estate   Agreement in which a living beneficiary receives use of, and income from, property. When the beneficiary dies, the property goes to the person who had given the life estate.

likely   More than 50% chance of occurring; same as *probable*; more than *possible*. A question about a rare event can be answered by saying that its occurrence is very unlikely, but anything can be said to be possible.

locality rule   Obsolete 'rule' that medical professionals should be held to the standard of care practiced in their own locality. Thus, if all physicians in a town were out of date in their practice, all would be excused. It is now recognized that practitioners in all parts of the country have access to education and consultants through transportation, telephone, tapes and other media.

loss of consortium   Loss of affection, companionship, sex and other benefits when a spouse or other close person dies or is severely injured. Payment for such loss is often sought in malpractice claims.

malice   Intentional wrongdoing against another person without justification, or wanton disregard for another's rights, welfare or reputation.

malicious prosecution   Difficult-to-prove counterclaim that a lawsuit has been brought without probable cause and with malicious intent.

malpractice   Negligence or misconduct on the part of a health-care practitioner, lawyer or other professional that causes injury and leads to a civil suit. Failure to use the degree of skill and knowledge exhibited by other professionals in similar circumstances is usually involved in the claim.

malpractice insurance   See *professional liability insurance*.

material   Substantial and important.

mental anguish Pain, fear and anxiety that follow a damaging or endangering physical or mental injury or loss.

meritorious Legally proper and deserving.

mistrial Invalid or erroneous trial.

motion Request made by an attorney. It may be accepted or denied by the court. Dozens of different motions may be made, whose purposes might not be apparent to the uninitiated at the time they are made.

neglect Failure to perform one's duties.

negligence Failure to act as a reasonable, prudent person would under similar circumstances.

non fit injuria See *assumption of risk*.

nurse practice acts State laws that define professional activities in which nurses may legally engage. Some states limit the right of nurses to diagnose problems and prescribe treatments.

objection Statement used to make the court aware that the objecting attorney believes a statement, procedure or evidence entered by the opposing attorney is not proper and should not be allowed.

occurrence policy Insurance for acts of alleged negligence that occur during the life of the policy, thus providing coverage even when a claim is filed after the policy has been terminated (see *claims-made policy*).

opening statements Verbal summaries given by opposing attorneys to the jury at the beginning of a trial.

pain and suffering All intangible damages, including discomfort and mental distress.

patient privilege Right of a patient to have information given to a practitioner held secret. This right is usually waived in court when the patient sues the practitioner.

perjury Lying under oath.

petition Written request.

plaintiff's attorney The lawyer of the person who is suing.

pleadings Formal statements of claims and defenses, including the complaint, answer and bill of particulars.

possible Anything that could happen under the circumstances (less than *likely* and *probable*).

precedent Previous court decision on a similar case. Courts try to follow principles used to decide previous cases.

prejudice Bias or preconception.

preponderance of evidence Enough testimony to prove something to be more probable than not. 'A fair preponderance of evidence' is the degree of proof needed in a civil (malpractice) case. In a criminal case, guilt must be proven 'beyond a reasonable doubt'.

prima facie   'At first glance'. Before further investigation.

prima facie **evidence**   That which seems to be correct and will be accepted by the court as fact if not contradicted in rebuttal by other evidence.

probable   Same as *likely* (see also *possible*).

professional liability insurance   Malpractice insurance. Policy covering legal counsel and costs of alleged lack of standard skill, misconduct or negligence in performing professional responsibilities to a client.

proof   Clear demonstration. That which causes people, or convinces a jury, to believe something.

proximate   Closely related or causative.

proximate cause   Malpractice implies that the damages suffered by the plaintiff were the direct result of the action, or inaction, or the defendant.

punitive damages   Funds awarded to a plaintiff, beyond the amount needed to compensate for injuries suffered, 'to make the person whole again' and to discourage the defendant from performing further negligent acts. Punitive damages are usually not covered by insurance policies.

reasonable doubt   See *preponderance of evidence*.

rebut   Contradict or oppose by countervailing proof or argument.

rebuttal evidence   Testimony given to disprove arguments given by the opposing party.

redirect examination   Re-examination of a witness by the attorney who called that person to testify. The questions are limited to material introduced by the opposing attorney during cross-examination.

refresh memory   Acceptable way in which a witness may admit inability to remember a detail at question during testimony in court, and ask to look at a medical record or other evidence to 'refresh my memory'. However, it is not acceptable to say you need to look up a detail because you do not remember it; you would then be accused of having no memory of what happened.

release   Giving up a right. When compensated for an injury, a plaintiff may sign a release barring further recovery for the injury, and releasing from liability any health-care practitioners who cared for the injury.

relevant   Concerning and related to the issue at hand.

remittitur   Order by a judge for a plaintiff to remit (give back) part of an unreasonably large award.

reorganization   An alternative to bankruptcy by which a debtor adjusts and sets up a payment schedule to honor at least part of the debts owed.

res ipsa loquitur   'The thing speaks for itself'. Means of proving negligence which depends on the fact, obvious to any lay person, that the injury would not have occurred in the absence of negligence. No expert witness is required to present complex arguments or facts proving guilt.

res judicata or *res adjudicata*   'The matter judged'. Decided by previous lawsuits whose precedents will be followed.

respondeat superior   'Let the master answer'. The employer (master) is responsible for the actions of employees (servants).

satisfaction   Compensation or payment of the damages set in a court decision.

servant   Employee or helper who is under the control of an employer or master.

settlement   Pre-trial agreement or court disposition concerning differences between parties in a lawsuit.

slander   Defamation by the spoken word (see also *libel*).

standard of care   The level or degree of competence under which a professional is expected to perform duties to a client (patient).

stare decisis   'Let the decision stand'. Follow previous court decisions on similar matters.

statute of limitations   The amount of time during which a lawsuit may be filed.

statutory law   Law enacted by a legislature (see *common law*).

subpoena   'Under penalty'. A written order to appear and testify in court, with a stated penalty for failure to do so.

subrogation   Substitution of one party for another (e.g. an insurance company may sue someone its client had the right to sue).

substantial   Of significant value (same as *material*).

suit   A legal action or case in court in which a plaintiff seeks compensation for injury.

summary judgment   Court decision based on the belief that there is no significant evidence or basis in law to support a claim for damages.

summations   Talks to the jury near the end of a trial in which each attorney, and sometimes the judge, reviews the main points of the case.

summons   Document which establishes that a court has jurisdiction over a defendant and orders the person to appear before the court.

superior   One who can direct another (e.g. employer to employee).

supersedeas bond   Money that must be paid by a defendant who is appealing a judgment. Even though an award for damages has been appealed, a fee (the *supersedeas bond*) must be paid by the defendant until the final judgment has been made.

testimony   Information given under oath.

theory   The legal foundation on which a case is based.

third-party complaint   Document (*impleader*) filed by the defendant stating that some other party is liable at least in part for the damages attributed to the defendant.

tort   A civil wrong other than a breach of contract (see *crime*).

tortfeasor   A party who commits a tort, a legal violation.

verdict   The veredictum is the 'true declaration' or decision made by a jury.

verification   Affirmation of accuracy.

vicarious liability   Responsibility for the acts of others (e.g. a hospital's accountability for the acts of its nurses).

vindictive damages   Punitive awards made because of anger.

voir dire   'To speak the truth'. The process of questioning and choosing jurors.

wanton   Malicious, immoral or reckless action that lacks consideration for others.

willful   Conscious or deliberate.

wrongful death   Statute allowing that the death of a person may be grounds for a civil suit.

wrongful life   Lawsuit that charges a health practitioner with being responsible for the life (undesired birth) of an individaul (e.g. following an unsuccessful sterilization procedure or failure to give genetic counseling).

BIBLIOGRAPHY

1. Alton WG. *Malpractice – A Trial Lawyer's Advice for Physicians (How to Avoid, How to Win)*. Boston: Little, Brown & Co., 1977
2. Illinois court rules against 'wrongful birth' suits. *Am Med News* 4 March 1983:17
3. MDs protest $4.4 million attorney's fee. *Am Med News* 24 December 1982:3
4. New York lawyers group sues to end liability screening panels. *Am Med News* 11 March 1983:3
5. Patient wins conspiracy suit, $5.1 million in damages. *Am Med News* 4 February 1983:14
6. Appleman JA. *Preparation and Trial*. Vienna, VA: Coiner, 1967
7. Bauer WB. Physicians losing respect; don't blame all of medicine's problems on lawyers. *Am Med News* 21 January 1983:60
8. Bayer MJ, Norton RL. Solving the clinical problems of phencyclidine intoxication. *ER Rep* 24 January 1983;4:2
9. Belli M. How doctors get sucked into malpractice suits. *Med Econ* 24 January 1983:76
10. Berlin L. Countersuit. In Everette JA, ed. *Legal Medicine*. Baltimore: Urban and Schwarzenberg, 1980

11. Birnbaum IM, Parker ES. *Alcohol and Human Memory*. New York: John Wiley & Sons, 1977

12. Black HC. *Black's Law Dictionary*. St. Paul: West Publishing Co., 1979

13. Blackwell BR. The drug defaulter. *Clin Pharmacol Ther* 1972;13:841

14. Boyd JR, Covington TR, Stanaszek WF. Drug defaulting II – analysis of noncompliance patterns. *Am J Hosp Pharmacol* 1974;31:485

15. Brodsky SL. *Psychologists in the Criminal Justice System*. Champaign: University of Illinois Press, 1972

Index

Acknowledgements

Without the help of a great number of people, this book would have been a lot shorter. First and foremost, I must thank the producers, executives, performers and writers who gave me their time and recollections: Elkan Allan, John Ammonds, Stanley Baxter, Alan Boyd, Bernie Clifton, Sir Bill Cotton, Jack Duncan, Noel Edmonds, Harold Fisher, John Fisher, Eric Geen, Richard Greenough, Johnnie Hamp, Terry Henebery, Steve Jones, John Kaye-Cooper, Jan Kennedy, Michael Leggo, David Liddiment, Yvonne Littlewood, Don Lusher, Ernest Maxin, Jim Moir, Stewart Morris, Roger Ordish, Jack Parnell, Marcus Plantin, Peter Prichard, Paul Smith, William G. Stewart, Brian Tesler and Rosalyn Wilder. Thanks are also due to David Clayton, Barry Cryer, Haldane Duncan, Colin Godman, Roy Holliday, Don Lawson, Jon Thoday and Big George Webley for other professional insights.

For generosity above and beyond the call of duty when it came to archive material and research pointers, as well as general advice, laughter and encouragement during the writing and research, my deepest thanks go out to Steve Arnold, Graham Barnard, Michael Bee, Mike Brown, Robin Carmody, Rory Clark, Martin and Janine Fenton, Ian Greaves, Simon Harries, Jack Kibble-White, Justin Lewis, Red O'Sullivan, Gareth Randall, Keith Skues, Gavin Sutherland and Richard Wyn Jones. For other valuable archive material and guidance, I am profoundly grateful to Ian Beard, Kif Bowden-Smith, Richard Elen, Lowestoft's Betamax guru Kevin Lambert, Greg McCaffrey, Kevin

Mulrennan, Jim Nugent, Ant Purvis, Cameron Yarde and the much-missed public version of the BBC's INFAX programme catalogue.

In the BBC's Written Archive Centre at Caversham, Jacqueline Kavanagh introduced me to the system, while Erin O'Neill (and, when she was away, Trish Hayes) dealt patiently with my enquiries over many months, digging out files and documents. Their contribution is immeasurable. I also spent a lot of very worthwhile hours in the London Library, the British Library – both at St Pancras and Colindale – and the BFI Library, so thanks go to their excellent staff.

Friends and relatives also served, sometimes without even realising it, among them: Richard Abram, Jane Anderson, Ralph Baxter, Claudia Bean, Ruby Cowling, Adam Cumiskey, Alastair Doughty, Professor Barry Fantoni, Ruth Ferris-Price, Bob Flag, Alex George, Stephen Gilchrist, Katy Guest, Geoff Hiscott, Patrick Humphries and Sue Parr, Ali Jackson, Terry James, Tanya Jones and John Hoare, Bill and Beth Kibby-Johnson, Charles Kennedy, Richard Lewis (whose family connections with the Delevines were an early inspiration), Hilary Lowinger, Sarah Lutyens, Maria McHale, Adam Macqueen, Andrew Malcolm, James Masterton, Hugh Mendl, Phil Norman, Allen Painter, Nick Parker, Nick Phillips, Paul Putner, Felicity Rubinstein, Kerry Swash, Kirsteen Thorne, Roger Tagholm (who said I should do a book on LE – happy now, Rog?), Ben Tisdall, Alan Wood and Francis Wheen. My mother and grandparents deserve recognition for letting me watch so much light entertainment in my formative years. My wife Susannah deserves similar credit for letting me watch just as much in adulthood.

Meanwhile, at Atlantic Books, thanks be to Clara Farmer for commissioning this book, Sarah Norman for taking on the editing when Clara fled, Daniel Scott for other services rendered and Toby Mundy for his usual support and ready supply of perspective.

Any errors are the fault of my dog, Lyttelton.

Lowestoft
August 2008